MISCELLANEOUS

ESSAYS AND REVIEWS.

By ALBERT BARNES.

IN TWO VOLUMES.—VOL. I.

CHICAGO:
PUBLISHED BY S. C. GRIGGS & CO.,
111 LAKE STREET.
NEW YORK: IVISON & PHINNEY.

1855.

STEREOTYPED BY L. JOHNSON AND CO.
PHILADELPHIA.

PREFACE.

THE Essays and Reviews in this volume are published in this form at the suggestion of others. They have been revised and corrected with such care as I could bestow upon them by having them read to me. Most of them were received favourably at the time when they were first published; and now, after the lapse of many years since they were first presented to the public, they have accomplished a purpose which was never contemplated at the time when they were written—by furnishing *occupation* when unable, by an afflictive dispensation of Providence, to read or write. I would hope, however, that they may subserve a higher end than this, and that they may do something to diffuse and perpetuate correct sentiments on the various points which are discussed.

Such as they are, they are now submitted to the public. Few men have greater occasion for gratitude for the manner in which their writings have been received, than I have had; and it is not improper, in this manner, to record the deep sense of the obligation which I feel. At a time of life, and in circumstances in which I can now hope to do little in what has occupied so many hours of my life, and filled up the interstices of professional pursuits, I may be permitted to hope, that these Essays, most of them the productions of earlier years, may be made useful, especially to those who are to occupy the places of men who are soon to pass away.

ALBERT BARNES.

Philadelphia, Dec. 14, 1854.

CONTENTS OF VOL. I.

V.

[CHRISTIAN SPECTATOR, 1834.]

VI.

[CHRISTIAN SPECTATOR, 1835.]

VII.

[NEW ENGLANDER, 1844.]

ESSAYS AND REVIEWS.

I.

[CHRISTIAN SPECTATOR, 1830.]

The Analogy of Religion, Natural and Revealed, to the Constitution and Course of Nature. By JOSEPH BUTLER, LL.D.

IN directing the attention of our readers to the great work whose title we have placed at the head of this article, we suppose that we are rendering an acceptable service chiefly to one class. The ministers of religion, we presume, need not our humble recommendation of a treatise so well known as Butler's Analogy. It will not be improper, however, to suggest that even our clerical readers may be less familiar than they should be with a work which saps all foundations of unbelief; and may, perhaps, have less faithfully carried out the *principles* of the Analogy, and interwoven them less into their theological system, than might reasonably have been expected. Butler already begins to put on the venerable air of antiquity. He belongs, in the character of his writings at least, to the men of another age. He is abstruse, profound, dry, and, to minds indisposed to thought, is often wearisome and disgusting. Even in clerical estimation, then, his work may sometimes be numbered among those repulsive monuments of ancient wisdom which men of this age pass by indiscriminately, as belonging to times of barbarous strength and unpolished warfare.

But our design in bringing Butler more distinctly before the public eye has respect primarily to another class of our readers. In an age pre-eminently distinguished for the short-lived productions of the imagination; when reviewers feel themselves bound to serve up to the public taste, rather the desserts and confectionaries of the literary world, than the sound and wholesome fare of other times; when, in many places, it is even deemed stupid and old-fashioned to notice an ancient book, or to speak of the wisdom of our fathers, we desire to do what may lie in our power to stay the headlong propensities of the times, and recall the public mind to the records of past wisdom. We have no blind predilection for the principles of other days. We bow down before no opinion because it is ancient. We even feel and believe, that in all the momentous questions pertaining to morals, politics, science, and religion, we are greatly in advance of past ages; and our hearts expand with joy at the prospect of still greater simplicity and clearness in the statement and defence of the cardinal doctrines of the Reformation. Most of the monuments of past wisdom we believe capable of improvement in these respects. Thus we regard the works of Luther, Calvin, Beza, and Owen. We look on them as vast repositories of learning, piety and genius. In the great doctrines which these works were intended to support we do firmly believe. Still, though we love to linger in the society of such men, and though *our* humble intellect bows before them, as in the presence of transcendent genius, yet we feel that in some things their views were darkened by the habits of thinking of a less cultivated age than this; that their *philosophy* was often wrong, while the doctrines which they attempted to defend by it were correct; and that even they would have hailed, on many topics, the increased illumination of later times. Had modern ways of thinking been applied to their works, had the results of a deeper investigation into the laws of the mind and the principles of biblical criticism, been in their possession, their works would have been the most perfect records of human wisdom which the world contains.

Some of those great monuments of the power of human thought, however, stand complete. By a mighty effort of genius, their authors seized on truth; they fixed it in permanent forms; they chained down scattered reasonings, and left them to be surveyed by men of less mental stature and far feebler powers. It is a proof of no mean talent now to be able to follow where they lead; to grasp in thought what they had the power to originate. They framed a complete system at the first touch; and all that remains for coming ages corresponds to what Johnson has said of poets in respect to Homer, to "transpose their arguments, new-name their reasonings, and paraphrase their sentiments."* The works of such men are a collection of *principles*, to be carried into every region of morals and theology, as a standard of all other views of truth. Such a distinction we are disposed to give to Butler's Analogy; and it is because we deem it worthy of such a distinction, that we now single it out from the great works of the past, and commend it to the attention of our readers.

There are two great departments of investigation respecting the "analogy of religion to the constitution and course of nature." The one contemplates that analogy as existing between the declarations of the Bible and ascertained facts in the structure of the globe, the organization of the animal system, the memorials of ancient history, the laws of light, heat, and gravitation, the dimensions of the earth, and the

---

* Johnson. Preface to Shakspeare.

form and motion of the heavenly bodies. From all these sources, objections have been derived against revelation. The most furious attacks have been made, at one time by the geologist, at another by the astronomer—on one pretense by the antiquarian, and on another by the chemist, against some part of the system of revealed truth. Yet never have any assaults been less successful. Every effort of this kind has resulted in the establishment of this great truth, that no man has yet commenced an investigation of the works of nature, for the purpose of assailing revelation, who did not ultimately exhibit important facts in its confirmation, just in proportion to his eminence and success in his own department of inquiry. We are never alarmed, therefore, when we see an infidel philosopher of real talents, commence an investigation into the works of nature. We hail his labours as destined ultimately to be auxiliary to the cause of truth. We have learned that here Christianity has nothing to fear; and men of science, we believe, are beginning to understand that here infidelity has nothing to hope. As a specimen of the support which Christianity receives from the researches of science, we refer our readers to Ray's Wisdom of God, to Paley's Natural Theology, and to Dick's Christian Philosopher.

The other department of investigation to which we referred is that which relates to the analogy of revealed truth to the actual facts exhibited in *the moral government of the world*. This is the department which Butler has entered, and which he has so successfully explored. It is obvious that the first is a wider field, in regard to the number of facts which bear on the analogy: the latter is more profound and less tangible, in relation to the great subject of theological debate. The first meets more directly the open and plausible objections of the blasphemer; the latter represses the secret infidelity of the human heart, and silences more effectually the ten thousand clamours which are accustomed to be raised against the peculiar doctrines of the Bible. The first is open to successive advances, and will be so, till the whole physical structure of the world is fully investigated and known. The latter, we may almost infer, seems destined to rest where it now is, and to stand before the world as complete as it ever will be, by one prodigious effort of a gigantic mind. Each successive chemist, antiquary, astronomer, and anatomist will throw light on some great department of human knowledge, to be moulded to the purposes of religion by some future Paley, or Dick, or Good; and in every distinguished man of science, whatever may be his religious feelings, we hail an ultimate auxiliary to the cause of truth. Butler, however, seems to stand alone. No adventurous mind has attempted to press his great principles of thought still further into the regions of moral inquiry. Though the subject of moral government is better understood now than it was in its day; though light has been thrown on the doctrines of theology, and a perceptible advance been made in the knowledge of the laws of the mind, yet whoever now wishes to know "the analogy of religion to the constitution and course of nature," has nowhere else to go but to Butler; or if he is able to apply the *principles* of Butler, he has only to incorporate them with his own reasonings, to furnish the solution of those facts and difficulties that "perplex mortals." We do not mean by this, that Butler has exhausted the subject. We mean only that no man has attempted to carry it beyond the point where he left it; and that his work, though not in our view as complete as modern habits of thought would permit it to be, yet stands like one of those vast piles of architecture commenced in the Middle Ages—proofs of consummate skill, of vast power, of amazing wealth, yet in some respects incomplete or disproportioned, but which no one since has dared to remodel, and which no one, perhaps, has had either the wealth, the power, or the genius requisite to make more complete.

Of Butler, as a man, little is known. This is one of the many cases, where we are compelled to lament the want of a full and faithful biography. With the leading facts of his life, as a parish priest and a prelate, we are indeed made acquainted. But here our knowledge of him ends. Of Butler as a man of piety, of the secret, practical operations of his mind, we know little. Now it is obvious that we could be in possession of no legacy more valuable, in regard to such a man, than the knowledge of the secret feelings of his heart; of the application of his own modes of thinking to his own soul, to subdue the ever-varying forms of human weakness and guilt; and of his practical way of obviating, for his personal comfort, the suggestions of unbelief in his own bosom. This fact we know, that he was engaged upon his Analogy during a period of twenty years. Yet we know nothing of the effect on his own soul; of the mode in which he blunted and warded off the poisoned shafts of infidelity. Could we see the internal organization of his mind, as we can now see that of Johnson; could we trace the connection between his habits of thought and his pious emotions, it would be a treasure to the world equalled perhaps only by his Analogy, and one which we may in vain hope now to possess. The true purposes of biography have been hitherto but little understood. The mere external events pertaining to great men are often of little value. They are *without* the mind, and produce feelings unconnected with any important purposes of human improvement. Who reads now with any emotion, except regret, that this is all he *can read* of such a man as Butler—that he was born in 1692, graduated at Oxford in 1721, preached at the Rolls till 1726, was made Bishop of Durham in 1750, and died in 1752. We learn, indeed, that he was high in favour at the university, and subsequently at court; that he was retiring, modest and unassuming in his deportment; and that his elevation to the Deanery of St. Paul's, and to the princely See of Durham, was not the effect of ambition, but the voluntary tribute of those in power to transcendent talent and exalted though retiring worth. An instance of his modest and unambitious habits, given in the record of his life, is worthy of preservation, and is highly illustrative of his character. For seven years he was occupied in the humble and laborious duties of a parish priest, at Stanhope. His friends regretted his retirement, and sought preferment for him. Mr. Secker, an intimate friend of Butler, being made chaplain to the king in 1732, one day, in conversation with Queen Caroline, took occasion to mention his friend's name. The queen said she thought he was dead, and asked Archbishop Blackburn if that was not the case. His reply was, "No, madam, but he is buried." He was thus raised again to notice, and ultimately to high honours in the hierarchy of the English church.

Butler was naturally of a contemplative and somewhat melancholy turn of mind. He sought retirement, therefore, and yet needed society. It is probable that natural inclination, as well as the prevalent habits of unbelief in England, suggested the plan of his Analogy. Yet, though retiring and unambitious, he was lauded in the days of his advancement, as sustaining the episcopal office with great dignity and splendour; as conducting the ceremonies of religion with a pomp approaching the grandeur of the Roman Catholic form of worship; and as treating the neighbouring clergy and nobility with the "pride, pomp, and circumstance," becoming, in their view, a minister of Jesus transformed into a nobleman of secular rank, and reckoned among the great officers of state. These are, in our view, spots in the life of Butler; and all attempts to conceal them have only rendered them more glaring. No authority of antiquity, no plea of the grandeur of imposing rites, can justify the pomp and circumstance appropriate to an English prelatical bishop, or invest with sacred authority the canons of a church that elevates the humble ministers of Him who had not where to lay his head, to the splendours of a palace or the pretended honours of an archiepiscopal throne—to a necessary alliance, under every danger to personal and ministerial character, with profligate noblemen or intriguing and imperious ministers. But Butler drew his title to memory, in subsequent ages, neither from the tinsel of rank, the staff and lawn of office, nor the attendant pomp and grandeur arising from the possession of one of the richest benefices in England. Butler the *prelate* will be forgotten: Butler the *author of the Analogy* will live to the last recorded time.

In the few remains of the Life of Butler, we lament, still more than any thing we have mentioned, that we learn nothing of his habits of study, his mode of investigation, and, especially, the *process* by which he composed his Analogy. We are told, indeed, that it combines the results of his thoughts for twenty years, and his observations and reading during that long period of his life. He is said to have written and re-written different parts of it, to have studied each word and phrase, until it expressed precisely his meaning, and no more. It bears plenary evidence that it must have been written by such a condensing and epitomizing process. Any man may be satisfied of this who attempts to express the thoughts in other language than that employed in the Analogy. Instinctively the sentences and paragraphs will swell out to a much greater size, and defy all the powers we possess to reduce them to their primitive dimensions, unless they be driven within the precise enclosures prescribed by the mind of Butler. We regret in vain that this is all our knowledge of the mechanical and mental process by which this book was composed. We are not permitted to see him at his toil, to mark the workings of his mind, and to learn the art of looking intensely at a thought until we see it standing alone, aloof from all attendants, and prepared for a permanent location where the author intended to fix its abode, to be contemplated, as he viewed it, in all coming ages. We can hardly repress our indignation that those who undertake to write the biography of such gifted men, should not tell us less of their bodies, their trappings, their honours, and their offices, and more of the workings of the spirit, the process of subjecting and restraining the native wanderings of the mind. Nor can we suppress the sigh of regret that he has not himself revealed to us what no other man could have done, and admitted subsequent admirers to the intimacy of friendship, and to a contemplation of the process by which the Analogy was conceived and executed. Over the past, however, it is in vain to sigh. Every man feels that hitherto we have had but little *biography*. Sketches of the external circumstances of many men we have—genealogical tables without number and without end—chronicled wonders, that such a man was born and died, ran through such a circle of honours, and obtained such a mausoleum to perpetuate his memory. But histories of *mind* we have not; and, for all the great purposes of knowledge, we should know as much of the *man*, if we had not looked upon the misnamed biography.

We now take leave of Butler as a man, and direct our thoughts more particularly to his great work.

Those were dark and portentous times which succeeded the reign of the Second Charles. That voluptuous and witty monarch had contributed more than any mortal, before or since his time, to fill a nation with infidels and debauchees. Corruption had seized upon the highest orders of the state, and it flowed down on all ranks of the community. Every grade in life had caught the infection of the court. Profligacy is alternately the parent and the child of unbelief. The unthinking multitude of courtiers and flatterers that fluttered around the court of Charles, had learned to scoff at Christianity, and to consider it as not worth the trouble of anxious thought. The influence of the court extended over the nation. It soon infected the schools and professions; and perhaps there has not been a time in British history when infidelity had become so general, and had assumed a form so malignant. It had attached itself to dissoluteness, deep, dreadful, and universal. It was going hand in hand with all the pleasures of a profligate court; it was identified with all that actuated the souls of Charles and his ministers; it was the kind of infidelity which fitted an unthinking age—scorning alike reason, philosophy, patient thought, and purity of morals. In the language of Butler, "it had come to be taken for granted, by many persons, that Christianity is not so much as a subject of inquiry, but that it is now, at length, discovered to be fictitious; and, accordingly, they treat it as if, in the present age, this were an agreed point among all people of discernment, and nothing remained but to set it up as a principal subject of mirth and ridicule, as it were, by way of reprisals for its having so long interrupted the pleasures of the world." In times of such universal profligacy and infidelity arose, in succession, Locke, Newton, and Butler; the two former of whom, we need not say, have been unsurpassed in great powers of thought and in the influence which they exerted on the sentiments of mankind. It needed such men to bring back a volatile generation to habits of profound thought in the sciences. It needed such a man as Butler, in our view not inferior in profound thought to either, and whose works will have a more permanent effect on the destinies of men than both, to arrest the giddy steps of a nation; to bring religion from the palace of a scoffing prince and court to the bar of sober thought, and to show that Christianity was not undeserving of sober inquiry. This was the design of the Analogy. It was not so much to furnish a complete demonstration of the *truth* of religion, as to show that it could not be proved to be false. It was to show that it accorded with a great system of things actually going on in the world, and that attacks made on Christianity were, to the same extent, assaults on the course of nature and of nature's God. Butler pointed the unbeliever to a grand system of things in actual existence, a *world* with every variety of character, feeling, conduct, and results—a system of things deeply mysterious, yet developing great principles, and bearing *proof* that it was under the government of God. He traced certain indubitable acts of the Almighty in a course of nature, whose existence could not be denied. Now, if it could be shown that Christianity contained like results, acts, and principles; if it was a scheme involving no greater mystery, and demanding a correspondent conduct on the part of man, it would be seen that it had proceeded from the same author. In other words, the objections alleged against Christianity, being equally applicable against the course of nature, could not be valid. To show this was the design of Butler. In doing this he carried the war into the camp of the enemy. He silenced the objector's arguments; or, if the objector still continued to urge them, he showed him that, with equal propriety, they could be urged against the acknowledged course of things; against his own principles of conduct on other subjects; against what indubitably affected his condition here, and what *might*, therefore, affect his doom hereafter.

We are fond of thus looking at the Bible as *part* of one vast plan of communicating truth to created intelligences. We know it is the fullest and most grand of all God's ways of teaching men, standing amidst the sources of information, as the sun does amid the stars of heaven, quenching their feeble glimmerings in the fulness of its meridian splendour. But, to carry forward the illustration, the sun does, indeed, cause the stars of night to "hide their diminished heads;" but we see in both but one system of laws; and whether in the trembling of the minutest orb that emits its faint rays to us from the farthest bounds of space, or the full light of the sun at noon-day, we trace the hand of the same God, and feel that "all are but parts of one stupendous whole." Thus it is with revelation. We know that its truths comprise all that the world elsewhere contains; that its authority is supreme over all the other sources of knowledge, and all the other *facts* of the moral system. But there *are* other sources of information—a vast multitude of facts that we expect to find in accordance with this brighter effulgence from heaven; and it is these *facts* which the Analogy brings to the aid of revelation. The Bible is in religion what the telescope is in astronomy. It does not contradict any thing before known; it does not annihilate any thing before seen: it carries the eye forward into new worlds, opens it upon more splendid fields of vision, displays grander systems, where we thought there was but the emptiness of space or the darkness of illimitable and profound night, and divides the milky way into vast clusters of suns and stars, of worlds and systems. In all the boundlessness of these fields of vision, however, does the telescope point us to any new laws of acting, any new principle by which the universe is governed? The astronomer tells us not. It is the hand of the same God which he sees, impelling the new worlds that burst on the view in the immensity of space with the same irresistible and inconceivable energy, and encompassing them with the same clear fields of light. So we expect to find it in revelation. We expect to see plans, laws, purposes, actions, and results, uniform with the facts in actual existence before our eyes. Whether in the smiles of an infant, or the rapt feelings of a seraph; in the strength of manhood, or the power of Gabriel; in the rewards of virtue here, or the crown of glory hereafter, we expect to find the

Creator acting on one grand principle of moral government, applicable to *all* these facts, and to be vindicated by the same considerations.

When we approach the Bible, we are at once struck with a most striking correspondence of plan to that which obtains in the natural world. When *we* teach theology in our schools, we do it by system, by form, by technicalities. We frame what we call a "body of divinity," expecting all its parts to cohere and agree. We shape and clip the angles and points of our theology, till they shall fit, like the polished stones of the temple of Solomon, into their place. So, when we teach astronomy, botany, or geography, it is by a regular system before us, having the last discoveries of the science located in their proper place. But how different is the plan which, in each of these departments, is pursued by infinite wisdom. The truths which God designs to teach us lie spread over a vast compass. They are placed without much apparent order. Those of revelation lie before us, just as the various *facts* do which go to make up a system of botany or astronomy. The great Author of nature has not placed all flowers in a single situation, nor given them a scientific arrangement. They are scattered over the wide world. Part bloom on the mountain; part in the valley; part shed their fragrance near the running stream; part pour their sweetness on the desert air, "in the solitary waste where no man is;" part climb in vines to giddy heights, and part are found in the bosom of the mighty waters. He that forms a theory of botany must do it, therefore, with hardy toil. He will find the *materials*, not the *system*, made ready to his hands. He will exhaust his life, perhaps, in his labour, before the system stands complete. Why should we not expect to find the counterpart of all this in religion? When we look at the Bible, we find the same state of things. At first but a ray of light beamed upon the dark path of our apostate parents, wandering from Paradise. The sun that had stood over their heads in the garden of pleasure, at their fall sunk to the west, and left them in the horrors of a moral midnight. A single ray, in the promise of a Saviour, shot along their path, and directed to the source of day. But did God reveal a whole system? Did he tell them all the truth that he knew? Did he tell all that we know? He did just as we have supposed in regard to the first botanist. The eye was fixed on one truth distinctly. Subsequent revelations shed new light; advancing facts confirmed preceding doctrines and promises; rising prophets gave confirmation to the hopes of men; precepts, laws, and direct revelations rose upon the world, until the system of revealed truth is now complete. Man has all he can have, except the facts which the progress of things is yet to develop in *confirmation* of the system, just as each new budding flower goes to confirm the just principles of the naturalist, and to show what the system is. Yet how do we possess the system? As arranged, digested, and reduced to order? Far from it. We have the book of revelation just as we have the book of nature. In the beginning of the Bible, for example, we have a truth abstractly *taught;* in another part it is *illustrated* in the life of a prophet; as we advance it is *confirmed* by the fuller revelation of the Saviour or the apostles, and we find its *full development* only when the whole book is complete. Here stands a law; there a promise; there a profound mystery, unarranged, undigested, yet strikingly accordant with a multitude of correspondent views in the Bible, and with as many in the moral world. Now, here is a mode of communication which imposture would have carefully avoided, because detection, it would foresee, must, on such a plan, be unavoidable. It seems to us that, if men had intended to *impose* a system on the world, it would have been somewhat in the shape of our bodies of divinity, and, therefore, very greatly unlike the plan which we actually find in the Bible. At any rate, we approach the

Bible with this strong presumption in favour of its truth, that it accords precisely with what we see in astronomy, chemistry, botany, and geography, and that the mode of constructing systems in all these sciences is exactly the same as in dogmatical theology.

We have another remark to make on this subject. The botanist does not shape his facts. He is the collector, the arranger, not the originator. So the framer of systems in religion *should* be, and it is matter of deep regret that *such* he has *not* been. He should be merely the collector and the arranger, not the originator of the doctrines of the gospel; and, though we think him of *some* importance, yet we do not set a high value on his labours. We honour the toils of a man who tells of the uses, the beauties, and the medicinal properties of the plant,—far more than of him who merely declares its rank, its order, its class in the Linnean system. So in theology, we admire the greatness of mind which can bring out an original truth, illustrate it, and show its proper bearing on the spiritual interests of our race, far more than we do the plodding chiseller who shape sit to its place in his system. It makes no small demand on our patience, when we see the system-maker remove angle after angle, and apply stroke after stroke to some great mass of truth which some mighty genius has struck out, but which keen-eyed and jealous orthodoxy will not admit to its proper bearing on the souls of men until it is located in a creed, and cramped into some frame-work of faith that has been reared around the Bible. Our sympathy with such men as Butler, and Chalmers, and Foster, and Hall, is far greater than with Turretine or Ridgely. With still less patience do we listen to those whose only business it is to shape and reduce to prescribed form; who never look at a passage in the Bible or a fact in nature, without first robbing it of its freshness, by an attempt to give it a sectarian location; who never stumble on an original and unclassified idea, without asking whether the system-maker had left any niche for the late-born intruder; and who apply to it all tests, as to a nondescript substance in chemistry, in order to fasten on it the charge of an affinity with some rejected confession or some creed of a suspected name. This is to abuse reason and revelation for the sake of putting honour on creeds. It is to suppose that the older creed-makers had before them all shades of thought, all material and mental facts, all knowledge of what mind *has been and can be,* and all other knowledge of the adaptedness of the Bible to every enlarged and fluctuating process of thought. It is to doom the theologian to an eternal dwelling in Greenland frost and snows, instead of sending him forth to breathe the mild air of freedom, and to make him a large-minded and fearless interpreter of the oracles of God.

It is not our intention to follow the profound author of the Analogy through his laboured demonstrations, or to attempt to offer an abridged statement of his reasoning. Butler, as we have already remarked, is incapable of abridgment. His thoughts are already condensed into as narrow a compass as the nature of language will admit. All that we purpose to do is to give a *specimen* of the argument from analogy in support of the Christian religion, without very closely following the book before us.

The main points at issue between Christianity and its opposers are, whether there is a future state; whether our conduct here will affect our condition there; whether God so controls things as to reward and punish; whether it is reasonable to act with reference to our condition hereafter; whether the favour of God is to be obtained with or without the mediation of another; whether crime and suffering are indissolubly united in the moral government of God; and whether Christianity is a scheme in accordance with the acknowledged laws of the universe, and is supported by evidence so clear as to make it proper to act on the belief of its truth.

Infidelity, in its proper form, approaches man with the declaration that there cannot be a future state. It affirms, often with much apparent concern, that there can be no satisfactory evidence of what pertains to a dark, invisible, and distant world; that the mind is incompetent to set up landmarks along its own future course; and that we can have no certain proof that *in* that dark abyss we shall live, act, or think at all. It affirms that the whole analogy of things is against such a supposition. We have no evidence, it declares, that one of all the millions who have died has lived beyond the grave. In sickness and old age, it is said, the body and soul seem alike to grow feeble and decay, and both soon to expire together. That they ever exist separate, it is said, has not been proved. That such a dissolution and separate existence should take place is affirmed to be contrary to the analogy of all other things. That the soul and body should be united again, and constitute a *single* being, is said to be without a parallel fact in other things to divest it of its inherent improbability.

Now let us suppose for a moment, that, endued with our present powers of thought, we had been united to bodies of far feebler frame, and much more slender dimensions, than we now inhabit. Suppose that our spirits had been doomed to inhabit the body of a crawling reptile, scarce an inch in length, prone on the earth, and doomed to draw out its little length to obtain locomotion from day to day, and scarce noticeable by the mighty beings above it. Suppose in that lowly condition, as we contemplated the certainty of our speedy dissolution, we should look upon our kindred reptiles, the partners of our cares, and should see their strength gradually waste, their faculties grow dim, their bodies become chill in death. Suppose now that it should be revealed to us that those bodies would undergo a transformation; that at no great distance of time they would start up into new being; that in their narrow graves there would be seen the evidence of returning life; and that these same deformed, prone, and decaying frames would be clothed with the beauty of gaudy colours, be instinct with life, leave the earth, soar at pleasure in a new element, take their rank in a new order of beings, be divested of all that was offensive and loathsome in their old abode in the eyes of other beings, and be completely dissociated from all the plans, habits, relations, and feelings of their former lowly condition. We ask whether against this supposition there would not lie all the objections which have ever been alleged against the doctrine of a resurrection and a future state? Yet the world has long been familiar with changes of this character. The changes which animal nature undergoes to produce the gay colours of the butterfly have as much antecedent improbability as those pertaining to the predicted resurrection, and, for aught that we can see, are improbabilities of precisely the same nature. So in a case still more in point. No two states which revelation has presented, as actually contemplated in the condition of man, are more unlike than those of an unborn infant and of a hoary man ripe with wisdom and honours. So far as appears, the state of the embryo, and that of Newton, Locke, and Bacon, in their mature powers, have, at least, as much dissimilarity as those between man here and man in a future state. Grant that a revelation could be made to such an embryo, and it would be attended with all the difficulties that are supposed to attend the doctrine of revelation. That this unformed being should leave the element in which it commences its existence; that it should be ushered in another element with powers precisely adjusted to its new state, and useless in its first abode—like the eye, the ear, the hand, the foot; that it should assume relations to hundreds and thousands of other beings at first unknown, and these, too, living in what, to the embryo, must be esteemed a different world; that it should be capable of traversing seas, of measuring the distances of stars, of gauging the dimensions of suns; that it could calculate with unerring certainty the conjunctions and oppositions, the transits and altitudes of the vast wheeling orbs of immensity, —is as improbable as any change which man, under the guidance of revelation, has yet expected in his most sanguine moments. Yet nothing is more familiar to us. So the analogy might be run through all the changes which animals and vegetables exhibit; nor has the infidel a right to reject the revelations of Christianity respecting a future state, until he has disposed of facts of precisely the same nature with which our world abounds.

But are we under a moral government? Admitting the probability of a future state, is the plan on which the world is actually administered one which will be likely to affect our condition there? Is there any reason to believe, from the analogy of things, that the affairs of the universe will ever, in some future condition, settle down into permanency and order? That this is the doctrine of Christianity none can deny. It is a matter of clear revelation; indeed, it is the entire basis and structure of the scheme, that the affairs of justice and of law are under suspense; that "judgment now lingereth and damnation slumbereth;" that crime is, for the present, dissociated from wo, for a specific purpose, viz. that mortals may repent and be forgiven; and that there will come a day when the native indissoluble connection between sin and suffering will be restored, and that they will then travel on hand in hand forever. This is the essence of Christianity, and it is a most interesting inquiry, whether any thing like this can be found in the actual government of the world.

Now it cannot be denied that, on this subject, we are thrown into a most remarkable, a chaotic mass of facts. The world is so full of irregularity—the lives of wicked men are so often peaceful and triumphant—virtue so often pines neglected in the vale of obscurity, or weeps and groans under the iron hand of the oppressor, that it appals men in all their attempts to reduce the system to order. Rewards and punishments are so often apparently capricious, that there is presumptive proof, in the mind of the infidel, that it will always continue so to be. And yet what if, amid all this apparent disorder, there should be found the elements of a grand and glorious system, soon to rise on its ruins? What if, amid all the triumphs of vice, there should still be found evidence to prove that God works by an unseen power, but most effectually, in sending judicial inflictions on men even now? And what if, amid these ruins, there is still to be found evidence that God rewards virtue even here, and is preparing for it more appropriate rewards hereafter—like the parts of a beautiful temple strewed and scattered in the ruins of some ancient city, but which, if again placed together, would be symmetrical, harmonious, and grand?

Christianity proceeds on the supposition that such is the fact; and, amid all the wreck of human things, we can still discover certain fixed results of human conduct. The consequences of an action do not terminate with the commission of the act itself, or with the immediate effect of that act on the body. They travel over into future results, and strike on some other, often some distant part of our earthly existence. Frequently the true effect of the act is not seen except *beyond* some result that may be considered as the accidental one: though for the *sake* of that *immediate* effect the act may have been performed. This is strikingly the case in the worst forms of vice. The immediate effect, for example, of intemperance is a certain pleasurable sensation, for the sake of which the man became intoxicated. The true effect, or the effect as *part of moral government*, travels *beyond* that temporary delirium, and is seen in the loss of health, character, and peace; perhaps not terminating in its consequences during the whole future progress of the victim. So the direct result of profligacy may be the gratification of passion; of avarice, the pleasurable indulgence of a grovelling propensity; of ambition, the glow of feeling in splendid achievements, or the grandeur and pomp of the monarch or the warrior; of duelling, a pleasurable sensation that revenge has been taken for insult. But do the consequences of these deeds terminate here? If they did, we should doubt the moral government of God. But in regard to their ultimate effects, the universe furnishes but one lesson. The consequences of these deeds travel over in advance of this pleasure, and fix themselves deep, beyond human power to eradicate them, in the property, health, reputation, or peace of the man of guilt; nay, perhaps the consequences thicken until we take our *last* view of him as he gasps in death, and all that we know of him, as he goes from our observation, is that heavier thunderbolts are seen trembling in the hand of God, and pointing their vengeance at the head of the dying man. What infidel can prove that some of the results, at least, of that crime, may not travel on to meet him in his future being, and beset his goings there?

Further, as a *general* law, the virtuous are prospered, and the wicked punished. Society is organized for this. Laws are made for this. The entire community throws its arms around the man of virtue; and, in like manner, the entire community, by its laws, gathers around the transgressor. Let a man attempt to commit a crime, and, before the act is committed, he may meet with fifty evidences that he is doing that which will involve him in ruin. He must struggle with his conscience. He must contend with what he knows to have been the uniform judgment of men. He must keep himself from the eye of justice. He must overcome all the proofs which have been set up that men approve of virtue. He must shun the presence of every man,—for, from that moment, every member of the community becomes, of course, his enemy. He must assume disguises to secure him from the eye of justice. He must work his way through the community, during the rest of his life, with the continued consciousness of crime; eluding by arts the officers of the law, fearful of detection at every step, and never certain that, at some unexpected moment, his crime may not be revealed, and the heavy arm of justice fall on his guilty head. Now all this proves that in *his* view he is under a moral government. How knows he that the same system of things may not meet him hereafter, and that in some future world the hand of justice may not reach him? The fact is sufficiently universal to be a proper ground of action, that virtue meets with its appropriate reward, and that vice is appropriately punished. So universal is this fact, that more than nine-tenths of all the world have confidently acted on its belief. The young man expects that industry and sobriety will be recompensed in the healthfulness, peace, and honour of a venerable old age. The votary of ambition expects to climb the steep "where fame's proud temple shines afar," and to enjoy the rewards of office or fame. And so uniform is the administration of the world in this respect, that the success of one generation lays the ground for the confident anticipations of another. So it has been from the beginning of time, and so it will be to the end of the world. We ask why should not man, with equal reason, suppose that his conduct now may affect his destiny at the next moment or the next year beyond his death? Is there any violation of reason in supposing that the soul may be active there, and meet there the results of conduct here? Can it be proved that death suspends or annihilates existence? Unless it can, the man who acts in his youth with reference to his happiness at eighty years of age, is acting most unwisely if he does not extend his thoughts to the hundredth or the thousandth year of his being.

What if it should be found, as the infidel cannot deny it *may be*, that death suspends not existence so much as one night's sleep? At the close of each day we see the powers of man prostrate. Weakness and lassitude come over all the frame. A torpor, elsewhere unknown in the history of animal nature, spreads through all the faculties. The eyes close, the ears become deaf to hearing, the palate to taste, the skin to touch, the nostrils to smell. All the faculties are locked in entire insensibility, alike strangers to the charms of music, the tones of friendship, the beauties of creation, the luxury of the banquet, and the voice of revelry. The last indication of *mind* is apparently gone, or the indications of its existence are far feebler than when we see man *die* in the full exertion of his mental powers, sympathizing in the feelings of friendship, and cheered by the hopes of religion. Yet God passes his hand over the frame when we sleep, and, instinct with life, again we rise to business, to pleasure, or to ambition. But what are the facts which meet us as the result of the doings of yesterday? Have we lost our hold on those actions? The man of industry yesterday, sees, to-day, his fields waving in the sun, rich with a luxuriant harvest. The professional man of business finds his doors crowded, his ways thronged, and multitudes awaiting his aid in law, in medicine, or in the arts. The man of virtue yesterday, reaps the reward of it to-day, in the respect and confidence of mankind, in the peace of an approving conscience, and the smiles of God. The man of intemperate living rises to nausea, retching, pain, and wo. Poverty, this morning, clothes in rags the body of him who was idle yesterday; and disease clings to the goings, and fixes itself in the blood of him who was dissipated. Who can tell but death shall be *less* a suspension of existence than this night's sleep? Who can tell but that the consequences of our doings here shall travel over our sleep in the tomb, and greet us in our waking in some new abode? Why should they not? Why should God appoint a law so wise and so universal here, that is to fail the moment we pass to some other part of our being?*

Nor are the results of crime confined to the *place* where the act was committed. Sin, in youth, may lay the foundation of a disease that shall complete its work on the other side of the globe. An early career of dissipation in America may fix in the frame the elements of a disorder that shall complete its work in the splendid capital of the French, or, it may be, in the sands of the Equator or the snows of Siberia. If crime may thus travel in its results around the globe; if it may reach out its withering hand over seas, and mountains, and continents, and seek out its fleeing victim in the solitary waste, or in the dark night,—we see not why it may not be stretched across the grave, and meet the victim there: at least we think the analogy should make the transgressor tremble, and turn pale as he flies to eternity.

But it is still objected that the rewards given to virtue and the pain inflicted on vice are not universal, and that there is not, therefore, the proof that was to have been expected that they will be hereafter. Here we remark that it is evidently not the design of religion to affirm that the *entire* system can be seen in our world. We say that the system is not fully developed, and that there is, therefore, presumptive proof that there *is* another state of things. Every one must have been struck with the fact, that human affairs are cut off in the midst of their way, and their completion removed to some other world. No earthly system or plan has been carried out to its full extent. There is no proof that we have *ever* seen

---

* ὕπνῳ κασιγνήτῳ θανάτοιο.

Iliad, Ξ. 231.

the full result of any given system of conduct. We see the effect of vice as far as the structure of the *body* will allow. We see it prostrate the frame, produce disease, and terminate in death. We see the effect on body and mind alike, until we lose our sight of the man in the grave. There our observation stops. But who can tell what the effect of intemperance, for example, would be in this world, if the body were adjusted to bear its results a little longer? Who can calculate with what accelerated progress the consequences would thicken beyond the time when we now cease to observe them? And who can affirm that the same results may not await the mind hereafter? Again we ask the infidel why they should not? *He* is bound to tell us. The presumption is against him.

Beside, the effect of vice is often arrested in its first stage. A young man suddenly dies. For some purpose, unseen to human eyes, the guilty man is arrested in his career, and the *effect* of his crimes is removed into eternity. Why is this more improbable than that the irregularities of youth should run on, and find their earthly completion in the wretchedness and poverty of a dishonoured old age? So virtue is often arrested. The young man of promise, of talent, and of piety dies. The completion of the scheme is arrested. The rewards are dispensed in another world. So says religion. And can the infidel tell us why they should *not* be dispensed there, as well as in the ripe honours of virtuous manhood? This is a question which infidelity *must* answer.

The same remarks are as applicable to communities as to individuals. It is to be remembered here that virtue has never had a full and impartial trial. The *proper* effect of virtue here would be seen in a perfectly pure community. Let us suppose such an organization of society. Imagine a community of virtuous men, where the most worthy citizens should always be elected to office; where affairs should be suffered to flow on far enough to give the system a complete trial; where vice, corruption, flattery, bribes, and the arts of office-seeking should be unknown; where intemperance, gluttony, lust, and dishonest gains should be shut out by the laws and by the moral sense of the commonwealth; where industry and sobriety should universally prevail and be honoured. Is there any difficulty in seeing that, if this system were to prevail for many ages, the nation would be signally prosperous, and gain a wide dominion? And suppose, on the other hand, a community made up on the model of the New Harmony plan, the asylum of the idle, of the unprincipled and the profligate. Suppose that the men of the greatest physical power and most vice should rule, as they infallibly would do; suppose there was no law, but the single precept enjoining universal indulgence; and suppose that under some miraculous and terrible binding together, by divine pressure, this community should be kept from falling to pieces or destroying itself for a few ages, is there any difficulty in seeing what would be the proper effect of crime? Indeed we deem it happy for the world that *one* founder of such a community has been permitted to live to make the experiment on a small scale, and but *one*, lest the record of total profligacy and corruption should not be confined to the singularly-named *New Harmony*. All this proves there is something either in the framework of society itself, or in the agency of some Great Being presiding over human things, that smiles on virtue and frowns on vice. In other words, there is a moral government.

It is further to be remarked, that, as far as the experiment has been suffered to go on in the world, it has been attended with a uniform result. Nations are suffered to advance in wickedness until they reach the point in the universal constitution of things that is attended with self-destruction. So fell Gomorrah, Babylon, Athens, Rome,—expiring, just as the drunkard does, by excess of crime, or by enervating their strength in luxury and vice. The body politic, enfeebled by corruption, is not able to sustain the incumbent load, and sinks, like the human frame, in ruin. So has perished every nation, from the vast dominions of Alexander the Macedonian, to the mighty empire of Napoleon, that has been reared in lands wet with the blood of the slain, and on the pressed and manacled liberties of man. In national, as well as in private affairs, the powers of doing evil soon exhaust themselves. The frame in which they act is not equal to the mighty pressure, and the nation or the individual sinks to ruin. Like some tremendous engine of many wheels and complicated machinery, when the balance is removed, and it is suffered to waste its powers in self-propulsion, without checks or guides, the tremendous energy works its own ruin, rends the machine in pieces, and scatters its rolling and flying wheels in a thousand directions. Such is the frame of society, and such the frame of an individual. So, if God gave up the world to unrestrained evil, it would accomplish its own perdition. We see in every human frame, and in the mingled and clashing powers of every society, the elements of ruin; and all that is necessary to secure that ruin is to remove the pressure of the hand that now restrains the wild and terrific powers, and saves the world from self-destruction. So, if virtue had a fair trial, it would be as complete in its results. In heaven it will secure its own rewards; like the machine which we have supposed, *always* harmonious in its movements. So in hell there will be the elements of universal misrule, and all the foreign force that will be necessary to secure eternal misery will be Almighty power to preserve the terrible powers in unrestrained being, and to press them into the same mighty prison-house; just like some adamantine enclosure that should keep the engine together, and fix the locality of its tremendous operations.

Long ago it had passed into a proverb, "that murder will out." This is just an illustration of what we are supposing. Let a murderer live long enough, and such is the organization of society, that vengeance will find him out. Such, we suppose, would be the case in regard to *all* crime, if sufficient permanency were given to the affairs of men, and if things were not arrested in the midst of their way. Results *in eternity*, we suppose, are but the *transfer to another state* of results which would take place here if the guilty were not removed. We ask the infidel, we ask the Universalist, why this state of things should be arrested by so unimportant a circumstance as death? Here is a uniform system of things—uniform as far as the eye can run it backward into past generations—uniform, so as to become the foundation of laws and of the entire conduct of the world—and uniform, so far as the eye can trace the results of conduct *forward* in all the landmarks set up along our future course. Unless God change, and the affairs of other worlds are administered on principles different from *ours*, it must be that this system will receive its appropriate termination *there*. It belongs to the infidel and the Universalist to prove that the affairs of the universe come to a solemn pause at death; that we are ushered into a world of different laws and different principles of government; that we pass under a new sceptre—a sceptre, too, not of *justice*, but of disorder, misrule, and the arrest of all that God has begun in his administration; that the *results* of conduct, manifestly but just commenced here, are finally arrested by some strange and unknown principle at our death; and that we are to pass to a world of which we know nothing, and in which we have no means of conjecturing what will be the treatment which crime and virtue will receive. We ask them, can they *demonstrate* this strange theory? Are men willing to risk their eternal welfare on the presumption *that God will be a different being there from what he is here, and that the conduct which meets with wo here will there meet with bliss?* Why not rather suppose, as Christianity does, according to all the analogy of things, that the same almighty hand shall be stretched across all worlds alike, and that the bolts which vibrate in His hand now, and point their thunders at the head of the guilty, shall fall with tremendous weight there, and close in eternal life and death the scenes begun on earth? We know of no men who are acting under so fearful probabilities that their views are false, as those who deny the doctrine that crime will meet with its appropriate reward in the future world. Here is a long array of uniform facts; all, as we understand them, founded on the presumption that the scheme of the infidel cannot be true. The system is continued through all the revolutions to which men are subject. Conduct, in its results, travels over all the interruptions of sleep, sickness, absence, delirium, that man meets with, and passes on from age to age. The conduct of yesterday terminates in results to-day; that of youth extends into old age; that of health, reaches *beyond* a season of sickness; that of sanity, *beyond* a state of delirium. Crime here meets its punishment, it may be, after we have crossed oceans, and snows, and sands, in some other part of the globe. Far from country and home, in lands of strangers where no eye may recognise or pity us but that of the unseen witness of our actions, it follows us in remorse of conscience, or in the judgments of the storm, the siroc, or the ocean. We are amazed that it should be thought that death will arrest this course of things, and that the mere act of crossing that narrow vale will do for us what the passage from yesterday to to-day, from youth to age, from the land of our birth to the land of strangers and of solitudes, can never do. Guilty man carries the elements of his own perdition within him; and it matters little whether he be in society or in solitude, in this world or the next, the inward fires will burn, and the sea, and the dry land, and the burning climes of hell, will send forth their curses to greet the wretched being who has dared to violate the laws of the unseen God, and to "hail" him as the "new possessor" of the "profoundest hell."

But the infidel still objects that all this is mere probability, and that, in concerns so vast, it is unreasonable to act without demonstration. We reply, that in few of the concerns of life do men act from demonstration. The farmer sows with the *probability* only that he will reap. The scholar toils with the probability, often a slender one, that his life will be prolonged, and that success will crown his labours in subsequent life. The merchant commits his treasures to the ocean—embarks, perhaps, all he has on the bosom of the deep—under the probability that propitious gales will waft the riches of the Indies into port. Under this probability, and this only, the ambitious man pants for glory; the votary of pleasure presses to the scene of dissipation; the youth, the virgin, the man of middle life, and he of hoary hairs, alike crowd round the scenes of honour, of vanity, and of gain. Nay more, some of the noblest qualities of the soul are brought forth only on the strength of probabilities that appear slight to less daring spirits. In the eye of his countrymen, few things were more improbable than that Columbus would survive the dangers of the deep, and land on the shores of a new hemisphere. Nothing appeared more absurd than his reasonings, nothing more chimerical than his plans. Yet, under the pressure of proof that satisfied his own mind, he braved the dangers of an untraversed ocean, and bent his course to regions whose existence was as far from the belief of the old world as that of heaven is from the faith of the infidel. Nor could the unbelieving Spaniard deny, that under the pressure of the *probability* of the existence of a western continent, some of the highest qualities of mind that the earth has seen were exhibited by the Genoese navigator; just as the infidel must admit that some of the most firm and noble expressions of soul have come from the enterprise of gaining a heaven and a home beyond the stormy and untravelled ocean on which the Christian launches his bark in discovery of a new world. We might add also, here, the names of Bruce, of Wallace, of Tell, of Washington. We might remark how they commenced the great enterprises whose triumphant completion has given immortality to their names, under the power of a probability that their efforts would be successful. We might remark how many *more* clouds of doubt and obscurity clustered around their enterprises than have ever darkened the Christian's path to heaven, and how the grandest displays of patriotism and prowess that the world has known have grown out of the hazardous design of rescuing Scotland, Switzerland, and America from slavery. But we shall only observe that there was just enough probability of success in these cases to try these men's souls; just as there is probability enough of heaven and hell to try the souls of infidels and of Christians, to bring out their true character, and answer the great ends of moral government.

But here the infidel acts on the very principle which he condemns. He has not *demonstrated* that his system is true. From the nature of the system he cannot do it. He acts, then, on a *probability* that his system *may* prove to be true. And were the subject one *less serious* than eternity, it might be amusing to look at the nature of these probabilities. His system assumes it as probable that men will not be rewarded according to their deeds; that Christianity will turn out to be false; that it will appear that no such person as Jesus lived, or that it will yet be proved that he was an impostor; that twelve men were deceived in so plain a case as that which related to the death and resurrection of an intimate friend; that they conspired to impose on men, without reward, contrary to all the acknowledged principles of human action, and when they could reap nothing for their imposture but stripes, contempt, and death; that religion did not early spread over the Roman empire; that the facts of the New Testament are falsehood, and, of course, that all the contemporaneous confirmations of these facts, collected by the indefatigable Lardner, were false also; that the Jews occupy their place in the nations by chance, and exist in a manner contrary to that of all other people without reason; that all the predictions of their dispersion, of the coming of the Messiah, of the overthrow of Babylon, and Jerusalem, and Tyre, are conjectures, in which men, very barbarous men, conjectured exactly right, while thousands of the predictions of heathen oracles and statesmen have failed; that the remarkable fact should have happened that the most barbarous people should give to mankind the only intelligible notices of God, and that a dozen Galilean peasants should have devised a scheme of imposture to overthrow all the true and all the false systems of religion in the world. The infidel, moreover, deems it probable that there is no God; or that death is an eternal sleep; or that we have no souls; or that man is but an improved and educated ape; or that all virtue is vain, and that all vice stands on the same level, and may be committed at any man's pleasure; or that man's wisdom is to disregard the future, and live to eat and drink and die; and all this, too, when his conscience tells him there *is* a God, when he *does* act for the future, and expects happiness or wo as the reward of virtue or vice; when he is palsied, as he looks at the grave, with fears of what is beyond, and turns pale in solitude as he looks onward to the bar of God. Now we hazard nothing in saying that the man who is compelled to act as the infidel is; who has all these probabilities to cheer him with the belief that infidelity is true, and this when it has no system to recommend as truth, and when it stands opposed to all the analogy of things,—is engaged in a most singular employment, when he denounces men for acting on the probability that there is a heaven, a God, a Saviour, and a hell. It seems to us that there is nothing more at war with all the noble and pure feelings of the soul than this attempt to "swing man from his moorings," and send him adrift on wild and tumultuous seas, with only the *infidel's* probability that he will ever reach a haven of rest. It is launching into an ocean, without a belief that there *is* an ocean; and weathering storms, without professing to believe that there *may be* storms; and seeking a port of peace, without believing that there *is* such a port; and acting daily with reference to the future, at the same time that all is pronounced an absurdity. And when we see all this, we ask instinctively, can this be man? Or is this being right, after all, in the belief that he is only a semi-barbarous ape, or a half-reclaimed man of the woods?

But we are gravely told, and with an air of great seeming wisdom, that all presumption and experience are against the miraculous facts in the New Testament. And it was, for some time, deemed proof of singular philosophical sagacity in Hume, that he made the discovery, and put it on record to enlighten mankind. For our own part, we think far more attention was bestowed on this sophistry than was required; and, but for the show of confident wisdom with which it was put forth, we think the argument of Campbell might have been spared. It might safely be admitted, we suppose, that all presumption and experience *were* against miracles before they were wrought:—and this is no more than saying that they were not wrought before they were. The plain matter of fact, apart from all laboured metaphysics, is, that there is a *presumption* against most facts until they actually take place, because, till that time, all experience was against them. Thus there were many presumptions against the existence of such a man as Julius Cæsar. No man would have ventured to predict that there *would* be such a man. There were a thousand probabilities that a man of that *name* would not live; as many that he would not cross the Rubicon; as many that he would not enslave his country; and as many that he would not be slain by the hand of such a man as Brutus; and all this was contrary to experience. So there were innumerable improbabilities in regard to the late Emperor of France. It was once contemplated, we are told, by a living poet who afterward wrote his life on a different plan, to produce a biography grounded on the *improbabilities* of his conduct, and showing how, in fact, all those improbabilities disappeared in the actual result. The world stood in amazement, indeed, for a few years at the singular grandeur of his movements. Men saw him ride, as the spirit of the storm, on the whirlwind of the revolution; and, like the spirit of the tempest, amazed and trembling nations knew not where his power would strike, or what city or state it would next sweep into ruin. But the world has since become familiar with the spectacle; men have seen that he was naturally engendered by the turbid elements; that he was the proper *creation* of the revolution; and that if *he* had not lived, some other master-spirit like him would have seized the direction of the tempest, and poured its desolations on bleeding and trembling Europe. So any great discovery in science or art is previously improbable, and contrary to experience. We have often amused ourselves with contemplating what would have been the effect on the mind of Archimedes, had he been told of the power of one of the most common elements—an element which men who see boiling water must always see:—its mighty energy in draining deep pits in the earth, in raising vast rocks of granite, in propelling vessels with a rapidity and beauty of which the ancients knew nothing, and in driving a thousand wheels in the minutest and most delicate works of art. To the ancient world all this was contrary to experience, and all presumption was against it,—as improbable, certainly, as that God should have power to raise the dead; and we doubt whether any evidence of divine revelation would have convinced mankind three thousand years ago, without the actual experiment, of what the school-boy may now know as a matter of sober and daily occurrence in the affairs of the world. So, not long since, the Copernican system of astronomy was so improbable, that, for maintaining it, Galileo endured the pains of the dungeon. All presumption and all experience, it was thought, were against it. Yet, by the discoveries of Newton, it has been made, to the great mass of mankind, devoid of all improbabilities, and children acquiesce in its reasonableness. So the Oriental king could not be persuaded that water could ever become hard. It was full of improbabilities, and contrary to all experience. The plain matter of fact is, that, in regard to all events in history, and all discoveries in science, and inventions in the mechanic arts, there may be said to be a presumption against their existence, just as there was in regard to miracles; and they are contrary to all experience until discovered, just as miracles are until performed. And, if this be all that infidelity has to affirm in the boasted argument of Hume, it seems to be ushering into the world, with very unnecessary pomp, a very plain truism—that a new fact in the world is contrary to all experience; and this is the same as saying that a thing is contrary to experience until it actually *is experienced.*

We have another remark to make on this subject. It relates to the *ease* with which the improbabilities of a case may be overcome by testimony. We doubt not that the wonders of the steam-power may be now credited by all mankind, and we, who have seen its application in so many forms, easily believe that it may accomplish similar wonders in combinations which the world has not yet witnessed. The incredulity of the age of Galileo, on the subject of astronomy, has been overcome among millions who cannot trace the demonstrations of Newton, and who, perhaps, have never heard his name. It is by *testimony* only that all this is done; and on the strength of this testimony man will hazard any worldly interest. He will circumnavigate the globe, not at all deterred by the fear that he may find, in distant seas or lands, different laws from those which the Copernican system supposes. We do not see why, in like manner, the improbabilities of religion may not vanish before testimony; and its high mysteries, in some advanced period of our existence, become as familiar to us as the common facts which are now the subjects of our daily observation. Nor can we see why the antecedent difficulties of religion may not as easily be removed by competent proof, as those which appalled the minds of men in the grandeur of the astronomical system, or the mighty power of the arts.

We wish here briefly to notice another difficulty of infidelity. It is, that it is altogether *improbable*, and against the analogy of things, that the Son of God, the equal of the Father of the universe, should stoop to the humiliating scenes of the mediation—should consent to be reviled, buffeted, and put to death. We answer, men are very incompetent judges of what a Divine Being may be willing to endure. Who would suppose, beforehand, that *God* would submit to blasphemy and rebuke? Yet what being has been ever more calumniated? Who has been the object of more scorn? What is the daily offering that goes up from the wide world to the Maker of all worlds? There is not a nation that does not daily send up a dense cloud of obscenity and profaneness as its offering.

Scarce a corner of a street can be turned but our ears are saluted with the sound of blasphemy—curses poured on Jehovah, on his Son, on his Spirit, on his creatures, on the material universe, on his law. To our minds, it is no more strange that the Son of God should bear reproach and pain with patience for thirty years, than that the God of creation should bear all this from age to age, and as an offering from the wide world. We have only to reflect on what the blasphemer *would* do if God should be imbodied, and reveal himself to the eye in a form so that human *hands* might reach him with nails, and spears, and mock diadems, to see an illustration of what they actually *did*, when his Son put himself in the power of blasphemers, and refused not to die. The history of the blasphemer has shown that, if he had the *power*, long ago the last gem in the Creator's crown would have been plucked away; his throne would have crumbled beneath him; his sceptre been wrested from his hand; and the God of creation, like his Son in redemption, would have been suspended on a "great central" cross! When we see the patience of God toward blasphemers, our minds are never staggered by any condescension in the Redeemer. We see something in the analogy so unlike what we see among men, that we are strongly confirmed in the belief that they are a part of one great system of things.

We have thus presented a *specimen* of the nature of the argument from analogy. Our design has been to excite to inquiry, and to lead our readers to cultivate a practical acquaintance with this great work. We deem it a work of *principles* in theology—a work to be appreciated only by those who think for themselves, and who are willing to be at the trouble of carrying out these *materials* for thought into a daily practical application to the thousand difficulties which beset the path of Christians in their own private reflections, in the facts which they encounter, and in the inuendoes, jibes, and blasphemies of infidels. We know, indeed, that the argument is calculated to *silence* rather than *convince*. In our view, this is what, on this subject, is principally needed. The question, in our minds, is rather, whether we *may* believe there is a future state, than whether we *must*. Sufficient for mortals, we think is it, in their wanderings, their crimes, and their sorrows, if they *may* believe there is a place where the wicked cease from troubling and the weary may be forever at rest; and if the thousand shades of doubt on that subject which thicken on the path of man, and which assume a deeper hue by infidel arts, *may be* removed. We ask only the *privilege* of believing that there is a world of purity; that the troubled elements of our chaotic abode *may* settle down into rest; and that from the heavings of this moving sea there may arise a fair moral system, complete in all its parts, where God shall be all in all, and where all creatures may admire the beauty of his moral character, and the grandeur of his sovereign control. We watch the progress of this system much as we may suppose a spectator would have watched the process of the first creation. At first, this now solid globe was a wild chaotic mass. Darkness and commotion were there. There was a vast heaving deep, a boundless commingling of elements, a dismal terrific wild. Who, in looking on that moving mass, would have found evidence that the beauty of Eden would so soon start up on its surface, and the fair proportions of our hills, and vales, and streams, would rise to give support to millions of animated and happy beings? And with what intensity would the observer behold the light bursting on chaos, the rush of waters to their deep caverns, the uprising of the hills clothed with verdure, inviting to life and felicity! With what beauty would appear the millions sporting with their new-created life in their proper elements! Myriads in the heaving ocean and gushing streams—myriads melodious in the groves—myriads joyful on a thousand hills and in a thousand vales. How grand the completion of the system! man, lord of all, clothed with power over the bursting millions; the *priest* of this new creation, rendering homage to its Great Sovereign Lord, and "extolling him first, him midst, and him without end." Like beauty and grandeur, we expect, will come out of this deranged moral system. Our eye loves to trace its development. With tears we look back on "Paradise Lost;" with exultation we trace the unfolding elements of a process that shall soon exhibit the beauty and grandeur of "Paradise Regained."

There is still a most important part of the subject untouched—the analogy of the Christian scheme, as we understand it, to the course of nature, and the fact that all the objections urged against *Calvinism* lie against the actual order of events. This part of the argument Butler has not touched. To this we propose now to call the attention of our readers—in some respects the most interesting and important part of "the analogy of religion, natural and revealed, to the constitution and course of nature."

Thus far we have had our eye fixed on the infidel. We wish now to direct our attention to the opponents of what we consider the Christian scheme, and inquire whether Butler has not furnished us materials to annihilate every objection against what are called the doctrines of grace. We say *materials*, for we are well aware that Butler did not complete the argument. We suppose, that had his object been to carry it to its utmost extent, there were two important causes which would have arrested its progress where it actually has stopped. The first is found in Butler's own views of the Christian scheme. We are not calling in question his piety, but we have not seen evidence that he had himself fully embraced the evangelical system, and applied his argument to the peculiar doctrines of the gospel. We fear that he stopped short of such a result in his own feelings, and that this may have been the reason why that system had not a more prominent place in his work. Still we would not apply the language of severe criticism to this deficiency in the Analogy. We know his design. It was to meet the infidelity of an age of peculiar thoughtlessness and vice. He did it. He reared an argument which infidels have thought it most prudent *to let alone.* They have made new attacks in other modes. Driven from this field, they have yielded it into the hands of Butler,—and their wisdom has consisted in withdrawing as silently as possible from the field, and losing the recollection both of the din of conflict and the shame of defeat. It has always been one of the arts of infidelity and error, to *forget* the scene of previous conflict and overthrow. Singular adroitness is manifested in keeping from the public eye the *fact,* and the monuments of such disastrous encounters. Thus Butler stands as grand and solitary as a pyramid of Egypt, and we might add, nearly as much forsaken by those for whose benefit he wrote. And thus Edwards on the Will is *conveniently* forgotten by hosts of Arminians, who continue to urge their arguments with as much self-gratulation, as though previous hosts of Arminians had never been prostrated by his mighty arm. Could we awaken the unpleasant reminiscence in the infidels of our age, that there was such a man as Butler, and in the opposers of the doctrines of grace, that there is extant in the English language such a book as "A Careful Inquiry into the Modern prevailing Notions on the Freedom of the Will," we should do more, perhaps, than by any one means to disturb the equanimity of multitudes, who live only to deal out dogmas as if they had never been confuted; and we might hope to arrest the progress of those destructive errors which are spreading in a thousand channels through the land.

The other cause of the deficiency which we notice in the Analogy is, that it was not possible for Butler, with the statements then made of the doctrines of grace, to carry out his argument, and give it its true bearing on those doctrines. The philosophical principles on which Calvinism had been defended for a century and a half were substantially those of the schoolmen. The system had started out from darker ages of the world; had been connected with minds of singular strength and power, but also with traits in some degree stern and forbidding. Men had been thrown into desperate mental conflict. They had struggled for mental and civil freedom. They had but little leisure, and less inclination to polish and adorn—to go into an investigation of the true laws of the mind, and the proper explanation of facts in the moral world—little inclination to look on what was bland and amiable in the government of God. Hence they took the rough-cast system, wielded in its defence the ponderous weapons which Augustine and even the Jansenites had furnished them, and prevailed in the conflict, not, however, by the force of their philosophy, but of those decisive declarations of the word of God, with which unhappily that philosophy had become identified. But when they told of imputing the sin of one man to another, and of holding that other to be *personally answerable* for it, it is no wonder that such minds as that of Butler recoiled, for there is nothing like this in nature. When they affirmed that men have no power to do the will of God, and yet will be damned for not doing what they have no capacity to perform, it is no wonder that he started back, and refused to attempt to find an analogy; for it is unlike the common sense of men. When they told of a limited atonement—of confining the original applicability of the blood of Christ to the elect alone, there *was* no analogy to this, in all the dealings of God toward sinners; in the sunbeam, in the dew, in the rain, in running rivulets or oceans; and here Butler must stop, for the analogy could go no farther upon the then prevalent notions of theology.

Still we record, with gratitude, the achievements of Butler. We render our humble tribute of thanksgiving to God that he raised up a man who has laid the foundation of an argument which *can* be applied to every feature of the Christian scheme.

We are not Hutchinsonians, but we believe there is a course of nature most strikingly analogous to the doctrines of revelation. We believe that all the objections which have been urged against the peculiar doctrines of the Christian scheme, lie with equal weight against the course of nature itself, and, therefore, really constitute no objections at all. This point of the argument Butler has omitted. To a contemplation of the outline of it we now ask the attention of our readers.

We are accustomed, in our ordinary technical theology, to speak much of the *doctrines* of Christianity; and men of system-making minds have talked of them so long, that they seem to understand, by them, a sort of intangible and abstract array of propositions, remote from real life and from plain matter of fact. The learner in divinity is often told that there is a species of daring profaneness, in supposing that they are to be shaped to existing facts or to the actual operations of moral agents. All this is metaphysics, and the moment he dares to ask whether Turretin or Ridgeley had proper conceptions of the laws of the mind, of moral agency, or of *facts* in the universe, that moment the shades of all antiquity are summoned to come around the adventurous theologian, and charge him with a guilty departure from dogmas long held in the church.

Now, we confess, we have imbibed somewhat different notions of the *doctrines* of the Bible. We have been accustomed to regard the word as denoting only an authoritative *teaching* (διδαχή, Matt. vii. 28, compare v. 19, xxii. 33, 2 Tim. iv. 2, 9,) of what *actually exists in the universe.* We consider the whole system of doctrines as simply a statement of *facts.* The doctrine of the Trinity, for example, is a statement of a fact respecting the mode of God's existence. The fact is beyond any investigation of our own minds, and we receive the statement as it is. The doctrine of the mediation is a statement of facts respecting what Christ did, and taught, and suffered, as given by himself and his followers. So of depravity, so of election or predestination, so of perseverance, so of future happiness and wo. What, then, are the doctrines of Christianity? Simply staments of what *has been*, of what *is*, and what *will be* in the government of God. In this every thing is as far as possible from abstraction. There is as little abstraction, and, why may we not add, as little sacredness, in these facts—we mean sacredness to prevent inquiry into their true nature—as there is in the science of geology, the growth of a vegetable, or the operations of the human intellect. We may add, that in no way has systematic theology rendered more essential disservice to mankind, than in drawing out the life-blood from these great facts—unstringing the nerves, stiffening the muscles, and giving the fixedness of death to them, as the anatomist cuts up the human frame, removes all the elements of life, distends the arteries and veins with wax, and then places it in his room of preparations, as cold and repulsive as are some systems of technical divinity.

In the doctrines of Christianity, as given us in the Bible, we find nothing of this abstract and unreal character. The whole tenor of the Scriptures prepares us to demand that theology be invariably conformed to the laws of the mind and the actual economy of the moral and material universe. The changes which have taken place in orthodox systems of divinity since the era of the Reformation have been chiefly owing to the changes in the system of mental and moral science. Whenever that system shall be fully understood, and established on the immovable foundation of truth, all who love the Lord Jesus Christ in sincerity, will be of one mind in their *mode* of stating the doctrines of the gospel, as they already are in their spiritual feelings. *Till* then, all that can be done by the friends of truth will be to show, that the objections which are urged against the doctrines of grace, can be urged, with equal power, against all the facts in God's moral government.

From the beginning, formidable objections have been brought against what are called the Doctrines of Grace, or the Evangelical System, or Calvinism. These objections have seldom, if ever, been drawn from the Bible. Their strength has consisted in the alleged fact, that these doctrines are in opposition to the established principles by which God governs the world. We concede that there is just enough of apparent irregularity in those principles to make these objections plausible with the great mass of men, just as there was enough of irregularity and improbability in the Copernican system of astronomy, to make it for a long time liable to many and plausible objections. Certain appearances strongly favoured the old doctrine, that the sun, moon, and stars travelled, in marshalled hosts, around our insignificant orb, just as, in the Arminian system, certain appearances may seem to indicate that man is the centre of the system, and that God, and all the hosts of heaven, live and act chiefly to minister to his comfort. But it is *now* clear that all the proper facts in astronomy go to prove, that the earth is a small part of the plan, and to confirm the system of Copernicus. So we affirm that the Calvinistic scheme, despite all Arminian appearances, is the plan on which this world is actually governed; and that all the objections that have been urged against it are urged against facts that are fixed in the very nature of things. And we affirm that a mind which could take in *all* these facts, could make up the Calvinistic scheme without the aid of revelation, from the actual course of events; just as in the ruins of an ancient city the skilful architect can discern in the broken fragments, pillars of just dimensions, arches of proper proportions, and the remains of edifices of symmetry and grandeur.

In entering on this subject, however, we cannot but remark,

that the evangelical scheme is often held answerable for that which it did not originate. We mean that, when opposers approach the Christian system, they almost universally hold it responsible for the *fall*, as well as the *recovery* of man. They are not willing to consider that it is a scheme proposed to *remedy an existing state of evil.* Christianity did not plunge men into sin. It is the system by which men are to be recovered from wo—wo which would have existed to quite as great an extent, certainly, if the conception of the evangelical system had never entered the Divine mind. The theory and practice of medicine is not to be held answerable for the fact that man is subject to disease and death. It *finds* men thus subject; and all that can be justly required of the art is, that to which it makes pretensions, viz. that it can do *something* toward removing or alleviating human suffering. So in Christianity. That men are, *in fact*, in the midst of sin, suffering, and death, is undeniable. The doctrine is common to the deist, the atheist, and the Christian. For that Christianity is not answerable. It proposes a remedy, and that remedy is properly the Christian system. Still we shall not, in our present discussion, avail ourselves of this very obvious remark; but shall proceed to notice the objections to the entire series of revealed facts, as if they constituted one system:—and the rather as the evangelical system proposes a statement respecting the exact *extent* of the evil, which has an important bearing on the features of the remedy proposed.

1. The first fact, then, presented for our examination is *the fall of man.* The Scriptures affirm that a solitary act—an act in itself exceedingly unimportant—was the beginning of that long train of sin and wretchedness which has passed upon our world. Now, we acknowledge that to all the mystery and fearfulness of this fact our bosoms beat with a full response to that of the objector. *We* do not understand the reason of it; and what is of more consequence to us and to the objector, is,

that *an explanation of this mystery forms no part of the system of revelation.* The only inquiry at present before us, is, whether the fact in question is so separated from all other events, as to be expressly contradicted by the analogy of nature.

We know there has been a theory which affirms that we are *one* with Adam—that we so existed in his loins as to *act* with him—that our *wills* concurred with *his* will—that his action was strictly and properly ours—and that we are held answerable at the bar of justice for that deed, just as A. B. at fifty is responsible for the deed of A. B. at twelve. In other words, that the act of Adam involving us all in ruin, is taken out of all ordinary laws by which God governs the world, and made to stand by itself, as incapable of any illustration from analogy, and as mocking any attempt to defend it by reasoning. With this theory we confess we have no sympathy; and we shall dismiss it with saying, that, in our view, Christianity never teaches that men are responsible for any sin but their own; nor can they be guilty, or held liable to *punishment*, in the proper sense of that term, for conduct other than that which has grown out of their own wills. Indeed, we see not how, if it were a dogma of a pretended revelation that God might at pleasure, and by an arbitrary decree, make crime pass from one individual to another—striking onward from age to age, and reaching downward to "the last syllable of recorded time,"—punished in the original offender; re-punished in his children; and punished again and again, by infinite multiples, in countless ages and individuals—and all this judicial infliction, for a single act performed cycles of ages before the individuals lived, we see not how any evidence could shake our intrinsic belief that this is unjust and improbable. We confess we have imbibed other views of justice; and we believe that he who can find the head and members of this theory in the Bible, will have no difficulty in finding there any of the dogmas of the darkest night that ever settled on the church.

But that the *consequences* or *results* of an action may pass over from one individual to another, and affect the condition of unborn generations, we hold to be a doctrine of the sacred Scriptures, and to be fully sustained by the analogy of nature.* And no one who looks at the scriptural account of the fall and recovery of man, can doubt that it is a cardinal point in the system. We affirm that it is a doctrine fully sustained by the course of events around us. Indeed, the fact is so common, that we should be exhausting the patience of our readers by attempting to draw out formal instances. Who is ignorant of the progressive and descending doom of the drunkard? Who is a stranger to the common fact that his intemperance wastes the property which was necessary to save a wife and children from beggary; that his appetite may be the cause of his family's being despised, illiterate, and ruined; that the vices which follow in the train of his intemperance often encompass his offspring, and that they, too, are profane, unprincipled, idle, and loathsome? So of the murderer, the thief, the highwayman, the adulterer. The result of their conduct rarely terminates with themselves. They are lost to society, and their children are lost with them. Nor does the evil stop here. Not merely are the *external* circumstances of the child affected by the misdeeds of a parent, but there is often a dark suspicion resting upon his very soul; there is felt to be in him a hereditary presumptive tendency to crime, which can be removed only by a long course of virtuous con-

* Rom. v. 12–19; 1 Cor. xv. 21, 22, 49; Josh. vii. 24, 25; Ex. xvii. 16; 1 Sam. xv. 2, 3; Matt. xxiii. 35. This view is by no means confined to revelation. The ancient heathen long since observed it, and regarded it as the great principle on which the world was governed. Thus Hesiod says, "*πολλάκι καὶ ξύμπασα πόλις κακοῦ ανδρὸς ἐπαυροῦ.*" And Horace says, "Quicquid delirant reges plectuntur Achivi."

duct, and which even then the slightest circumstance re-excites. Is an illegitimate child to blame for the aberration of a mother? Yet who is ignorant of the fact that, in very few conditions of society, such a son is placed on a level with the issue of lawful wedlock? So the world over, we approach the son of the drunkard, the murderer, and the traitor, with all these terrible suspicions. The father's deeds shut our doors against him. Nor can he be raised to the level of his former state, but by a long course of purity and well-doing. Now in all these cases, we see a general course of things in divine providence corresponding in important respects to the case of Adam and his descendants. We do not deem the child guilty, or ill-deserving, *but society is so organized, and sin is so great an evil, that the proper effects cannot be seen, and the proper terror be infused into the mind to deter from it, without such an organization.* It is true, that these results do not take place with undeviating certainty. It is not *always* the case that the child of a drunkard is intemperate, idle, or illiterate, while it is always the case, that a descendant of Adam is a sinner. In the former case, there may be other laws of government to prevent the regular operations of the plan. In the latter, God has not seen fit wholly to interrupt the regular process in a single instance. Even when men are renewed—as the child of the drunkard may be removed from the regular curse of the parent's conduct—the renewed man still is imperfect, and still suffers pain and death.

But, we know, there is an appearance of much that is formidable in the difficulty, that a single act, and that a most unimportant one, should result in so many crimes and calamities. But the objection, as we have seen, lies against the course of nature as truly as against the revealed facts resulting from the connection of Adam and his descendants. To lessen the objection, we would further remark, that it is not the outward form of an action which determines its character and results. The blow which, in self-defence, strikes a highwayman to the earth, may have the same physical qualities as that which reached the heart of the venerable White of Salem. It is the *circumstances*, the attendants, the relations, the links that bind the deed to others, the motives, which determine the character of the action. Adam's act had this towering pre-eminence, that it was the *first* in the newly-created globe, and committed by the first of mortals; the prospective father of immense multitudes. In looking at it, then, we are to turn from the mere physical act, to run the eye along the conduct of his descendants, and to see if we can find any other deeds that shall be *first* in a series, and then to mark their results, and in them we shall find the proper analogy. Now it is evident, that here we shall find no other act that will have the same awful peculiarity as the deeds of our first father. But are there no acts that can be "set over against" this to illustrate its unhappy consequences? We look, then, at the deed of a man of high standing whose character has been blameless, and whose ancestry has been noble. We suppose him, in an evil moment, to listen to temptation, to fall into the wiles of the profligate, or even to become a traitor to his country. Now who does not see how the fact of this being the *first* and characteristic deed may entail deeper misery on his friends, and stain the escutcheon of his family with a broader and fouler blot? Or take an instance which approaches still nearer to the circumstances of our first parent's crime. One false step, the first in a before-virtuous female of honourable parentage, and high standing, spreads sackcloth and wo over entire families, and sends the curse prolonged far into advancing years. It needs no remark to show how much that deed may differ in its results, from any subsequent acts of profligacy in that individual. The *first* act has spread mourning throughout every circle of friends. Lost now to virtue, and disowned by friends, the subsequent conduct may be regarded *as in character*, and the results terminate only in the offending individual. It is impossible, here, not to recur to the melancholy case of Dr. Dodd. His crime differed not from other acts of forgery except in his circumstances. It was a *first* deed, the deed of a man of distinction, of supposed piety, of a pure and high profession, and the deed stood out with a dreadful pre-eminence in the eyes of the world; nor could the purity of his profession, nor the eloquence of Johnson, nor the voice of thirty thousand petitioners, nor the native compassion of George III., save him from the tremendous malediction of the law—a death as conspicuous as the offence was primary and eminent.

We think, from this peculiarity of a first offence, we can meet many of the objections which men allege against the doctrines of revelation on the subject. If further illustration were needed, we might speak of the opposite, and advert to the well-known fact, that a first distinguished act in a progenitor may result in the lasting good of those connected with him by the ties of kindred or of law. Who can reflect without emotion on the great deed by which Columbus discovered the Western world, and the glory it has shed on his family, and the interest which, in consequence of it, has arisen at the very name, and which we feel for any mortal that is connected with him? Who can remember without deep feeling the philanthropy of Howard, and the deathless lustre which his benevolence has thrown over his family and his name? Who thinks of the family of Washington without some deep emotion running back to the illustrious man whose glory has shed its radiance around Mount Vernon, around his family, around our capitol, and over all our battle fields, and all the millions of whom he was the constituted political father? There is a peculiarity in the great first deed which sheds a lustre on all which, by any laws of association, can be connected with it.

Compared with other deeds having, perhaps, the same physical dimensions, it is like the lustre of the sun diffusing his beams over all the planets, when contrasted with the borrowed, reflected rays of the moon which shines upon our little globe.

Now we think there is an analogy between these cases and that of Adam, because we think it is a fixed principle in moral as in natural legislation, that the same law is applicable to the same facts. We find a series of facts on the earth, and a similar series in the movement of the planets, and we have a single term to express the whole—gravitation. We deem it unphilosophical to suppose that nature is there, in the same facts, subjected to different laws from what passes before our own eyes. So when we find one uniform process in regard to moral conduct—when we find *results, consequences,* and not *crimes,* travelling from father to son, and holding on their unbroken way to distant ages, why should we hesitate to admit, that to a great extent, at least, the facts respecting Adam and his descendants fall under the same great law of Divine providence? We do not here deny, that there may have been beyond this a peculiarity in the case of Adam, which must be referred to the decisions of Divine wisdom, and justified on other principles than those of any known analogy. But we never can adopt that system which tramples on all the analogies which actually exist, and holds men to be personally *answerable,* and actually *punished* by a just God, for an act committed thousands of years before they were born. Such a doctrine is nowhere to be found in the Scriptures.

2. As the result of this act of Adam, Christianity affirms that man is depraved. It has marked the character and extent of this depravity, with a particularity which we wonder has ever been called into debate.* It affirms that man is by

* Rom. i. 21–32; iii. 10–19; v. 12; viii. 6, 7; Gen. viii. 21; Ps. xiv. 1–3; Eph. ii. 1–3; 1 John v. 19; John iii. 1–6.

nature destitute of holiness, and it is on the ground of this fact that the Christian scheme was necessary. There is one great principle running through the whole of this scheme, which renders it what it is, viz.—*the appointment of a Mediator.* It regards man as so fallen, and so helpless, that but for an extraordinary intervention—the appointment of some being that should interpose to save—it was impossible that any native elasticity in the human powers or will, or any device which human ingenuity might fall on, should raise him up, and restore him to the favour of God. Now the thing which most manifestly characterizes this system is the doctrine of *substitution*—or the fact that Jesus Christ lived for others, toiled for others, and died for others; or, in other words, that God bestows upon us pardon and life in consequence of what his Son has done and suffered in our stead.* The peculiarity which distinguishes this system from all others, is, that man does not approach his Maker *directly*, but only through the atonement of the Son of God.

Now in recurring to the analogy of nature, we have only to ask, whether calamities which are hastening to fall on us are ever put back by the intervention of another? Are there any cases in which either our own crimes or the manifest judgments of God are bringing ruin upon us, where that ruin is turned aside by the intervention of others? Now we at once cast our eyes backward to all the helpless and dangerous periods of our being. Did God come forth *directly* and protect us in the defenceless period of infancy? Who watched over the sleep of the cradle, and guarded us in sickness and helplessness? It was the tenderness of a mother bending over our slumbering childhood, foregoing sleep, and rest, and ease, and hailing toil and care that *we* might be defended.

---

* John i. 29; Eph. v. 2; 1 John ii. 2; iv. 10; Isa. liii. 4; Rom. iii. 24, 25; 2 Cor. v. 14; 1 Peter ii. 21.

Why, then, is it strange, when God thus ushers us into existence through the pain and toil of another, that he should convey the blessings of a higher existence by the groans and pangs of a higher mediator? God gives us knowledge. But does he come forth to teach us by inspiration, or guide us by his own hand to the fountains of wisdom? It is by years of patient toil in others, that we possess the elements of science, the principles of morals, the endowments of religion. He gives us food and raiment. Is the Great Parent of benevolence seen clothing us by his own hand, or ministering directly to our wants? Who makes provision for the sons and daughters of feebleness or gayety or idleness? Who but the care-worn and anxious father and mother, who toil that their offspring may receive these benefits from their hands? Why, then, may not the garments of salvation, and the manna of life, come through a higher mediator, and be the fruit of severer toil and sufferings? Heaven's highest, richest benefits are thus conveyed to the race through thousands of hands acting as *mediums* between man and God. It is thus, through the instrumentality of others, that the Great Giver of life breathes health into our bodies and vigour into our frames. And why should he not reach also the sick and weary *mind*—the soul languishing under a long and wretched disease, by the hand of a mediator? Why should he not kindle the glow of spiritual health on the wan cheek, and infuse celestial life into our veins, by Him who is the great physician of souls? The very earth, air, waters, are all channels for conveying blessings to us from God. Why, then, should the infidel stand back, and all sinners frown, when we claim the same thing in redemption, and affirm, that, in this great concern, "there is *one* mediator between God and man, the man Christ Jesus, who gave himself a ransom for all?"

But still it may be said, that this is not an *atonement*. We admit it. We maintain only that it vindicates the main principle of the atonement, and shows that it is according to a *general law*, that God imparts spiritual blessings to us through a mediator. What, we ask, is the precise objectionable point in the atonement, if it be not, that God aids us in our sins and woes, by the self-denial and sufferings of another? And we ask, whether there is any thing so peculiar in such a system, as to make it intrinsically absurd and incredible? Now we think there is nothing more universal and indisputable than a system of nature like this. God has made the whole animal world tributary to man. And it is by the toil and pain of creation that our wants are supplied, our appetites gratified, our bodies sustained, our sickness alleviated; that is, the impending evils of poverty, famine, or disease are put away by these substituted toils and privations. By the blood of patriots he gives us the blessings of liberty; that is, by *their* sufferings in our defence we are delivered from the miseries of rapine, murder, or slavery, which might have encompassed our dwellings. The toil of a father is the price by which a son is saved from ignorance, depravity, want, or death. The tears of a mother, and her long watchfulness, save from the perils of infancy, and an early death. Friend aids friend by toil; a parent foregoes rest for a child; and the patriot pours out his blood on the altars of freedom, that *others* may enjoy the blessings of liberty; that is, that others may not be doomed to slavery, want, and death.

Yet still it may be said, that we have not come, in the analogy, to the precise point of the atonement, in producing *reconciliation* with God by the sufferings of another. We ask, then, what is the Scripture account of the effect of the atonement in producing reconciliation? Man is justly exposed to suffering. He is guilty, and it is the righteous purpose of God that the guilty should suffer. God is *so* opposed to him, that he will inflict suffering on him unless by an atonement it is prevented. By the intervention of the atonement, therefore, the Scriptures affirm that such sufferings shall be averted. The man shall be saved from the impending calamity. Sufficient for all the purposes of justice, and of just government, has fallen on the substitute, and the sinner may be pardoned and reconciled to God. Now, we affirm, that in every instance of the substituted sufferings, or self-denial, of the parent, the patriot, or the benefactor, there occurs a state of things so analogous to this, as to show that it is in strict accordance with the just government of God, and to remove all the objections to the peculiarity of the atonement. Over a helpless babe—ushered into the world naked, feeble, speechless, there impends hunger, cold, sickness, sudden death—a mother's watchfulness averts these evils. Over a nation impend revolutions, sword, famine, and the pestilence. The blood of the patriot averts these, and the nation smiles in peace. Look at a particular instance. Xerxes poured his millions on the shores of Greece. The vast host darkened all the plains, and stretched towards the capitol. In the train there followed weeping, blood, conflagration, and the loss of liberty. Leonidas almost alone stood in his path. He fought. Who can calculate the effects of the valour and blood of that single man and his compatriots in averting calamities from Greece, and from other nations struggling in the cause of freedom? Who can tell how much of rapine, of cruelty, and of groans and tears it turned away from that nation?

Now we by no means affirm that this is *all* that is meant by an atonement as revealed by Christianity. We affirm only, that there is a sufficient similarity in the two cases, to remove the points of objection to an atonement made by the infidel,—to show that reconciliation by the offerings of another, or a putting away evils by the intervention of a mediator, is not a violation of the analogies of the natural and moral world. Indeed, we should have thought it an argument for the rejection of a system, if it had not contemplated the removal of evils by the toils and pains of substitution. We maintain that the system of the Unitarians, which denies all such substitution, is a violation of all the modes in which God has yet dispensed his blessings to men. In the nature of the case, there is all the antecedent presumption there *could* be, that, if God intended to confer saving blessings on mankind, it would be by the interposition of the toils, groans, and blood of a common mediating friend. The well-known case of the King of the Locrians, is only an instance of the way in which reconciliation is to be brought about among men. He made a law that the adulterer should be punished with the loss of his eyes. His son was the first offender. The feelings of the *father* and the justice of the *king* conflicted. Reconciliation was produced by suffering the loss of one eye himself, and inflicting the remainder of the penalty on his son.

But still, there are two points in the atonement so well substantiated, and yet apparently contradictory, that it becomes an interesting inquiry, whether *both* positions can find an analogy in the course of events. The first is, that the atonement was originally applicable to all men—that it was not limited by its nature to any class of men, or any particular individuals—that it was an offering made for the race,* and is, when made, in the widest and fullest sense, the property of man; and the second is, that it is actually applied to only a portion of the race, and that it was the purpose of God that it should be so applied.†

Now in regard to the first aspect of the atonement suggested, we can no more doubt that it had this original, uni-

---

* 2 Cor. v. 14, 15; 1 John ii. 2; Heb. ii. 9; John iii. 16, 17; vi. 51; 2 Peter ii. 1.

† Isa. liii. 10; John xvii. 2; Eph. i. 3–11; Rom. viii. 29, 30; ix. 15–24; John vi. 37, 39; 2 Tim. i. 9.

versal applicability, than we can any of the plainest propositions of the Bible. If this is not clear, nothing *can* be clear in the use of the Greek and English tongues—and we discern in this, we think, a strict accordance with the ordinary provisions which God has made for man. We look at any of his gifts—from the smallest that makes life comfortable, to the richest in redemption, and we shall not find one that *in its nature*, is limited in its applicability to any class of individuals. The sun on which we look sheds his rays on all—on all alike; the air we breathe has an original adaptation to all who may inhale it, and is ample for the want of any number of millions. From the light of the feeblest star, to full-orbed day; from the smallest dew-drop, to the mountain-torrent; from the blushing violet, to the far-scented magnolia; there is an original applicability of the gifts of Providence to all the race. They are fitted to *man as man*, and the grandeur of God's beneficence appears in spreading the earth with fruits and flowers, making it one wide garden, in place of the straitened Paradise that was lost. We might defy the most acute defender of the doctrine of limited atonement to produce an instance in the provisions of God, where there was a designed limitation in the nature of the thing. We shall be slow to believe that God has not a *uniform plan* in his mode of governing men.

But still it will be asked, what is the use of a universal atonement, if it is not actually applied to all? Does God work in vain? Or would he make a provision, in the dying groans of his Son, that was to be useless to the universe? We might say here, that in our view, there is no waste of this provision,—that the sufferings which were requisite for the race were only those which were demanded in behalf of a single individual; and that we are ignorant of the way of applying gauges and decimal admeasurements and pecuniary computations to a grand moral transaction. But we reply, that it is according to God's way of doing things that many of his provisions should appear to *us* to be vain. We see in this, the hand of the same God that pours the rays of noon-day on barren sands, and genial showers on desert rocks, where no man is—to *our* eye, though not to *his*, in vain. Who knows not that the sun sheds his daily beams on half the globe covered with trackless waters; and around thousands of dungeons where groans in darkness the prisoner? But some Solon or Cadmus may yet cross those oceans, to bear law and letters to the barbarian; some Howard to pity and relieve the sufferer; some Xavier or Vanderkemp to tell benighted men of the dying and risen Son of God. So we say of the atonement. It is *not* useless. Other ages shall open their eyes upon this Sun of righteousness; shall wash in this open fountain; shall pluck the fruit from this tree of life; shall apply for healing to the balm of Gilead, and find a physician there.

But still it was the purpose—the decree of God, that this atonement should be *actually* applied to but a part—we believe ultimately *a large part*—of the human family. By this we mean, that it is *in fact* so applied, and that *this fact* is the expression of the purpose or decree of God. So it is with all the objects we have mentioned. Food is not given to all. Health is not the inheritance of all. Liberty, peace, and wealth, are diffused unequally among men. We interpret the decrees of God, so far as we can do it, *by facts;* and we say that the actual *result*, by whatever means brought about, is the expression of the *design* of God. Nor can any man doubt that the dissemination of these blessings is to be traced to the ordering of God. Is it owing to any act of man, that the bark of Peru was so long unknown, or that the silver of Potosi slept for ages unseen by any human eye? Is there not evidence that it was according to the good pleasure of the giver, that the favour should not be bestowed on men till Columbus crossed the main, and laid open the treasures and the *materia medica* of the West, to an avaricious and an afflicted world? We are here struck with another important analogy *in the manner* in which God's plans are developed. Who would have imagined that so important a matter as the discovery of a new world, should have depended on the false reasonings and fancies of an obscure Genoese? Who would have thought that all the wealth of Potosi should have depended, for its discovery, on so unimportant a circumstance as an Indian's pulling up a shrub by accident in hunting a deer? So in the redemption of man—in the applicability of the atonement. Who is ignorant that the Reformation originated in the private thoughts of an obscure man in a monastery? A Latin Bible fallen on as accidentally, and a treasure as much unknown, as Hualpi's discovery of the mines of Potosi, led the way to the most glorious series of events since the days of the apostles.

But it is still said, that it is unreasonable for men to *suffer* in consequence of not being put in possession of the universal atonement; and that Christianity affirms there is no hope of salvation but in the Son of God.* So it does. But the affirmation is not that men are *guilty* for not being acquainted with that scheme, but that they lie under the curses of the *antecedent state* before mentioned, from which Christianity came to deliver. The Hindoo suffers and dies under the rage of a burning fever. The fault is not that he is ignorant of the virtues of quinine, nor is he punished for this ignorance of its healing qualities; but he is lying under the operation of the previous state of things, from which medicine contemplates his rescue. Half the world is shut out from benefits which they might enjoy by being made acquainted with the provisions for their help. Their sufferings are not a *punishment* for this want of knowledge. They are the operation of

* Acts iv. 12.

the system from which they might be delivered by the provisions made for their welfare. How much suffering might have been saved had Jenner lived a century earlier. Is it contrary, then, to the analogy of nature, to suppose that men may suffer in consequence of the want of the gospel, and even that in eternity they may continue under the operation of that *previous* state of things to which the gospel has never been applied to relieve them? He who opposes Christianity because it implies that man may suffer, if its healing balm is not applied, knows not what he says, nor whereof he affirms. He is scoffing at the analogy of the world, and calling in question the wisdom of all the provisions of God to aid suffering man.

3. On the ground of man's depravity, and of the necessity of an atonement for sin, the gospel declares that without a change of heart and life, none can be saved.* It affirms that contrition for past sins, and confidence in the Son of God, are indispensable for admission to heaven. Now we scarce know of any point on which men so reluctate as they do here. That so sudden, thorough, and permanent a revolution should be demanded, that it should be founded on things so unmeaning as repentance and faith, that all which man *can* enjoy or suffer forever, should result from a change like this, they deem a violation of every principle of justice. And yet, perhaps, there is no doctrine of revelation which is more strongly favoured by the analogy of nature. Can any one doubt that men often experience a sudden, and most important revolution of feeling and purpose? We refer not here to a change in religion, but in regard to the principles and the actions of common life. Who is ignorant that from infancy to old age, the mind passes through many revolutions—that as we leave the confines of one condition of our being, and advance to

* John iii. 3, 5, 36; Mark xvi. 16.

another, a change, an entire change, becomes indispensable, or the whole possibility of benefiting ourselves by the new condition is lost. He who carries with him into youth the playfulness and follies of childhood, who spends that season of his life in building houses with cards, or in trundling a hoop, is characterized by weakness, and *must* lose all the benefits appropriate to that new period of existence. He who goes into middle life with a "bosom that carries anger as the flint bears fire"—who has not suffered his passions to cool, and his mental frame to become fixed in the compactness of mature and vigorous life, gives a pledge that the bar, the bench, or the desk—the counting-room, the office, or the plough, have little demand for *his* services, and that his hopes will be forever blasted. The truth is, that at the beginning of each of these periods, there was a *change* demanded—that on that change depended all that followed in the next succeeding, perhaps in every succeeding period, and that when the change does not exist, the period is characterized by folly, indolence, ignominy, or vice. The same remark might be extended to old age, and to all the new circumstances in which men may be placed. We ask, then, why some revolutions similar *in results*—we mean not in nature—should not take place in reference to the passage from time to eternity?

But our argument is designed to bear on the great moral change called *regeneration*. Now no fact, we think, is more common than that men often undergo a complete transformation in their moral character. It would be difficult to meet, in the most casual and transitory manner, with any individual, who could not remark that his own life had been the subject of many similar revolutions, and that each change fixed the character of the subsequent period of his existence. At one period he was virtuous. Then temptation crossed his path, and the description which we would have given of him yesterday, would by no means suit him to-day. Or at one time, he was profligate, profane, unprincipled. By some process of which he could, perhaps, scarce give an account, he became a different man. It might have been gradual—the result of long thought,—of many resolutions, made and broken,—of many appeals, of much weeping, and of many efforts to break away from his companions. Now, what is important for us to remark is, that *this change* has given birth to a new course of life, has initiated him into a new companionship, and has *itself* fixed all the joys or sorrows of the coming period. Such revolutions in character seem like the journeyings of the Arabian, wandering he knows scarcely whither, without compass, comfort, or food, till in his progress he comes to a few spreading *oases* in the desert. His reaching this paradise in the wide waste of sand decides, of course, the nature of his enjoyments till he has crossed it, and secures a release from the perils of the burning desert. In human life, we have often marked an ascent to some such spot of living green; we have seen the profligate youth leaving the scene of dissipation, and treading with a light heart and quick step, the path of virtue, beside cool, living streams, and beneath refreshing bowers. Christianity affirms that a similar change is indispensable before man can tread the broad and peaceful plains of the skies. And it affirms that such a change will fix the condition of *all that new state of being*,—or, in other words, will secure an eternal abode beneath the tree of life, and fast by the river of God. We wait to learn, that in this, religion has made any strange or unreasonable demand.

It is a further difficulty in Christianity, that it should make such amazing bliss or wo dependant on things of apparently so little consequence as repentance and faith. We shall not here attempt to show the philosophy of this, or even to set up a vindication. We affirm only that man's whole condition in this life often depends on changes as minute, apparently as unphilosophical, and as unimportant. What is seemingly of less consequence in our view, when we tread the vale of years, than the change from infancy to childhood—and again to boyhood—and then even to manhood—a change from one unimportant object to another? What is often apparently a matter of less magnitude, than for a young man to withdraw from some haunt of pleasure—a thing requiring but little resolution; but it may be stretching in its results to all his coming life? A change of an opinion, or a habit, or a companion, may be often a most unimportant circumstance; and yet it may determine one's character for the entire life. It is recorded of Paley, one of the acutest and most powerful men of the Christian church, that he was, when in college, idle and a spendthrift. One morning a rich and dissipated fellow-student came into his room with this singular reproof: "Paley, I have been thinking what a fool you are. *I* have the means of dissipation, and can afford to be idle. *You* are poor, and cannot afford it. *I* should make nothing if I were to apply myself. *You* are capable of rising to eminence,—and, pressed with this truth, I have been kept awake during the whole night, and have now come solemnly to admonish you." To this singular admonition, and to the change consequent upon it, Paley owes his eminence, and the church some of the ablest defences of the truth of religion. Now who, beforehand, would have thought that the labours of such a man, perhaps his eternal destiny, and so many of the proofs of Christianity, would have been suspended on a change wrought in a manner so singular and surprising. If, as no one can deny, man's doom in this life may depend on revolutions of such a nature, we are ignorant of any reason why the doom of another state may not be fixed by a similar law.

Perhaps the doctrine which has appeared to most infidels entirely unmeaning and arbitrary, is that which demands *faith* as the condition of salvation. Repentance is a doctrine of more obvious fitness. But the demand of faith seems to be an arbitrary and unmeaning appointment. And yet we think it indubitable, that on man's *belief* depends his whole conduct and destiny in this life. What enterprise would have been more unwise, than that of Columbus, if he had not had a *belief* that by stretching along to the West, he might reach the Indies? What more foolish than the conduct of Tell, and Wallace, and Washington, if not sustained by a persuasion that their country might be free? What more mad than the toils of the young man bending his powers to the acquisition of learning, if he were not sustained by *faith* in some yet unpossessed honour or emolument? What more frantic than for the merchant to commit his treasures to the deep, if he did not *believe* that prosperous gales would re-waft the vessel, laden with riches, into port? We might also say, that *faith* or *confidence* in others is demanded in every enterprise that man ever undertakes, and is the grand principle which conducts it to a happy result. We need only ask what would be the condition of a child, without faith or confidence in a parent; of a pupil, without reliance on the abilities of his teacher; of a subject, distrusting the sovereign; of a soldier, doubting the skill or prowess of his commander; of a tradesman, with no reliance on those whom he employs? What would be the condition of commercial transactions, if there were no established confidence between men of different nations? What the condition of arts, and of arms, if this great pervading principle were at once cut off? In all these instances, moreover, this principle of faith is the *index* and *measure* of the aid to be expected from others. Is it any new principle that the child who has no confidence in a father, usually fails of his favour; or that the pupil should fail of benefit, if he doubts the qualifications of his teacher? And would any single desolating blow so cripple all enterprises, and carry such ruin into the political, the military, and the commercial world, as to destroy the *faith* which one man reposes in another? Is it, then, a strange and unknown doctrine, when religion says, that the most important benefits are suspended on faith? Is it any thing more than one instance of a general principle, which confers peace and wealth on children; learning on the scholar; success on the tradesman; liberty on those who struggle for it; and even laurels and crowns on those who pant in the race for honour and in the conflicts of war? We do not deem it strange, therefore, that God should have incorporated faith into a scheme of religion; and proclaimed from pole to pole, that he who has no confidence in counsellors and guides, shall be without the benefit of counsel and guidance; and that he who has no confidence in the Son of God, shall be dissociated from all the benefits of his atonement.

Let it be remembered, also, that the faith which is demanded in the business of life is very often reposed in some persons whom we have never seen. How few subjects of any empire have ever seen the monarch by whom they are governed? Nay, perhaps the man who holds our destiny in his hand may be on the other side of the globe. Under his charge may be the property which we embarked on the bosom of the deep; or, it may be, the son whom we have committed to him for instruction. Mountains may rise, or oceans roll their billows forever to separate us; but the bonds of faith may be unsevered by the coldest snows, unscathed by the most burning sun, and unbroken amid all the rude heavings of ocean, and the shocks of nations. We ask, why may not a similar bond stretch toward heaven, and be fixed to the throne of the Eternal King? Is it more absurd that *I* should place my confidence in the unseen Monarch of the skies, whom I have not seen, than that my neighbour should place reliance on the king of the Celestial Empire, or of Britain, or of Hawaii, alike unseen by him?

But there is an amazing stupidity among men on the subject of religion; and it cannot be, we are told, that God should make eternal life dependant on matters in which men feel so little interest. We might reply to this, that it is not the fault of God that men are so indifferent. He has done enough to arouse them. If the thunders of his law, the revelation of his love in redemption, and the announcement that there is a heaven and a hell, are not adequate to arouse the faculties of man, we know not what further could be demanded. God has no other system of wrath to bear on human spirits; and heaven and hell embosom no other topics of appeal. But we reply further, that no fact is more familiar to us, than that all men's interests in life suffer for want of sufficient solicitude concerning them. By mere heedlessness a man may stumble down a precipice, nor will the severity of the fall be mitigated by any plea that he was thoughtless of his danger. Thousands of estates have been wrecked by want of timely attention. Character is often ruined by want of proper solicitude in selecting companions. Nay, the king of terrors comes into our dwellings, perfectly unmoved by any inquiry whether we were awaiting his approach or not; and stands over our beds, and wields his dart, and chills our life-blood, with as much coolness and certainty as if we were paying the closest attention to the evidences of his approach. And why should we expect that mere *indifference*, or want of anxiety, should avert the consequences of crime in the eternal world?

It is also, we think, an undoubted doctrine of the Christian scheme, that the great change required in man is the work of God.* And it is no small difficulty with the infidel, that so important results are dependant on a change which owes its existence to the will of a distant being. Yet we cannot be

* John i. 13; iii. 5, 8; Rom. ix. 16, 18; Eph. ii. 1; 1 Peter i. 3; 1 John v. 1; Ezek. xi. 19; John vi. 44, 45.

insensible to the fact that *all* our mercies hang on the will of this great, invisible God. When we say that the salubrity of the air, the wholesomeness of water, the nutrition of plants, and the healing power of medicine, all owe their efficacy to his will, we are stating a fact which physiology is, at last, coming to see and acknowledge. At all events, man does not feel himself straitened in obligation or in effort, by the fact that the *success* of his exertions depends on causes unseen and unknown? All but atheists acknowledge that health flows through the frame of man because God is its giver. Infancy puts on strength and walks; childhood advances to youth; man rises from a bed of sickness, or fractured limbs again become compact, because God sits in the heavens, and sends down his influence to rear, to strengthen, and to heal. Yet, does any one hesitate to put forth his energy for wealth, or his kindness to his children, to take medicine, or to set a bone, because all these will be inefficacious without the blessing of God? But in all this, he is as invisible, and for aught that Christianity teaches to the contrary, as truly efficient, as in the work of saving men. And against all exertion in these matters, lie the same objections that are urged against efforts in religion.

Nor do we deem the doctrine that man may be changed suddenly, and by an influence *originating from some other source than his own mind*, at variance with the analogy of nature. We have already spoken of the fact that sudden changes often take place in the minds of men; and that it is a doctrine of the Scriptures that such a change is indispensable to an admission into heaven. We now proceed to remark, that such revolutions often bear the marks of being brought about by an external, and often an invisible agency; and that there *are* revolutions where it is not unphilosophical to ascribe them to the great and eternal Being in the heavens. Changes of opinion are almost uniformly the result of an influence *foreign* at first to our minds. It is the parent, the friend, the advocate, the flatterer, or the infidel, that has *suggested* the train of thought which results in an entire revolution in our ways of thinking. It is some external change in our business; some success or disappointment; some cutting off our hopes by an agency not our own; or some sudden enlargement of the opportunities for successful effort, that fixes the purpose and revolutionizes the principles or the life. Or it is a voice from the tomb—the remembered sentiment of the now speechless dead—that arrests the attention, and transforms the character. Zeno and Epicurus have thus spoken to thousands of men in every age. Cicero in the forum, and Plato in the schools, still put forth an influence, stretching down from age to age, and in tongues unspoken by them and unknown. Voltaire and Hume still lift their voices, and urge the young to deeds of shame and crime, and Volney and Paine still mutter from their graves, and beckon the world to atheism and pollution. Man may send an influence round the globe, and command it to go from age to age. Now, in all these instances, the influence is as *foreign*, and as *certain*, as in any power of God contemplated in revelation. To our view, it is quite as objectionable as a part of moral government, that men should thus dispose each other to evil, and ultimately to ruin, as that God should incline them to an *amendment* of character, and a deliverance from the "ills which flesh is heir to."

But how is man's freedom affected by all this? We reply, equally in both cases, and not at all in either. Who ever felt that he was fettered in deriving notions of stern virtue from Seneca, or of profligacy from Epicurus? Who dreams that there is any compulsatory process in listening to the voice of Hume, or imbibing the sentiments of Volney? Peter the Hermit poured the thousands of Europe, and almost emptied kingdoms caparisoned for battle, on the plains of Asia. But he moved none against their will. Patrick Henry struck the notes of freedom, and a nation responded, and were changed from subjects of a British king to independent freemen; but all were free in renouncing the protection of the British crown, and their reverence for a British ruler. God influences countless hosts; pours upon darkened minds the love of more than mortal freedom; opens upon the soul the "magnificence of eternity," and the renewed multitude treads the path to life. Prompted to intense efforts by the voice that calls to heaven—as he is who is led by the voice of his country to the field of blood, and who is changed from the peaceful ploughman to the soldier treading in the gore of the slain—they dream not that there is any violation of their moral freedom. In *all* these cases the *foreign* influence exerted (from whatever quarter it may have come) has only convinced them as to the path of duty and honour, and secured a conformity of their wills to that of the unseen and foreign power.

Nor does it alter the case that in regeneration a higher influence is exerted than that of mere moral suasion, since that influence operates in perfect conformity with the laws of moral action and the freedom of the will. In all the cases supposed, the mind acts equally under the impulse of a *foreign*, unseen influence; and in all these cases we know, by the testimony of consciousness, that we are equally free. Any objection, therefore, against the existence of such an influence in regeneration, lies with equal force against the analogy of nature, in the whole world of mind around us.

4. Religion affirms that God exerts the power which *he* puts forth, in pursuance of a plan, or purpose, definitely fixed before the foundation of the world. It affirms, in as intelligible a form as any doctrine was ever expressed in any of the languages of men, that in regard to the putting forth of his power in saving sinners, there is no chance, no hap-hazard; that the scheme lay before his eyes fully; and that his *acts*

are only the *filling up* of the plan, and were contemplated distinctly when God dwelt alone in the stillness and solitude of his own eternity.* If such a doctrine is not revealed, we think it impossible that it *could* be revealed in any language; and we know of no single doctrine that has been more universally *conceded* by infidels to be in the Scriptures; none in the Bible that has been so often brought forward among their alleged reasons for rejecting it as a revelation; none that has so frequently crossed the path of wicked men and revealed the secret rebellion of their hearts; none that has called forth so much misplaced ingenuity from Socinians, and Arminians, and timid men who were afraid to trust the government of the world in the hands of its Maker, as if he were not qualified for universal empire; and none, therefore, which has, in our view, such *primâ facie* proof that it is manifestly a doctrine of truth and excellence. But the outcry, it seems to us, against this doctrine has been altogether gratuitous and unwise. For who is a stranger to the fact that, from infancy to old age, we are more or less influenced by the *plans* or *purposes of others?* The plan or purpose of a parent may determine almost every thing about the destiny of a child. The purpose to remove from regions of pestilence and *malaria* may secure his health; the change from one clime to another may determine the liberty he shall enjoy, the measure of his intelligence, the profession he shall choose, and ultimately his doom here and hereafter. Nay, the parent's *plan* may fix the very college where he shall study; the companions he shall choose; the law office, or the seminary where he shall prepare for professional life; and, finally, every thing which may establish his son in the world. So the *plan* of the infidel is successful in corrupting thousands of the young; the *purpose* of Howard

* Eph. i. 4, 5; Rom. viii. 29, 30; ix. 15, 16, 18, 21: John xvii. 2; 2 Thess. ii. 13; John vi. 37–39; 2 Tim. i. 9.

secured the welfare of thousands of prisoners; the determination of Washington resulted in the independence of his country. In all these, and ten thousand other cases, there is a *plan* formed *by other beings* in respect to *us* which finally enters as a *controlling element* into our destiny. If it be said that they all leave us free, so we say of the decrees of God, that we have a like consciousness of freedom. In neither case does the *foreign purpose* cripple or destroy our freedom. In neither case does it make any difference whether the plan was formed *an hour* before the act, or has stood fixed for ages. All that could bear on our freedom would be the fact that the purpose was *previous to the deed*—a circumstance that does not alter the *act itself*, whether the decree be formed by ourselves, by other men, or by God.

But we remark, further, that it is perfectly idle to object to the fact that a plan or decree is contemplated in revelation; and that God should confer benefits on some individuals which are withheld from others. Did any man, in his senses, ever dream that the race are in all respects on an equality? Has there ever been a time when one man has had just as much health as another; when one has been as rich as another, or as much honoured? To talk of the perfect equality of men, is one of the most unmeaning of all affirmations respecting the world. God has made differences, is still making them, and will continue to do so. The very framework of society is organized on such a principle that men *cannot* be all equal. Even if the scheme of modern infidelity should be successful—if all society should be broken up, and all property be meted out in specific dollars and cents to the idle and the industrious alike, and every man should lose his interest in his own wife and daughter, and they should become the common inheritance of the world, and all law should be at an end,—if this scheme should go into disastrous accomplishment, what principle of perpetuity could be devised? Who knows not that such a chaotic mass would settle down into some kind of order, and men be put in possession again of property, and some of the benefits of social life be again restored? Man might better attempt to make all trees alike, and all hills plains, and all fountains of the same dimensions, than to attempt to *level* society, and bring the race into entire equality. To the end of time it will be true that some will be poor while others are rich; that some will be sick while others are well; that some will be endowed with gigantic intellects, and enriched with ancient and modern learning, while others will pine in want, or walk the humble but not ignoble vale of obscurity.

Now we might as well object to this fixed economy of things as to that which affirms that God dispenses the blessings of redemption according to his good pleasure. If God may confer *one* blessing on one individual which he withholds from another, we ask why he may not be a sovereign also in the dispensation of other favours? We ask what principle of justice and goodness is violated, if he imparts penitence and faith to one individual, that is not violated also if he gives him health, while another pines in sickness? We ask with emphasis, where is there more of partiality in giving the Christian's hope to Brainerd or Martyn, than there is in giving great talents to Newton or great wealth to Crœsus? And we put it to the sober thoughts of those who are so fond of representing the doctrine that God bestows special grace on one, and not on another, as unjust, tyrannical, and malignant, whether they are not lifting their voice against the manifest analogy of nature, and all the facts in the moral and material world? We ask such a man to tread the silent streets of one city where the pestilence spreads its desolations, and then another filled with the din of business, and flushed with health and gain; to go through one land and see the fields smile with golden grain, and rich with the vine and the orange, or fragrant with aromatics, and then through another where the heavens are brass, and the earth dust, and every green thing withers, and every man weeps while the horrors of famine stare him in the face; to go amid one people and hear the clangor of arms, or another and see the squalidness of poverty, or another and see every river studded with villages, and every village pointing its spire to heaven, and universal peace in all its borders, and education diffusing its blessings there— such observers we ask to tell us whether the destiny of *all* men is equal, and *why* in religion God may not do as he does in respect to health, to freedom, and to law?

We go further. We affirm that unless this doctrine of *election* were found in the Scriptures, the scheme would be taken out from all the analogy of the world. No man could recognise a feature of the plan on which God *actually* governs the universe, unless he found there the distinct affirmation that God had "chosen us in Christ before the foundation of the world," and that it is "not of him that willeth, nor of him that runneth, but of God that showeth mercy." The system of conferring favours as he pleases, of giving wealth, and vigour, and talent, and success, is so much a matter of sovereignty, and the secret who shall possess these endowments is so completely lodged in his bosom, that any scheme, to be conformed to the constitution and course of nature, *must* recognise this great principle, or we are shut up to the alternative that the *present* doings of God are wrong, or the constitution of nature one of decisive evil. To us it seems, therefore, that they strike a blow of no ordinary violence and boldness, who denounce the purposes of God in the Bible as dark, partial, and malignant. Nor can we conceive a more rude assault on the whole framework of things, than the popular scheme which denies that God has any purposes of special mercy, and that he confers any spiritual blessings on one which he does not on all,—or, in other words, which attempts to separate the scheme of redemption from the whole analogy of things actually carried on in the world.

But on this point the entire movement of the world bears the marks of being conducted according to a *plan*. We defy a man to lay his finger on a fact which has not such a relation to other facts as to show that it is part of a scheme—and if of a scheme, *then of a purpose formed beforehand*. Alexander the Great, in the vigour of life, and in the full career of conquest, was cut off by the act of God. Julian the Apostate, in the same regions found also an early death, and gigantic plans were arrested by the hand of God with reference to other great purposes in the liberty or religion of man. Napoleon met the mighty arm of God in the snows of the North, and the vast purpose of his life was defeated by a purpose superior to his own. In the midst of daring schemes, man often falls. God wields the dart to strike in an unusual manner, and the victim dies. He falls in with the great plans of the Deity, meets snows, or lightnings, or burning heats, or piercing colds that come round by the direction of the Governor of the world, and the man sinks and *his* plans give way to the higher purposes of the Almighty.

Now we know that at any particular stage of this process we could not discover that there was a plan or a scheme. And we know also that all the objections to such a scheme result from looking at single portions of the plan,—parts dissociated from the whole. In this world we think there is this universal principle to be discovered—APPARENT IRREGULARITY, RESULTING IN ULTIMATE ORDER. During any one of the six days of creation we should scarcely have seen even the *outlines* of the world that ultimately started up. Fix the eye on any *single* hour of the state of the embryo, the egg, or the chrysalis, and who would suppose there was any plan or purpose with reference to the man of godlike form and intelligence; or the beauty of the peacock, the speed of the ostrich, the plaintive melody of the nightingale, or the gay colours of the butterfly? We might illustrate this fully by a reference to the process of digestion. Who could suppose, from the formation of the chyle, that there was any thing like a *plan* laid to supply a *red* fluid, or to give vigour to sinews, or firmness to the bones? So in all the works of God. We are not surprised that unthinking men have doubted whether God had a plan or decree. So unlike the termination is the *actual process*, and so little apparent reference is there to such a termination, that we are not amazed that men start back at the annunciation of a decree. The truth is, that God has laid the *process* of his plan and decrees much deeper than his common acts. They require more patient thought to trace them—they are more remote and abstruse—and they cannot be seen without embracing *at once* the commencement and termination, and the vast array of improbable *media* by which the result is to be secured. Yet to deny that God *has* a plan; that his plan may be expressed by the word *purpose* or *decree*, is as absurd as to deny that the embryo is formed with reference to the future man, or the chyle to future blood, muscles, and bones. Who, in looking upon a complicated piece of machinery, would suppose that a *plan* was in operation tending to the manufacture of cloth, or the propelling of vessels, or the minuter works of art? What strikes the eye is a collection of wheels moving without apparent order. Two wheels shall be beside each other moving in contrary directions; yet all shall ultimately combine to the production of the contemplated result. Thus move the events of the world—and so apparently irregular and unharmonious, but ultimately fixed and grand, are the ways of God. As in a rapid, swollen stream, while the current rolls onward, here and there may be observed in the heaving waters a small portion that seems to be setting in a contrary direction—an eddy that revolves near the shore or that fills the vacancy made by some projecting tree or neck of land, yet *all* setting towards the ocean; so roll on the great events in God's moral and material universe—setting onwards toward eternity in furtherance of a plan, awful, grand, benevolent.

A large field is still open on which we can make but a passing remark—we mean the analogy of the *laws* of Christianity to those suggested by the constitution and course of nature. If our remarks in the former part of this article were correct, then it is fair to expect that religion would reveal such a set of laws as would be in accordance with the course of nature; that is, such as the actual order of events would show to be conducive to the true interest and welfare of man. We think it could be shown that the actual process of things has conducted mankind, after the shedding of much blood, and after many toils of statesmen and sages, to just the set of rules which are revealed in the Old and New Testaments to regulate human conduct. And it would be no uninteresting speculation to inquire into the changes in opinions and laws suggested by the history of events among nations, to see how one set of enactments struck out by the toils of some philosopher and applied by some moralist or statesman, were persevered in until set aside by some opposing event in the government of God, and exchanged for a better system—for one more in accordance with the course of nature—until the revolutions of centuries have brought men to the very laws of the Scriptures, and the profoundest wisdom has been ascertained to be to sit at the feet of Jesus of Nazareth and receive the law from his lips. We might remark on the law of theft in Lacedæmon; on the views in relation to rapine and war; on the seclusion from the world which guided the Essene of Judea, and the monk of the early and Middle Ages; on the indulgence of passion, recommended by the Epicureans; on the annihilation of sensibility, the secret of happiness among the Stoics; on the law of universal selfishness, the *panacea* of all human ills recommended by infidelity; and on the laws of honour that have guided so many men to fields of disgrace and blood, and filled so many dwellings with weeping. In all the different codes, we think we could show that the *course of nature* has ultimately driven men from one set of laws to another, from one experiment to another, until every scheme terminated in its abandonment, or in shaping itself to the peculiar laws of the Bible. But on this point, which is capable of very ample illustration, we can do no more than simply point out the *principle*, and leave the reader to pursue the subject for himself.

We now take our leave of the Analogy of Butler. We have endeavoured to state the nature of the argument on which it rests. We would say, in conclusion, that it is one of easy and universal application. We know of no argument that is so potent to still the voice of unbelief in the heart—to silence every objection to all the doctrines of Christianity—or to subdue the soul to a humble, reverential belief, that the God of creation is the God of redemption; and that he who clothes the sunbeam with light, and the flower with its beauty, is the same All-present Being that goes forth to the grander work of delivering the soul from sin. As God will continue the process of his government, as he will make the genial shower to rise and fertilize the earth, as he will clothe the hills and vales with verdure and beauty, despite of all the blasphemies of men; as he will cause new flowers to spring forth, however many the foot of hard-hearted man may crush, and as he will cause the glory of the *material* system to roll on from age to age, in spite of all the opposition and malice of devils and men, so, we believe, he will also cause this more glorious system to ride triumphantly through the earth, and to shed its blessings on all the nations of the world. Man can triumph over neither. They are based on the solid rock. The plans of men reach them not. Parallel systems of providence and redemption, liable to the same objections, and presenting the same beauties, testify that they have come from the same God, and are tending to the same high development.

We are of the number of those who do not shrink from avowing the opinion, that the system of Christianity, as it has been held in the world, is capable of progressive improvements in the mode of its exhibition. This system, in the mind of the Son of God, was complete, and was so given to mankind. But we think that the world has availed itself fully of the scheme. No earthly being ever yet so well understood the laws of the mind as the Son of God; and the system as held *by him* was adapted to the true nature of created spirits, and to the regular course of things. But Christianity has often been attached to schemes of mental and moral philosophy as remote from the true one as "from the centre thrice to the utmost pole." Now, the improvement which we anticipate, is, that men will consent to lay aside their systems of mental science; and with them, much also of the technicalities of their theology—and suffer religion to speak in the words expressive of what Locke calls "large, round-about sense;" that they will be willing to inquire, first, what philosophy *religion* teaches, and then ask, if they choose, whether that philosophy is to be found in the schools. Could all the obstructions in the way of correct mental philosophy and natural science be at one removed, we have no doubt that the Christian system would be seen to fall at once into the scheme of material and mental things. Now this is the kind of improvement which we expect will take place in theology. An analogy could never be established between theology as it *has* been held, and the common course of events. Religion, as it has been often presented, has been *unlike* all other things—so cold, distant, unliving, and formal, that we wonder not that men who have had tolerably correct notions of the laws of the mind and of facts, should have shrunk from it; nor do we wonder that the preaching of no small number of ministers should have been fitted to make men Arminians, Socinians, or Deists.

We have sat down in pensive grief, when we heard from the lips of tyros in divinity (as the first message which they bring us) solemn and measured denunciations of *reason* in religion. We have asked ourselves, whence the herald has derived his commission to commence an assault on what has been implanted in the bosom of man by the hand of the Almighty? Has the book which he holds in his hand told him to utter unfeeling and proscriptive maledictions on all just views of mental operations? Has God commissioned him to summon the world to a rejection of all the lessons taught by the investigations of the mind, the decisions of conscience, and the course of events? Is the God who has hitherto been thought to be the God of creation and providence, coming forth in the old age and decrepitude of the world, to declare that the fundamental principles of civil society, the judicial inflictions of his hand, the lessons taught us in parental and filial intercourse, and in the reasonings of sober men with the eye upturned to heaven, have all been delusive; and that the new revelation is to set at defiance all that has been ascertained to be law, and all that the world has supposed to be just maxims in morals? We marvel not that thinking men shrink from such sweeping denunciations. Nor do we remember that the ministry is often despised, the sanctuary forsaken, and the day-dreams of any errorist adopted, who *professes* to give them proper place to the inferences drawn from the government of God.

It is a maxim, we think, which should rule in the hearts of Christian men, and

> "Most of all in man that ministers,
> And serves the altar,"

that the world is to be convinced, *that Christians are not of necessity fools.* And, in doing this, we care not how much of sound reason, and true philosophy, and the analogies of nature, are brought into the sacred desk. The truth is, that religion sets up its jurisdiction over all the operations of mind. And the truth is, also, that those who have done most to vilify and abuse the use of reason, have been the very men who have incorporated the most of false philosophy into their own systems of divinity. It is not to be concealed, that the most ardent desire of the enemies of religion is that its ministers and friends should deal out fierce denunciations against *reason*, and set up the system of Christianity as something holding in fixed defiance all the discoveries of knowledge and all the schemes of philosophy. More than half the work of Atheism is done, if the world can be persuaded that Christianity contemplates the surrender of the deductions of reason, and the course of the world, into the hands of infidel philosophers; nor do we know a more successful artifice of the enemy of man, than the schemes which have been devised to effect such a disjunction, and to set up the Christian plan as something that stands in irreconcilable opposition to the course of nature and the just process of thought.

But, if the view which we have taken of this matter is correct, then all the works of God, far as the eye can reach, and far on beyond, are in strict accordance with the Christian scheme. One set of laws rules the whole; one set of principles reigns everywhere; one grand system of administration is going forward. Apparent differences between the Christian scheme and the course of events, are daily becoming rarer, and soon the whole will be seen to harmonize. The laws of mental action are becoming better understood, and are found to coincide more and more with the plain, unperverted declarations of the Bible. The laws of nations are growing more mild, tender, bloodless, and forbearing. The great principles of morals are laying aside the ferocity of the darker ages, disrobing themselves of the principles of the Goth and the Vandal, and returning more and more to the simplicity of primeval life—to the principles of Abraham, "that beauteous model of an Eastern prince, of David the warrior-poet, of Daniel the far-sighted premier, of Paul the mild, yet indomitable apostle, and of Jesus the meek Son of God."

We anticipate that the order of events, and the deductions of reason, and the decisions of the gospel, will yet be found completely to *tally;* so that Christianity shall come armed with the *double power* of having been sustained by miracles when first promulgated, and when appearing improbable, and of falling in at last with all the proper feelings, and just views of the world. As one evidence that the world is hastening to such a juncture we remark, that the views entertained of moral character have undergone already a transformation. "What mother would now train her sons after the example of Achilles, and Hector, and Agamemnon, and Ulysses?" Other models, more like the Son of God, are placed before the infant mind. Society in its vast revolutions has brought itself into accordance, in this respect, with the New Testament. And we cannot doubt, that though the affairs of the church and the world may yet flow on in somewhat distinct channels, yet they will finally sink into complete and perfect harmony; like two streams rising in distant hills, and rendering fertile different vales, yet at last flowing into the bosom of the same placid and beautiful ocean. Men will go on to make experiments in geology, and chemistry, and philosophy, in order to oppose the Bible, till scheme after scheme shall be abandoned. They will frame theories of mental science, until they arrive at the scheme of the New Testament. They will devise modes of alleviating misery, until they fall on the very plan suggested more than two thousand years before them. And they will form and abandon codes of morals, until they shall come at last, in their international and private affairs, to the moral maxims of the New Testament—and the world shall arrive at the conclusion, that the highest wisdom is to sit down like children at the feet of the Son of God.

And here we conclude by saying, that the men who promulgated this system were Galilean peasants and fishermen. They had indubitably little learning. They were strangers to the doctrines of the schools, to ancient and modern science, to the works of nature and of art. No infidel can prove that they knew more than the science necessary for the skilful management of a fishing-boat, or the collection of taxes. And yet they have devised the only scheme which turns out to be in accordance with the course of nature : a scheme which has survived the extinction of most others prevalent in their day, a system *in advance* still,—no one can tell how much,—even of our own age. Now it is a well-known fact, that in the progress of discovery hitherto, no man has gone much in advance of his own generation. Society and science work themselves into a state for the discoveries which actually take place, and hence it happens that, about the same time, the same invention is often made on both sides of the globe. A controversy still exists respecting the discovery of the art of printing, and gunpowder, the application of steam, the invention of the quadrant, and many of the improvements in chemistry. We ask, then, how it has happened that these Galileans stepped over all the science of their own age; established a system in strict accordance with the course of nature; disclosed elementary principles of morals, entirely unknown to the philosophy of that age, and arrived at, in the history of man, only by long and painful experiments of many thousand years! Why, let the skeptic tell us, has not science struck out principle after principle, that could long since have been organized into a system which should accord with the constitution and course of nature? To our minds, the greatest of all miracles would be, that unaided and uninspired fishermen should have projected such a scheme of Christianity.

Revealed religion, then, is in accordance with the course of nature. To reason against or reject it, on the principles commonly adopted by infidels, is to call in question the whole system of things around us. Nor will it answer any valuable purpose to laugh or mock at it. "There is argument neither in drollery nor in jibe." If, in spite of this striking accordance with the course of nature, it can be proved false, let the evidence be fairly brought forward. Let its miracles be set aside. Let its prophecies be shown not to have been uttered. And then let it be shown *how it is* that such a system has originated from such a source—a system which has bowed the intellects of such men as Bacon, and Locke, and Boyle, and Hale, and Boorhave, and Newton, and Edwards, and Dwight. But if the demonstration cannot be made out,—if a single doubt remains, it will not do to deride this religion. It will no more do to meet the announcement of hell with a jeer, than to stand and mock at convulsions, fevers, and groans;—nor should men laugh at the judgment any more than at the still tread of the pestilence, or the heavings of the earthquake; —nor will it be at all more the dictate of wisdom to contemn the provisions of redemption than to mock the pitying eye of a father, or to meet with contempt the pensive sigh of a mother over our sufferings, or to jeer at the physician who comes reverently, if it may be, to put back from us the heavy, pressing hand of God.

II.

[CHRISTIAN SPECTATOR, 1832.]

The Christian Ministry, with an Inquiry into the Cause of its Inefficiency. By the Rev. CHARLES BRIDGES, B.A., Vicar of Old Newton, Suffolk, and Author of "Exposition of Psalm cxix." New York: Jonathan Leavitt. Boston: Crocker and Brewster, 1831. In two vols., 12mo.

THIS work has been republished in this country, with a recommendatory notice by the Rev. Dr. Milnor of New York. We invite the attention particularly of our clerical readers to it, as a practical work of high value on the duties of their calling. It is plain, simple, and thorough in its character; evidently the production of a man ardently attached to the ministry; abounding in scriptural views of the nature of this great office; and illustrating those views, in a full and interesting manner, by the sentiments of eminent ministers of the gospel, and by pertinent anecdotes from the lives of distinguished pastors and preachers. It is not such a work, indeed, as we should expect from those profound British thinkers, Foster and Hall; but it is such a book as we most love to peruse in those moments of care and perplexity, of doubt and despondency, when we seek not for profound discussion, or new views, but when we wish for scriptural encouragement in our work, and ask for the friendly aid and counsel of an experienced pastor, and the voice of Christian friendship to cheer us in the arduous toils of this self-denying office. To induce our readers to become possessed of a book eminently adapted, we believe, to do good, we shall give its outlines by recording the titles of the chapters, and by a single extract—presenting views which we wish particularly to commend to the attention of our readers, and which may serve as a fair specimen of the general style of the work. The volume contains a discussion of the following subjects:—General view of the Christian ministry—General causes of the want of success in the Christian ministry—Causes of ministerial inefficiency, connected with our personal character—The public work of the Christian ministry—The pastoral work of the Christian ministry—Recollections of the Christian ministry.

The extract which we shall present relates to habits of study:

"Nor let it be thought, that studious habits must necessarily infringe upon the more active employment of our work. What shall we say to the nine ponderous folios of Augustine, and nearly the same number of Chrysostom,—volumes not written like Jerome's, in monastic retirement, but in the midst of almost daily preaching engagements, and conflicting, anxious, and most responsible duties,—volumes not of light reading—the rapid flow of shallow declamation, but the results of deep and well-digested thinking? The folios, also, of Calvin, the most diligent preacher,* and of Baxter, the most laborious pastor of his day, full of thought and matter, bearing the same testimony to the entire consistency of industrious study with devoted ministerial diligence. The secret of this efficiency seems to have much consisted in a deep and important sense of the value of that most precious of all talents—*time*, and of an economical distribution of its minutest particles for specific purposes. Mr. Alleine would often say, 'Give me a Christian that counts his time more precious

---

* "What shall I say of his indefatigable industry, even beyond the power of nature, which, being paralleled with our loitering, I fear will exceed all credit? and may be a true object of admiration, how his lean, worn, spent, and weary body could possibly hold out. He read every week in the year three divinity lectures, and every other week over and above; he preached every day, so that (as Erasmus says of Chrysostom) I do not know whether more to admire the indefatigableness of the man, or his hearers. Yea, some have reckoned up that his lectures were yearly one hundred and eighty-six, his sermons two hundred and eighty-six, besides Thursday he sat in the presbytery," &c.—*Clark's Lives.*

than gold.' Mr. Cotton would express his regret after a departure of a visitor, 'I had rather have given this man a handful of money, than have been kept thus long out of my study.' Melancthon, when he had an appointment, expected not only the hour, but the minute to be fixed, that time might not run out in the idleness of suspense. Seneca has long since taught us, that time is the only thing of which 'it is a virtue to be covetous.' And here we should be like the miser with his money—saving it with care, and spending it with caution. It is well to have a book for every spare hour, to improve what Boyle calls the 'parentheses or interludes of time, which, coming between more important engagements, are wont to be lost by most men, for want of a value for them: and even by good men, for want of skill to preserve them. And since goldsmiths and refiners,' he remarks, 'are wont all the year long to save the very sweepings of their shops, because they may contain in them some filings of dust of those richer metals, gold and silver, I see not why a Christian may not be as careful not to lose the fragments and lesser intervals of a thing incomparably more precious than any metal—time; especially when the improvement of them by our meletetics may not only redeem so many portions of our life, but turn them to pious uses, and particularly to the great advantage of devotion.'" pp. 58–60.

The work is designed evidently for the clergy of Great Britain, and particularly those of the Established Church. Coming from the bosom of that church, and designed for its members, we hail it as an omen of great advancing good. We regard it as an indication of no small progress toward a better state of things there, that such a work as this is patronized, and that, in less than five months, a second edition has been demanded. But though intended particularly for that church, it is adapted to Christian ministers of all denominations. Indeed, it contemplates the work of the ministry as it was appointed by the Lord Jesus, and, wherever read, it will do good.

With one thing we have been particularly struck in its perusal, viz. that no small part of its illustrations, and of the anecdotes and authorities introduced on the subject of the ministry, are taken from this side the ocean. This fact is a voluntary tribute to the descendants of the Puritans, which we were not quite prepared to expect from England, and especially from the bosom of the Established Church. As a people, we are young. We have no established religion. We have been without ecclesiastical patronage, without the fostering care of government, without sinecures, and without such independent provision for the ministry as to give leisure for that intellectual advancement which might be expected under an established religion. Preachers in this land are doomed to toil; and one of the most laborious and active occupations here is, without doubt, the Christian ministry. It is a tribute of which we would speak with deep interest;—it is a voice which we desire all men to hear in favour of our free institutions, when foreigners turn their eyes to this country for illustrations of the true nature of the pastoral office, and for examples of self-denying industry and faithfulness among the heralds of salvation. We turn instinctively to our free institutions, and look over our history with new gratitude and delight, to trace the moulding power of their organization in this country, in forming the ministry. We ask ourselves whether the nature of our institutions is fitted to give appropriate beauty and largeness to the embassy which the preacher bears? And what is the kind of ministry which is best adapted to our civil and religious organization, and connected with the preservation of our civil rights, and the welfare of the church of God?

Commending the book which is the occasion of our remarks to the cordial notice of our readers, we desire, at this interesting period of the history of our republic, to do as much as in us lies to hold before our countrymen what we deem to be the appropriate character of this class of men, and from the memory of the past, the aspect of the present, and the anticipations of the future, to keep full in the public eye a subject on which we mean frequently to dwell—the importance of an able and well-educated clergy.

It is impossible to contemplate the history of this republic without feeling that the whole of its organization has been such as to give development to the proper powers and influence of the Christian ministry. From its settlement a series of events has been in progress demanding profound wisdom, indefatigable activity, rich and varied learning, and indomitable courage and integrity. Every one knows that the whole system of society in New England was framed under the auspices of the Christian religion, and, of course, under the direction, in no small degree, of those whose office it was to preach the gospel. Nor was it possible that ignorant or inactive ministers should have been adapted to that state of things, or that they *could* have met the crises which occurred in the foundation of a mighty empire. The constitution of a vast civil polity was to be framed. The formation of churches was an object of deep solicitude, and required profound wisdom. Laws adapted to a new and peculiar community were to be enacted. The earth was to be subdued and cultivated. Morality, chastity, industry, intelligence, and order, were to be promoted among the people. The eye of the lawgiver and the Christian could not but run along future ages, and anticipate the grandeur of a mighty Christian empire. For the enjoyment of freedom, they had sought the dreariness and solitude of a vast wilderness, and they were conscious of living to mould the destiny of countless millions.

Many would have thought that to preach to a handful of people on the shores of Plymouth, to instruct the little flock that came across the waters, and who were encountering all the perils of the wilderness and the privations of a life in a strange and inhospitable country, an ignorant ministry would have been sufficient. Thus many think now about our Western *World*. But our Puritan fathers had different conceptions of the nature of this office. Profoundly learned when they came to these shores, they have been unequalled in this country or any other for patient study and toil, even after their arrival. Till within a few years, there were no men in this country, and scarcely in any other, who have been so profoundly skilled in the Oriental and ancient languages, or so laborious in writing books, as the men who came first to New England.

Here we are happy to record the high eulogium of a man than whom no one in our country is better qualified to speak, or whose opinions in the literary and political world have more the authority which, by common consent, has been conceded to him on the bench.

"They were so fortunate," says Chancellor Kent, "as to enjoy the presence and guidance of one man who had been early initiated in university learning, and proved to be one of those superior and decided characters, competent to give a permanent direction to human affairs. No sage of antiquity was superior to him in wisdom, moderation, and firmness; none equal to him in the grandeur of his moral character, and the elevation of his devotion. This learned audience will have perceived that I allude to the Rev. Thomas Hooker, whom his distinguished biographer has termed *the light of the Western churches, and oracle of the Connecticut colony*."* "The leading Puritans of New England, and the great body of Protestant clergy everywhere, no less than the fathers of the primitive church, were scholars of the first order. Let us take as a sample from among ten thousand, the Rev. John Cotton, styled *the father and glory of Boston*. He was advanced in early life, by reason of his great learning as a scholar, to a fellowship in the English University of Cambridge. His skill in the Hebrew, Greek, and Latin languages, as well as in textual divinity, was unrivalled. His industry was extraordinary. He wrote and spoke Latin with ease, and with Ciceronian eloquence. He was distinguished as a strict and orthodox preacher, pre-eminent among his contemporaries for the sanctity of his character, and the fervour of his devotion. He died, as he had lived, in the rapturous belief that

* Address before the Phi Beta Kappa Society, 1831. p. 9.

he was in reality to join in the joys and worship of the saints in glory."*

Nor did they deem any of their acquisitions to be useless in the wilderness. One of the first of their measures was to found Harvard College. Never did a Puritain conceive that a minister of the gospel could be fitted, even for the Western wilds, without a long and profound training in the schools. Every idea which he had of the perpetuity of liberty was blended indissolubly with the thought that the ministry should be profoundly trained for their work.

Under auspices such as these our country rose. There are few subjects from which the mind less willingly departs, than from the contemplation of that peculiar and wonderful race of men. We feel that the ministers and people of that age had been formed for each other, and both had been formed to meet the toils and hardships connected with the subjugation and culture of the rocky soil to which God directed them. And though they were a sect which has been "everywhere spoken against," yet their memorial is the virtue, the order, the intelligence, and the piety of the Northern States, and no small part of the results of the effort to spread the knowledge of the gospel, and religious freedom, among all the empires of the earth.

It would almost seem as if the conceptions of our fathers on this subject, had been formed by a prophetic anticipation of what this republic is destined yet to be. One can hardly help reflecting on what *might* have been the state of things in this land, if they had possessed different views respecting the nature of the gospel ministry. Had they believed that an ignorant ministry would be adapted to the New World;—had they been men of limited views, or weak judgment, or slender learning and piety, these qualities would have gone into all

* Address before the Phi Beta Kappa Society, 1831. pp. 25, 26.

the veins and sinews of our empire. Had the Catholic placed his foot on the rock of Plymouth, instead of the Puritan, New England would have been *now* what South America is. Ignorance and superstition would have spread over all the hills and vales, and the intellect, now so free, so enlightened, so manly, would have been prostrate beneath a base and grovelling superstition. We cannot but add, had they possessed the views which have prevailed among some Protestant denominations in our country, in regard to the Christian ministry, those views would have done more than all the subsequent efforts of the statesman could have *undone*, to form a wild and fanatic population, and to shed over all this nation the elements of ignorance and misrule.

It was the glory of New England, that her first preachers were fitted to any possible intellectual or moral growth of this republic. There has not been, and there will not be, a state of the public mind, in which the first preachers of New England would not have been competent to meet all that could be demanded of ministers of the gospel. First in industry, first in toil, first in piety, they stood at the head of this republic, not only as leading the way to this Western World, but as illustrating most impressively, what America *must have,* and *must be,* if her institutions are to be free; if her schools are to flourish; if her science and arts are to be under a mild and wholesome discipline; and if her broad fields and streams are to continue to invite from afar the stranger, the oppressed, and the fatherless, to the hospitalities of freedom, and the dwelling-place of virtue and peace. Our eyes delight to dwell on the wonderful sagacity of those men, in foreseeing what our country would demand in her religious teachers; and upon that stern and indomitable firmness which sustained them in the perils of the Western wilderness, that *we* might be blessed with the labours of a ministry which should blend all that is profound in learning, courteous in refined life, eloquent in persuasion, bold in investigation, and mild and lovely in the religion of the Son of God. We give humble and hearty thanks to the great King of Zion, that we are permitted to look back to an early history like this. And we cannot but be struck here with the indications in our national infancy, that the God of nations contemplated in the formation of our republic some gigantic purpose respecting the future condition of all mankind. Under what different auspices has our country risen, from those of the Greek, the Roman, and even the German, the French, and the British people. Age after age, in all those nations, rolled away with no such commanding elements of formation as we have seen here. Their early history was amid fables and poetry, and day-dreams, and a wild and fanciful mythology; and even after the lapse of centuries, there has not existed among any other people, though enjoying all their laws, and learning, and religion, any power to mould advancing generations, to be compared with what attended the very first touch given to the principles and destiny of Americans. Here, a sun rose bright and full to shed its beams all along the path of those who were laying the foundation of a mighty empire; there, millions toiled age after age, in "disastrous twilight," and scarcely did centuries disclose on their lands what shot by one steady effulgence, frcm *the beginning*, across the bosom of the dark Western forest.

The extraordinary circumstances under which the American church has gone forward, have changed somewhat the views of the ministry, and given a new direction to the minds of our countrymen. Our country is fitted for enterprise. Every active power is called into requisition. Boundless Western prairies stretch out their uncultivated bosoms, to be traversed and tilled by civilized man. Vast streams roll their waters to the oceans, rising in the interior of yet unpenetrated forests, and laving by their rolling floods lands unequalled in fertility on the banks of the Nile or the Jordan. On the borders of those streams, men are invited to plant towns and cities; and the bosoms of those internal floods they seek to cover with the fruits of husbandry, and the productions of art. Over lands fertile beyond the conception of the ancient Roman and the colonizing Greek, still repose the shades of a dark wilderness, where have not yet been heard the axe of the pioneer, or the song of the ploughman. But soon those forests will disappear, and the habitations of men will take the place of the lair, and the cry of the beast of prey give way to the busy scenes of commerce, of husbandry, and of art. Never have the powers of a people expanded so rapidly as in America since the War of Independence. The energies of the nation were before *pent up*, and confined to the states that now merely skirt the Atlantic. Once free, American enterprise burst every barrier. The flood rolled westward; and all the previous conceptions of political economists were outstripped by what an amazed world has seen to be *fact*, in peopling the new hemisphere.

It was impossible but that this state of things should affect the ministry. Men began to inquire, whether the somewhat staid and leaden habits of the pulpit should not be broken up; whether the active powers might not be put to greater tension, and gain an ascendency over the contemplative habits of our fathers; and whether it was not demanded that the ministry should keep pace with the state of things that has unexpectedly grown up around us. Rules which apply to the fixed and Gothic habits of the darker ages, apply with but little force to our own times. Guages with which we could measure the ministerial duties of other days, little befit our own country. We have, in law and in legislation, broken up the older habits of thinking among men. We are striking out new modes of freedom; new tracks of thought; new measures to be applied to the capabilities of men. We are forming a state of things, in this republic, very much as if we had not the memorials of past ages. The maxims of the Roman do not apply to us, for his purpose was conquest, and monuments, and laurels. *We* have nothing to conquer but the sturdy oaks of our mountains, and the obstructions of our streams, and the barriers to the free access to a soil given to us fresh from the hand of God. The principles of the Greek have as little applicability to us. He adorned the stinted territory which God gave him with temples, and arches, and altars, and then sought adjacent lands where to place the monuments of his wisdom, and the proofs of his art,—the beauteous forms which the hands of Praxiteles and Phidias taught to start breathing from the marble. *We* have no such breathing forms of statuary; we are not pent up in a straitened territory; we need not seek other lands to proclaim our wisdom, or to deposit the monuments of our art. Least of all do the maxims of the schools, the thoughts that have received their forms beneath the eye of monarchs, and amid the remains of Gothic grandeur, apply to us. We have emerged in our learning, our laws, and our religion, from the dark cells of the monastery, and bid farewell to the lucubrations of the anchorite. Man stands here erect in all the dignity of the purest freedom that God has ever conferred on mortals. In his habits, his religion, and his laws, he has broken away from the iron sceptre and stern usages that tyrannize over all other men. This change has come into the church. An unusual spirit of religious enterprise has marked the present age. All former habits are broken up; and in our religion as well as in our liberty and laws, we are developing principles to which all other men have been strangers. Every thing is laid bare to this spirit of active exertion. Every opinion which has hitherto been held sacred among men, is to be subjected to the test of a new investigation. The result of this active state of things will be, probably, like that of applying the fires of the compound blowpipe to mineral substances. What shall be found to abide the test of this scrutiny may be regarded as safe from the investigations of future ages of men. What shall be dissipated or converted into dross, however long it may have been venerated, and however sacred the names that have been applied to it, will hereafter be rejected and forgotten.

Now, to many pious and thinking men, it has become a matter of deep deliberation, whether, in this state of things, it is proper to occupy eight or ten of the most vigorous years of life in the mere *training* of the ministry for future labour. It has been made a question whether it were not best to abstract a large part of these years from the college and the seminary, to be employed in the active business of winning souls to Christ. And especially has this been pressed with great weight on the mind, when it is remembered that the whole process of education is expensive; when there are, perhaps, not more than seven millions of our population who are in any tolerable way supplied with the preaching of the gospel, and when almost the entire Pagan and Mohammedan world is open for the speedy and rapid propagation of Christianity, if more were ready to bear to them the message of life. It is not wonderful, therefore, that the sentiments of men on the subject of preparation for the ministry are undergoing a rapid change. And it is an interesting subject of investigation, whether there should be an effort to arrest the progress of that change, or whether the efforts to educate more thoroughly for this work should be abandoned. We wish to state some of the reasons which should influence Christians still to seek for a laborious and profound preparation in those who are trained up for the gospel ministry. Those views have originated from the nature of the ministerial office, and from the state of our country.

The ministry is appointed to explain and vindicate the

Christian religion. That religion, like every other system, may be contemplated in a variety of aspects. A man may look at it with the cold eye of speculation; he may regard the historical documents which contain its record; he may contemplate it as fitted to make external changes in society; he may survey it as an assemblage of moral precepts; or he may look on it as fitted to make an *immediate* and *permanent* impression on the spirits of men. He may contemplate it as the fairest system of morality which the world has known, or as a grand and amazing plan to produce immediate reconciliation between God and man, through the blood of the Mediator, offered in atonement for the sins of the world.

Those who are preparing for the ministry may also look at Christianity in all these lights; and from this point of observation, they will judge of the *kind* of qualifications which are indispensable to fit them for their work. Nor can it be doubted, that candidates for the ministry may make of themselves whatever they wish, and come into this work with just such aims and attainments as they choose. It is easy, for example, for a young man to fix his eye on the profound acquisitions of mental science, and in religious themes he shall find ample scope for subtle distinctions; and this propensity shall give the entire cast to his studies and his ministry: or he may contract a fondness for a dry and lifeless system of divinity, having just the same relation to the Christianity of the Bible which the stiff and frightful preparations in the room of the anatomist have to real life; and every truth that comes under his eye shall be divested of half its freshness and its power by the process of giving it its location in his arrangement of doctrine. Every lineament of beauty and of strength, every thing that speaks of life, and raciness, and vigour, shall vanish under the mere anatomy of the theological system; and the preaching shall be known only by dry detail, and minute dissections, and the cold and heartless laying bare of bones and sinews and muscles. Or he may strike into the regions of fancy, and cultivate the graces of elocution, and all that shall be known of him is, that he is a splendid declaimer, followed and admired by multitudes, but most unsuccessful in winning souls to Jesus. Or he may deal only in moral precepts, like those of Seneca, and call in the name of Jesus to give sanction to the cold and unmeaning *essays* which his own mind has originated. Or he may be a warm-hearted friend of the conversion of sinners. He may mingle together just as much of the other characteristics which have been suggested as shall be necessary to *fill up* this single purpose of his soul. And this design *to save souls,* and to labour for revivals of religion, and to advance the latter-day glory of the church, will be the best of all guages in his inquiries how much of the other qualifications he should seek :—just as the great purpose of a warrior to make a permanent aggression on a marshalled foe shall measure the nature of his studies; the amount of his repose; and the character of the force he shall bring into the field—the heavy, slow-moving, dense column of artillery, or the light squadron of dragoons, or the well-disciplined infantry.

This, then, is the starting-point from which we are to contemplate the kind of preparation needed in the ministry. If Christianity is a mere system of morals, as many would persuade us, then let our days and nights be spent in frozen and distant climes of thought, having as little to do with the Bible, and as much converse as possible with the shades of pagan men. If it is a system of teaching men that they have no capacity to repent and believe; that men are bound by adamant; that laws are enacted which cannot be obeyed, and a heaven offered which cannot be won; and that diadems of glory are offered as if to mock our helplessness; and harps of praise as if to deride our groans and tears; that men are to wait God's time for conversion, and are *bound* to make no effort till a foreign power reaches the heart, as the lightning rives the oak, then the right kind of training is to discipline the mind—unhappily the easiest of all modes of training for this work—to this posture of inactivity and delay:—then let it be the design of preaching to repress the ardour of the soul; to clip the wings of faith; and to keep back from every process of investigation founded on a belief that man has a conscience; that he is a moral agent; that he is under obligation to repent, and that he is invested with any power to do his duty.

If it is a system whose power was appropriately displayed on the day of Pentecost, and under the labours of Luther, and Edwards, and the Tennants, then it demands in the ministry *all* the culture which can find mind to conflict with mind, which can so shape and direct truth that it shall reach the conscience, and shall make the sinner tremble when the law speaks out its thunders, and be filled with joy when the gospel whispers peace. Our belief is that the gospel is such a system, and that its general characteristic is, that it is a scheme fitted to make an *immediate* impression on the souls of men. It is an annunciation of a plan of mercy which supposes a decided *act* of the mind in its reception, or its rejection. It can never be presented without calling forth such an act. It is the proclamation of a Sovereign, demanding an immediate return of revolted subjects; the tender voice of a Father, inviting his wandering children to the parental arms; the mandate of the Lawgiver, prescribing the way of obedience; and the awful annunciation of a great Prophet, lifting the veil from the future, and disclosing the tremendous realities of hell, and the unutterable glories of heaven. It appeals to the sober judgment of the mind, to the voice of conscience, to the inextinguishable desire of happiness, to the dying love of the Son of God, to all our hopes and all our fears, and solemnly commands men to turn and live. This is the message which the ministry bears. Compared with the inducements to become Christians, and Christians *at once*, how feeble are those things which *do* actually influence and control men! Man, for the hope of gain, will brave all the dangers of the seas, and all the colds of the north, and the fiery sands of the burning zone. The clarion of battle, or the sweet name of liberty, will rouse nations to arms, and fire the most listless with the hope of victory. The hard-hearted man melts at the pleading of the orphan; the stern brow is relaxed at the tears of impoverished age; the iron nerves of the guilty tremble as the lips of a witness sworn to declare the truth open to hasten his condemnation; the rebel son is humbled at the pleadings of a father, or the tears of a mother. But, in all these cases, how powerless are the motives which press men to action, compared with those which the ministry should use to urge them to enter into heaven. Yet, what advocate, patriot, parent, or even pauper, hesitates to approach men with the expectation that an immediate impression may be effected by the eloquence of argument, and the tears of persuasion? Why, we ask, should not the ministers of religion appeal to men to rouse them with like decisiveness to action, and with like success?

When John the Baptist proclaimed the message of God, he expected an immediate movement on the minds of a wicked generation, and thousands encompassed the man rudely attired, and trod penitent in his footsteps to the waters of Jordan. When the Son of Man came, he also proclaimed the need of immediate repentance. Every word he spake took effect. Every reproof was felt. His voice always found its way to the human heart. Thousands gnashed upon him with their teeth, and indignantly turned away from the Prophet of Galilee; but thousands also mourned in bitterness over their sins, and came for salvation to the meek and lowly Lamb of God. A single interview with him seemed to seal the character. The Scribe turned away more indignant. The Sadducee sought not his presence again. The fishermen of Galilee heard his voice at once, and followed him. Was the gospel proclaimed in Jerusalem, in Arabia, in Corinth, in Philippi, in Rome? Who is stranger to the fact that it made its way at once to the heart, and that the apostles never admitted a debate, or a moment's deliberation, about putting away idols, and turning to God? When Luther, and Calvin, and Knox rose from the oppression of the Romish hierarchy, they pursued their labours with the *expectation* that their voice would be heard in all the vales and in all the mountains of the Old World. It *was* heard. It sounded in the glens and glaciers of Switzerland; it was borne over the plains of France, and along the banks of the Rhine and the Danube; it shook the throne of England's king, and echoed along the Highlands of Scotland, and moved in all Europe a heavy mass on which had been recumbent the shades of a long and chilly night, and roused no small portion of the world to life, to energy, to regeneration. When Whitefield spoke, when Edwards reasoned, when the Tennants pleaded, no small portion of the people of America were roused to seek the path of life, and pæans of thanksgiving rose from thousands of tongues taught to sing the power of the gospel, brought to bear *directly* on the consciences of men. We might add to their honoured names those of many living men, who, like them, have come into the ministry with a belief that the gospel is *fitted* to make an impression on men. Few are the older villages in our country which have not been blessed with the labours of such men; and from their labours and the attending agency of the Holy Ghost, an awful sacredness seems to encompass the rising towns in this land. Seldom do we tread the streets of a city, or town, or peaceful hamlet, that has not been hallowed by revivals of religion; and in this fact we mark the evidence, at once, that a God of mercy presides over the destinies of this people, and that the gospel is indeed "the *power* of God unto salvation." And while *we* live, an unusual power has gone forth in illustration of this great point, that the gospel is fitted to make an impression on the souls of men *at once*, and that in the hands of a faithful ministry, it can draw men with a *resistless power*, weeping, to the cross.

Now, if this is the nature of the ministry, and if every man who enters upon this work bears a message thus fitted to make an impression at once on the heart, fitted completely to revolutionize the man, and stamp the features of that revolution eternally on his soul,—then it is proper to ask, whether this is a work which demands any special training, or whether men are formed for it by native endowments, or by any extraordinary communication of the Holy Spirit. Here we shall call the attention of our readers to a few principles on which the world has hitherto acted.

A comparatively long and tedious training, involving often an apparently great waste of time, is the allotment of man. What would seem to be a greater waste of more precious time, than that twenty years, or one-third of the ordinary life of man, should be employed in infancy and youth in the slow and cumbersome process of learning to talk, to move, to read, to think, and to become acquainted with the elements of the mechanic arts? Yet the humblest occupations, the professions demanding the lowest amount of intellect and skill, are subjected to this long and tedious pupilage. Is it, then, a departure from the established laws of the world, when men are called to prepare, by long and weary toils, for the momentous work of leading sinners, weeping and humbled, to the altar and the cross? In every other department of action, in all the mechanic arts, in every thing demanding strength, and skill, and power over men,—from the child, the ancient wrestler, and the soldier, to the advocate, the physician, and the senator,—there is but one process of training men, and that is by long and weary years of probation and toil.

Who knows not how much more was gained on the field of Waterloo, or in the strife at Trafalgar, by regular and disciplined troops, than could have been done by raw and undisciplined men? And who, when the banners of victory float over the fields of the slain, or the acclamations of emancipated freemen greet the returning conqueror, regrets the days of discipline, or the time spent in preparing for conflict?

We may weep over the desolations of our country; we may wish that many more heralds of the cross were in the field; we may be disposed to chide the dilatory steps of those who devote years of preparation to this work; but we should not be unmindful that in like manner every father might weep that so many years are requisite to fit his son to aid him, or that so tedious a process had been appointed by God to fit him to adorn the walks of public or private life.

Let it be remembered that it is a great law of nature, that eminent success is not to be measured by the *years* that men occupy in the field. It is by the power of *concentration* which men possess, by the direct and efficient might which they bring to bear on a particular object, that their conquests are marked. The power of the blowpipe is not from the length of time during which it is applied to metals; it is the intensity and condensation of the flame. The power of an army is not from the time it has been in the field; it is in the nature of its discipline, and the concentrated energy of its leaders. Alexander and Napoleon gained their chief laurels while yet young; one decisive action gave immortality to the name of Nelson, and in our own country, to those of Macdonough and Perry. Yet who would aver that the time spent in preparation for these scenes of victory was lost, or should have been employed for years in feeble and misdirected sallies. So Newton turned the concentrated power of his mind, with amazing intensity, on the subjects of science, and before the age of thirty, had almost completed his discoveries, and given a finish to the glories of his imperishable name; and Milton devoted a long and toilsome life in slow preparation for writing a book, which, he foresaw, "the world would not willingly let die." We might remark, also, that our Saviour judged in this manner of the power of concentrated action; and of the time when men should labour in the gospel. In three years, his voice and his omnipotent arm made an impression on the condition of mankind, that gave a new and ever-abiding direction to human things. Nor has that example been unblessed in the ministry of those who have proclaimed his gospel. It remains *yet* to be proved that they who go forth in the fulness of their strength, and the maturity of a long preparation for their work, accomplish *less* in the ministry, than they who diffuse their work over more years, and enter this great office with diluted powers and feeble preparation, with acquisitions which scarce remind us that learning or discipline are in any way connected with the gospel.

Now, let it be remembered, that this ministry is called to act on *mind;* that it is sent forth to encounter every class of men; that it meets every form of prejudice; that it falls in with all the power of sophistry, all the art of sin, all the pride of intellect and of passion, all the sottishness and brutality of life; all the forms of learning, and all the subtlety of schools, and all the pedantry of the world; and that they who are to proclaim the gospel are required to *teach* all nations, and the necessity of such a training as we advocate will be at once apparent. How shall *he* seek to bear the gospel to the minds of men, who is ignorant of the laws of the mind? How is he to answer the cavils of skeptics, who is ignorant alike of their cavils, and the sources of their plausibility? How shall he meet their prejudices, and surmount their real difficulties, who has yet to learn what they are, and what is their strength; and how shall he present a system who knows not what the system is, or tell men of laws, and usages, and claims in the Bible, who has yet himself to look into those laws, to learn the existence of those usages, or to see arguments which support those claims?

Every man who stands before others to preach the gospel, stands there professing his ability to explain, defend, and illustrate the book of GOD; to meet the cavils of its enemies, and to press its great truths on the hearts and consciences of men. His very profession implies that he not merely *believes*, but is able to show to thinking men that this is a revelation of God. Why should he attempt to explain a book which he can neither vindicate nor understand? It implies that he is familiar with the ever-varying forms of objection and cavil; that he is not merely convinced, but is able to convince others, that this is a book of GOD, and that Christians are not of necessity fools, but that religion commends itself to the sober judgment and conscience of men. What right has a man in this holy office to *assume* that *his* word is law, and *his* opinion infallible? What right have we to advance to our fellow-men, and claim that what *we* say is to be received without argument, and that men are not to call it in question without being charged with fighting against God? The age has gone by when declamation could be passed off for argument, when dogmatism could sit down in the place of thought, and when pride and pomp could bow the souls of men to the dictation of the priesthood. Men *will* think, and will reason henceforward; and the truth has gone forth, never more to be recalled, that there are henceforth to be no trammels on the freedom of the mind, but such as reason, and conscience, and thought can fasten there. And if we, with all the advantages of learning and science, and the amazing but just power of a Christian pulpit, in "its legitimate and sober use," cannot persuade men, by the blessing of God, *to think as Christians*, they will be persuaded by others *to think like infidels.* Thought will be untrammeled, and an age has arrived when the refuse of other professions will not do for the ministry; when the man who at the bar, or in the senate, could not gain a livelihood, might perform the office of a mendicant or a curate.

Far from us, and from our friends, and from this age, be the ministration of men of dull and stupid intellects; of cold and phlegmatic hearts; of a dogmatical and aristocratic cast of mind; of lofty and self-assuming dictation; of barren and technical statements of dogmas, unsustained by thought and unsupported by sound argumentation. The world is becoming more and more sensitive to the truth that he who enters not upon this work with somewhat of the fixedness of purpose that characterized the youthful conqueror of Italy, or Washington struggling for freedom, or that gave firmness to the indomitable minds of Hancock, or Henry, or Hamilton, or rather to the burning ardour of Paul, has fallen below the aim demanded of the heralds of salvation, and had better find an occupancy and a livelihood in any of the less conspicuous kinds of employment.

It might seem almost needless to add, that the man who goes forth to proclaim the gospel should be able to *read* it, at least, in the language in which it was originally penned. Why should a man go to expound a message to others, which he can neither read nor understand, as it came from the hand of Him who commissions him? Can there be a more evident unfitness in regard to qualification for a work, than to be ignorant of the very document which it is the main business of his life to present to others? It is almost too absurd for grave remark, to speak of an ambassador who cannot, except by an interpreter, read his credentials; of a lawyer who cannot read the laws which he expounds; of a teacher who cannot read even the books which he professes to teach. And yet the melancholy fact has existed in this land, and still exists, that to multitudes of those who are public teachers, the original languages of the Scriptures are unapproached treasures; and that the confidence with which they speak, is that of men who depend on the testimony of others, for a knowledge of that which it is their appointed business to explain.

Who knows not how reluctantly this whole subject is approached even in the seminaries of Christian theology? And who knows not how it is laid aside as soon as the departing evangelist has bid adieu to the place of his theological training? And who knows not that the whole arrangement of the study afterward contemplates the removal of all books written in the Greek and Hebrew tongues, into the most remote and unfrequented departments of the library? And who knows not how much there is to excite compassion, if not ridicule, ever afteward, in the effort to trace out the meaning of a Hebrew word, or to catch the thought couched in the phraseology of the forgotten Greek?

The main business of the ministry is to study and to explain the Bible; and it is idle to talk of *studying* the Bible, unless the language of its original composition can be understood. The great truth is impressing itself more strongly on this generation—that sublime truth which achieved, under God, the glories of the Reformation—that the Bible is the foundation of theological knowledge. And it has not failed to attract attention, that, in proportion as the Scriptures have been brought into view, systems of technical divinity have retired into the back ground; the mind has been unloosed from trammels; and new views of truth have presented themselves to the understanding and the heart. Indeed, from age to age, the propensity to bury the Bible under a cumbrous load of standards and systems of divinity has been so great; so much care has been taken to shape and direct every great mass of truth; so solicitous have men been first to form the *mould* of the system, and then to run the system into it, that it has ceased to be matter of marvel that Christianity has been so little free and unfettered in its movements, and that the growth of knowledge in this grandest of all departments of science, has been so slow and stinted. One great truth is standing before this age. It will be in vain for us to refuse distinctly to contemplate it. It will work its way into all our schools; it will occupy all our seats of learning; it will seize upon all our seminaries. It is not that the sentiments of the past are to be treated with contempt and disregard. It is not that men are indignantly to trample on all the monuments of wisdom and all the standards of Christian doctrine. It is *that the Bible is the great original source of truth in this world;* that it is to be investigated by all the aid which learning, and piety, and toil can bring to bear on it; that its great and unchanging decisions are to be listened to with profound deference, and without theological gainsaying; and that its unbending sentiments are to give shape to every system of truth; to remould, if necessary, every form of doctrine; to repress every vagary of ancient imagination; and to chain down every fancy of daring metaphysics, of theological poetry, romance, and knight-errantry; and to demolish every Gothic pile that stands to awe the human mind, or that stretches its lengthened shadows over any of the paths of human thought. Let the ministry, as they *will*, and must, and should do, in this and every coming age, approach the book of God as Bacon, and Boyle, and Newton approached the world of matter and of mind before them, as simple interpreters, and the outer limit of theological attainment will have been gained. The human mind will be emancipated, and the strength of the human faculties in theology will be demonstrated by sitting at the feet of *Christianity*, evincing the higher laws of the universe, just as men who sat down before the works of God, evincing its *lower laws*, with childlike simplicity, learned what was the order of his material creation.

Now we know not a stronger argument for education than this. The mind *will be free.* It is the charter of this age. Shall it be a wild and erratic freedom? Shall it be suffered to rove undisciplined over all the works and word of God? Or shall it be disciplined and subjected to sober laws, and bound by the restraints of a thorough education—the only proper restraints of thought? Shall men be taught to approach the Bible, subjected to just rules of exegesis, fitted to defend the truth, and commend it to every man's conscience; or shall men start forth by hundreds as they will into the ministry, exalting every vagary of the fancy into a Scripture truth; deeming every crudity of the mind a revelation from heaven, and subjecting the Scriptures to every vain, foolish interpretation that a heated fancy and fanaticism may engender? The truth is, men *must* be educated, or the very principles on which the world is acting, will work its ruin. Fix a vast wheel in complicated machinery, for a check and balance, and it produces equality and order. Loosen that same wheel from its axis, and send it with the same momentum at random, and it will carry desolation to the entire fabric.

We shall close this discussion with a reference to the singular aspect of our land, in other respects bearing on this subject. The star of our freedom moves westward. It has gone from the graves of our fathers, and now stands over the valleys of the Mississippi. The hand that is to guide us, is henceforward to be stretched out far beyond the mountains; or the chains that are to bind us will be forged in the regions of the setting sun.

We remark, then, that the ministry is called to act on the destinies of an age, a predominant characteristic of which, we fear, is likely to be, that it will be infidel. Every man who can cast an eye over this land, knows that infidelity here will not be of a character that can be encountered by those who are not trained for the conflict. It is not merely that ancient infidelity which loved to sit among ruins, like the satyr and the owl, and the bittern and the cormorant, in the lonely palaces of Babylon. It is not simply that of France, whose fabric was reared and cemented by the blood of millions, and which traced its eulogium in a nation's tears and pollution. It is not merely the sentiment of Hobbes, that all property is the right of every man, and may be taken if it can; nor the dying maxim of Hume, that precious legacy which the historian of England left—that suicide is lawful, that adultery must be practiced, if a man would secure all the benefits of life. It is not merely the unbelief which visits the palace in the writings of Voltaire and Gibbon, or which travels down into the brothel and the sty in the works of Paine. It is all combined; the precious offering of entire ages of infidelity, poured, in the fulness of its measure, on our shores, and rearing its temples of pollution and crime in our villages, our cities, our theatres, our palaces, our schools, and our prisons. It comes to us with the learning of the past, and the scoffing of the present; arrayed in wealth and in rags; now seating itself in the place of power, and now uttering its oracles from the dunghill; now flowing in rills of oily eloquence; now putting on the aspect of reason and learning; now seen in the pleadings for licentious indulgence; now lurking in the smile of polished contempt; and now pouring forth its piteous wailings in the name of liberty, and rallying our countrymen to the standards of freedom, when it has known no freedom, and attempting to sit down in the abodes of learning, when its reign there has been always that of ignorance and death.

The inquiry is, whether we shall send forth young men untrained and unfitted to grapple with this hydra, or whether we shall act on what has hitherto been deemed the dictate of common sense, to *train* them for their work, and *fit* them for the portentous aspect of the times? It is too late to dream that ignorance can cope with learning, or unskilfulness with cunning; or that darkness can supply the place of light; or dogmatism can settle questions in religion; or men be overawed by the terrors of anathemas and chains. Men will be free. And unless you can train your ministers to meet them in the field where the freedom of mind is *contemplated*, and let argument meet argument, and thought conflict with thought, and sober sense and learning overcome the day-dreams and dotage of infidelity, as it has done the strength of its manhood, you may abandon the hope that religion will set up its empire over the thinking men of this age.

Again: Ministers act in an age remarkable for the subtilty and cunning of error. It weaves itself into our learning. It is intrenched in the ramparts reared to confine thought, and to fetter the human faculties, in a darker age. Ancient systems raise their affrighting forms over the men who dare to break away from the consecrated modes of thought and expression. Error hides itself in specious pretences. It comes in the glow of pious feeling. It awes us by telling of the venerated names of men that the world loves and delights to honour. It summons to its aid authority, law, ecclesiastical censures; profound regard for order; veneration for the past, and great apprehensions of the future. On the other hand, it calls to its defence new modes of reasoning; the latest forms of mental science; the philosophy of the schools, and the profound learning of an age unequalled in power of thought, rapidity of conception, grandeur of enterprise, and deep researches into the laws of matter and of mind. If there ever was an age when a man, to be any thing, must think for himself, this is that age. Yet who is he that thinks for himself? Only he whose mind you discipline; whose fancy you chain down to sober investigation; whose veneration for names and systems you merge in the grand enterprise of looking at things *as they are.* This object is contemplated in every design of education; and our only security against error, under God, is to train men to habits of sober and patient thought; to teach them that argument is not in names; nor religion in dictation; nor piety in cant phrases and stereotyped expressions of regard for what the world has admired, "time whereof the memory of man runneth not to the contrary," but in a conscience made quick to love the truth, and habits of industry, and patience, and prayer that shrink from no obstacles, and that persevere until the mind is fixed in the truth, and the message is borne to the soul fresh from God.

Again: No eye can be closed to the fact that the emissaries of a church which, in much darker times than ours, called for all the skill of Luther, the learning of Calvin, and the eloquence of Melancthon, are coming in upon this land. Nor do we send forth many men into the field, who will not encounter others trained for the conflict; plausible in argument; smooth and winning in eloquence; mild in manners; rich in learning; subtle in sophistry; and commanding in talent; schooled in the nurseries of the delusive arts, and in colleges formed to teach the *real* cunning of the serpent, and the *apparent* harmlessness of the dove. Who knows not that the Jesuit is at our doors, and is hastening to embrace the pillars of the state, and enter into the temple of our liberty? Who knows not that, with skill adapted *to our times*, he comes with art, with eloquence, and with power; that he selects the richest vales for his abode, and draws to the places of fascination and ruin, our sons and daughters? And shall Protestants go forth to meet him unapprized of his arts, unskilled for conflict, unguarded with the panoply with which teaching and prayer can furnish the champion of truth in this holy war? Our countrymen may slumber over this. Our churches may repose in security. But if there is an eye to catch the prospect of danger, or an ear open to alarm, the Christian will feel that they who are defenders of the truth, cannot be fitted for this conflict by ignorance, or marshalled for the battle by piety alone, however ardent.

We before remarked on the prodigious expanse of the active powers in this land. We might dwell on this, and show that this untiring activity demands correspondent learning and discipline, in our ministry. Our countrymen stretch their way to the West, and found cities, and towns, and colleges there. Who is to attend them? Who to counsel, who to sit in the seats of learning? Shall ignorance; shall infidelity? Counsellors they will have, and men of learning they will have to teach their youth, and lay the foundation of their own society. Can any American, any man who has ever cast a glance at Plymouth, doubt whether they should be men of learning and talent who are to direct the destinies of the West, and mould the character of that population? Be ignorance and fanaticism anywhere else rather than in the ministry of the rising empire of the West. He that by a *touch*, may control the destiny of millions, should *not* be a pedant, a conceited fanatic, or a stranger to the power of moulding the elements of political and religious society, with reference to the destinies of the rising empire.

Our country is connected with the world. We owe a debt to all nations. Our name is everywhere known. Our influence stretches across the waters. Every nation looks to us; and it must be ours to furnish men who shall bear the gospel from pole to pole. The name of an American *preacher* should be *in religion*, what the name of an American *citizen* is, a passport to all climes, and an honour in all the kingdoms of the earth. Let men be trained as they should be, and it will. Even now it is an honoured name, and is beginning to be known in all the empires of men. Missionaries, nurtured by our education societies, are encountering the dangers of every ocean; treading every region of sand, or snows; ascending every hill, and going down into every valley; exploring every island, and in almost every language proclaiming the wonderful works of God.

Whose heart does not beat with holier and happier emotion, when he remembers that America is rearing men to carry the gospel through every zone? And who would limit the efforts of any association that sought to fit heralds of salvation to go forth to benighted nations, and to tell of a dying Saviour in the snows of Siberia, and on the banks of the Senegal and the Ganges? Every American Christian must love his religion and his country more when he remembers, that even now the voice of the American is heard in the islands of the ocean, and that our country's blood, consecrated by piety and learning, flows amid all the people of the earth. We live with reference to future times, and distant men. We know how the voice of the American is heard abroad. We love our country more when we remember that the example and the eloquence, the learning and piety of the Mathers, and of Eliot, and Hooker, and Edwards, and Davies, and Brainerd, and Dwight, and Payson, strike across the waters, and shall be borne on to other ages and other men. It shows that we are not unmindful of our birthright, and that we remember that we are the descendants of the people honoured by the names of Baxter, and Owen, and Barrow, and Taylor. We love our country more when we remember, too, that Fisk, and Parsons, and Hall went from our shores, and have not been deemed unworthy coadjutors in the cause for which Martyn, and Swartz, and Vanderkemp toiled and died. To furnish more such men is the noblest object of the toils and prayers of American Christians.

There is an entire field of thought connected with this subject, into which we cannot now enter. We refer to the question, whether this object will not take care of itself; whether there is need to aid those who are coming forward; or whether numbers sufficient would not of themselves seek a preparation for the holy ministry. We can only advert to the well-known facts,—1. That true worth is retiring and modest, and needs to be sought out, and urged onward. 2. That talent and piety are often found in humble life, and encompassed with poverty. 3. That there is an alarming want of ministers in this land, of those who are qualified for their work, and that the increase by no means keeps pace with that of our population. 4. That the way to prevent the land from being overrun with preachers of every character and qualification, *except the right*, is to raise the standard of the ministerial character, to diffuse knowledge, and make the people restless and dissatisfied under an ignorant or a bigoted ministry; to *fit* men for their office, and to furnish the churches with men of sense, and piety, and learning. Ministers enough of *some order* there will be. Every land is furnished with priests of religion; and the number of *such* priests is in exact ratio to the ignorance of the people, and the corruption of the form of religion. Infidelity has its priest in every man, who is sworn, by his talent and influence, to propagate the scheme. Paganism has its thousands of altars, and its array of priests to attend on every altar. In France, under the Romish Church, four hundred thousand, or one man in every sixty-two of the inhabitants, are ecclesiastics; in Spain, one hundred and eighty thousand, or one in every sixty-one of the population, are supported by the church; and so, under the same system, it will be in this country, unless Protestants betake themselves to their duty, and train up men well qualified for the ministry. Every man knows, also, that ignorant and unqualified preachers abound in all Christian denominations. The question is not, whether there will be ministers of religion. It is, whether they shall be qualified for their work; whether the Protestant churches of this land will train men for the holy office; or whether the disciples of fanaticism and of ignorance, the high-priests of infidelity, and the vast array of secular clergy, and monks, and nuns, under the guidance of the Jesuit, shall take possession of the country, and prey like the locust on the avails of our toil, and abide in the dwelling-places of our wealth and our arts. The Christian world has but to take its choice. The churches have the great question before them. It is, whether this land shall submit to the teachings of ignorance, the ravings of fanaticism, the dogmatisms of infidelity, the guidance and support of numberless hordes of Jesuits; or to the instructions of a pious, educated, and sober ministry.

Our land has been blessed hitherto with the toils of holy men. They live in memory, and in the fruits of their deeds.

> "We give in charge
> Their names to the sweet lyre. The historic muse,
> Proud of the treasure, marches with it down
> To latest times."

We seek that other men may be reared to occupy the place of the illustrious and the pious dead; to spread the triumphs of the gospel through all the vales, and in all the hills of this land, and throughout the world. No more deep-felt and ever-abiding desire dwells in our bosoms, than that revivals of religion may diffuse their rich and peaceful fruits in all the mansions, and schools, and towns of our republic. We have no more fervent prayer to offer for the land which gave us birth, and which has been rendered sacred by the blood shed by our fathers, and by the prayers which they offered, and by the descent of the Holy Ghost, than that it may be continually blessed with the ministrations of the gospel of peace, producing its appropriate, its *immediate* effect on the souls of men. In all our visions of the future glory of America; all our conceptions of the magnificence of our power; the monuments of our arts; the blessings of our liberty; we anticipate, as chiefest and brightest in the splendid prospect, the time when the gospel of peace shall be borne from the lips of every herald of salvation, with the directness and power which have crowned it in the days of our Edwardses, our Tennants, our Dwights, and our Paysons.

III.

[CHRISTIAN SPECTATOR, 1832.]

The Works of Lord Bacon. Four vols. fol. London: 1730.

THE connection between philosophy and theology has been felt and acknowledged in all ages. Most Christians have deplored the influence of the former upon the latter; but even those who have been loudest in their complaints, and strongest in their expressions of grief on this account, have given often the most melancholy proofs of this very influence. In view of this long and intimate union, however, and of the fact that philosophy may take its complexion from religion, as well as religion from philosophy, it becomes a question of no ordinary interest, whether God did not intend that the one should be perpetually a check upon the other? Did he not design that the strange tendency in philosophic minds to perverseness, pride, and atheism, should be continually restrained by the overawing influence of the proofs of religion everywhere present? And did he not intend, also, that the vagaries of the human mind in religion, the romance and knight-errantry of theology—the tendency to fanaticism, and dogmatism, and mysticism, should be held in check by the influence of common sense, the knowledge of the true laws of mind, and the investigations of science from age to age? The relation of the sciences—the *vinculum commune* between them, was long ago remarked by Cicero. The mutual influence of *modern* sciences on each other, and of all on religion, is a much more important inquiry to a Christian.

We have neither the time nor ability to enter into a full investigation of this subject. Nor indeed do we conceive that a *detailed* inquiry would so effectually answer the end we have proposed to ourselves in our work, as some other mode. To meet the demands of the present state of theological science, and to turn theological inquiries to the best practical account, it is not necessary, in our view, to proceed into much actual detail. We address ourselves to an age of inquiry. We speak in our pages to those who, we believe, are qualified, and are disposed, to think for themselves. We contemplate the existence of no barriers to investigation; no fetters to free inquiry; nor want of diligence or disposition to follow out any train of thought which may be suggested for practical use. It is our province to furnish topics for such inquiries; and the design which we have in view in our labours in the Christian Spectator, will not have been accomplished unless we have laid the foundation for investigation, and for active Christian effort, long after our humble labours on earth have closed.

It is under the influence of reflections like these, that we wish to call the attention of our readers to the works of Lord Bacon. Our object will be accomplished if we can briefly exhibit his character; and can state the influence of his writings on science, and the kind of influence which the inductive philosophy is destined to exert, particularly on the science of theology.

"For my name and memory," said Bacon in his will, "I leave them to men's charitable speeches, and to *foreign nations, and to the next ages.*" The reason of a part of this remarkable bequest is to be found in the melancholy fall of this illustrious man, to which we shall have occasion again to advert. In the close of the bequest—the legacy of his name to future times—we discover proofs of the same consciousness of immortality that prompted Milton to compose a work that the world "should not willingly let die." Yet more than two centuries have passed away, and we have as yet no well-written biography of this greatest of British philosophers.

Till within a year, indeed, we had nothing that deserved to be called a life of Newton. Still it is not a little remarkable, that no one, prompted either by fame or usefulness, has presented to us a biography of such a man as Bacon. In the whole range of literature there is not a finer unoccupied field than would be presented in the attempt to give the public a well-written account of the author of the Novum Organum; of the state of science at the time he lived, and of his influence on the interests of science, of literature, and of religion. Yet, perhaps, we shall ever be compelled to regret, in regard to him,—a thing by no means uncommon in biography,—that of his peculiar habits of life, his changes of opinion, the progress of his discoveries, and their immediate influence on men, we are to know nothing but a few most meagre facts which have been rescued from oblivion.

There is another remark which we are here compelled to make respecting the works of Bacon. Few modern scholars, we fear, are acquainted with them,—even with the *Novum Organum*. The study of them requires more time, patience, industry, perhaps *conscience*, than most men of modern habits are willing to appropriate to them. Bacon is regarded as belonging to a distant age and to long-past times, and though his *name* is in every one's mouth, and his praises in all nations; yet how few are there who could give an intelligent account of his principles of philosophy! How few theologians, we are compelled to ask, have ever looked for a moment at the Novum Organum? Yet we are aware of its difficulty; and we are not disposed to utter the language of complaint against the men of our own times. We are convinced that though our generation should not sit down to the *formal* perusal and study of this profound work, yet there has gone forth from it an influence which reaches our age, and that we are, though unconsciously, reaping its benefits, as the Nile long shed fertility on the fields of Egypt, while the source of its waters was unknown; and as the rain and light of heaven diffuse their influence over the earth, while that influence may be unnoticed or forgotten. It has been asked with emphasis, "who now reads the *Rambler?*" And it is indubitable that this book, which once exerted so mighty an influence on the English language and people, has given place, at least in general reading, to works of far inferior merit and interest. The reason seems to be, that its object is well-nigh accomplished. It commenced with a standard of morals and language elevated far above the prevailing style of morals and of writing. It has elevated both, and has brought the English language and notions of morality to its *own level.* Nor is it wonderful that men should regard with less interest a work which *now* is seen to have no very extraordinary elevation. It is a component part of English literature, having *fixed* itself in the language, the style, and the morals of the English people, and taken its place as an integral and almost undistinguished part of the national principles of writing and morality. The result is, that while the *benefits* of the Rambler may be diffusing themselves, unperceived, to almost all the endearments of the fireside and virtues of the community, the book itself may be very imperfectly known, and unfrequently perused. Johnson may be almost forgotten, except in praise; but his mighty power is yet sending forth a mild influence over lands and seas, like the gentle movements of the dew and the sunbeam. The same is true of Bacon. He has *incorporated himself* into all our science. He has imbedded his principles in the very foundation of all our improvements in astronomy, natural philosophy, and chemistry, and, to a great extent, of mental science and theology. It is related of Phidias, that in constructing the statue of Minerva at Athens, he so wrought *his own image* into her shield that it could not be removed without destroying the statue. Thus Johnson has wrought himself into our language and morals;—and Bacon into our science. We have often endeavoured to follow out the effect of his labours, by taking our present science and literature, and attempting to go back and remove step by step, year by year, and age by age, all that may have resulted from the influence of the "Instauration of Learning," by Bacon.—No one can be aware of what he owes to that man, who is not able to thread all these mazes, and to trace all the unseen progress of his principles that have thus found their way, though from an unknown benefactor, into English science and literature.

The leading facts of Bacon's life are soon told. He was born on the 22d day of January, 1560. At an early age he graduated at Cambridge, and after having travelled for some time on the Continent, became a student at law, and was at the usual period admitted to practice. During the reign of Elizabeth, in consequence of having rivals and enemies at court, he was either overlooked, or purposely prevented from obtaining offices of standing and honour. This period of his life was passed chiefly in the practice of the law; in writing some treatises on jurisprudence; and in preparation for the more elevated offices in the government which he afterward filled, and the more important advances in the sciences which he was destined ultimately to make. But though he was thus neglected by Elizabeth, and undistinguished by any external and substantial marks of her favour, he was often admitted as her counsellor, and enjoyed to a considerable degree her confidence. On the accession of James I., Bacon advanced rapidly through various offices in the gift of the crown. Of James he says in a letter to him, that "he had raised and advanced him nine times: thrice in dignity, and six times in office." He was successively counsellor extraordinary to his majesty; king's solicitor-general; attorney-general; counsellor of state; lord-keeper of the great seal; and lord chancellor. From this last office he was degraded for corruption, after having held it two years, and devoted the remainder of his life to the pursuits of philosophy. During this period of four years, his principal philosophical works were written. He died on the 9th of April, 1636.

There is little pertaining to the early life and actions of this illustrious man, on which we wish to offer any remarks. Indeed, it would be difficult to present to our readers any thing like a just biography of his early years. There are no memorials of those years; no records of his mode of study, and his advances in science; of his changes of views, and his projects of ambition; nothing that will acquaint us with the manner by which his mind was trained to the amazing stature which it afterward obtained. Nothing could be more interesting or useful than to follow out the development of such an intellect, and to trace the influence of external causes, and internal principles and emotions, in framing a character whose influence has been already felt in all the departments of science and of morals. But we are doomed to sigh unavailingly over the lamentable defects of the biography of illustrious men. One *hint* only is recorded, which sheds some light on the development of his early powers. It is said of him that at the early age of sixteen years, while at the university, "he fell into the dislike of the philosophy of Aristotle; not for the worthlessness of the author, to whom he would ever ascribe all high attributes, but for the unfruitfulness of the way, being a philosophy only strong for contentions and disputations, but barren of the productions of works for the benefit of the life of man." At a time when the philosophy of Aristotle was enthroned in the universities of Europe; when his decision was law in all the investigations of philosophy; when for almost two thousand years he had swayed an undisputed sceptre over all that part of the world which claimed to be civilized, it was no slight indication of independence of mind even to *doubt* the infallibility of his decisions, and no unpromising omen of the advance which was afterward to be made by him in the sciences. Aristotle and Bacon now stand at the head of the two great sects of philosophers that have divided mankind. It was the high honour of the one, that mankind for ages yielded their heads and hearts to his decisions, and bowed to his authority. It was the unrivalled glory of the other, that he displaced him from his proud elevation, and introduced a *new method* of investigating truth, that has forever broken the sceptre which the philosopher of Greece so long swayed over mankind.

It is not our purpose to offer any remarks on the character of Bacon as a lawyer. He was the rival of Coke; and it is not easy to estimate which of the two was the more eminent man in this department of human science. Had Bacon confined his researches to that which seems to have limited the ambition of Coke, it would be a matter of more moment to institute the comparison. The admirers of legal attainments might then delight to inquire which of these two men was entitled to the highest honours of his profession. But the name of Bacon naturally suggests to us far different attainments from those which adorned the bar or the bench. We forget the robes of the lawyer, and the dignity of the ermine. The advocate, the counsellor, the chancellor, the titles of nobility are lost in the profound attainments of the man of science, and the restorer of learning. We may just remark, however, that the united testimony of Bacon's contemporaries award to him the highest attainments as a lawyer, and a full, rich, and flowing eloquence, that placed him deservedly beside the Roman pleader; and that, while he was speaking, "the only fear was lest he should make an end." Of the correctness of his legal opinions and decisions, as chancellor, we have the highest proof that has ever been furnished in any case. Though he was accused and convicted of receiving bribes; though he confessed the crime, and was sentenced to a heavy penalty; and though some were given *pendente lite*, and probably with the express intention on the part of those who offered them to influence his decision in their favour, yet it is recorded to his lasting honour, and it comes to us as a solace when we think of the fate of this illustrious man, that not one of his decisions was reversed or called in question as unjust.

Bacon was not only a man of profound legal attainments, but also eminent in the various departments of general literature. With the classic purity and elegance of his Latin style, every man must be struck who has read the Novum Organum. But we feel more interest in remarking, that there is nowhere to be found a better exhibition of the power of the English language, than in his prose writings. For manliness and strength; for purity and occasional elegance of diction; for copious and varied illustration; for terseness, compactness, and the absence of all expletives, and the use of such words and phrases as leave the thought clear and transparent to the view, we know not where there can be found better models than his Essays. Less full and flowing than Milton; less dense and compact, perhaps, than Butler; less filled with varied imagery, and the creations of fancy, than Taylor; less argumentative and stately, it may be, than Barrow; and less majestic and pompous than Johnson, he had yet in a rare union what we most admire in all. He has placed on his pages, in wonderful combination, those excellencies of style which have given immortality to so many other men. And if any one wishes to understand the beauty and force of the English language, we know not how he can better do so than by becoming familiar with the writings of this illustrious man. Nor was his excellence in this respect apparently a matter of particular study. His mind was full of thought, and he gave utterance to his thoughts in pure and majestic English, that makes us love our language more, and exult in the possession of so noble a medium of conveying the loftiest conceptions and the most enlarged philosophy to mankind.

But it is not as a lawyer, or a man of literature, that we wish now to contemplate this illustrious man. We wish to look at the influence of his philosophy on that holy cause to which our pages are consecrated. We believe that this influence has gone far, and is destined to go still farther, into all the departments of Christian theology. We believe it is inevitable that the prevailing philosophy shall exert a wide influence over the theology of our age. We do not doubt that it ought to do so. Not that it is to control the Bible, or set aside its decisions, but that it is to hold in check certain vagaries of the human mind, which bigots, and zealots, and theological antiquarians would persuade us are conformed not only to the tradition of the elders, but to the testimony of the Scriptures themselves. There is a wonderful charm to many minds in a theological dogma, where it can be *pretended* that it has been held "time whereof the memory of man runneth not to the contrary." And there is a marvellous shrinking, and expression of abhorrence, when philosophical dogma is summoned to meet dogma, and the rules of a correct philosophy are employed to uncanonize and dethrone these elements of ecclesiastical tyranny. Our remarks, then, are designed to lead to a just estimate of the influence of the philosophy of Bacon on the science of Europe; of his religious character; of the applicability of his philosophy to theology; and the effect which would be produced by an unsparing application of those principles to the theology of modern times.

We do not deem it necessary to enter at large into the inquiry about the state of science when Bacon wrote his Novum Organum. There are two great departments of knowledge on which such a mind would act—the one pertaining to the physical sciences, the other embracing the vast department comprehended under the general term of metaphysics. We have given a full statement of the condition of the latter when we say, that this entire department was, till the time of Bacon, under the influence of the philosophy of Aristotle.* He reigned in the schools; he controlled the systems recorded in the books; he fixed the metes and bounds of inquiry; he swayed a sceptre over the entire invisible world into which man might be disposed to push his investigations. More than all, this philosophy had incorporated itself with all the *religious* dogmas of Europe, and was imposed on the belief of men with all the sanctions of the most terrific and iron-featured superstition that has ever extended a sceptre of night over the world. During centuries of darkness this system had been compacted, and with infinite toil of profound metaphysicians had received its shape,

> "If shape it might be called, that shape had none
> Distinguishable in member, joint, or limb;
> Or substance might be called that shadow seemed."

It is common now to speak of the system with contempt. We

* "Toward the close of the fifth century, the influence of Aristotle began to prevail over that of Plato in the Christian world. After considerably declining in the sixth century, it again revived; and in another century it had gained such an ascendency, that Aristotle seems everywhere to have been triumphant. Glosses, paraphrases, summaries, arguments, and dissertations on his works, were composed without end, as if to make darkness visible. Many of the inhabitants of the West learned Arabic, in order to read a translation of them into that language. Men were everywhere taught to believe in *matter, form,* and *privation,* as the origin of all things; that the heavens were self-existent, incorruptible, and unchangeable; and that all the stars were whirled around the earth in solid orbs. Aristotle's works were the great text-book of knowledge, and his logic was the only weapon of truth. Christians, Jews, and Mohammedans united in professing assent to the great lawgiver of human opinions; not Europe alone, but also Africa and Asia, acknowledged his dominion; and while his Greek originals were studied at Paris, translations were read in Persia and Samarcand."—*Brougham's Account of Bacon's Novum Organum.*

despise it because it has passed out of view, and we deem it not worth inquiry. We look on it as we do on desert sands which we are not bound to traverse; and on dark and pestilential and frightful abodes which we are afraid to enter. But they who have looked at the system are the last to hold it in contempt as an effort of profound and subtle argumentation, and the last to wonder that it exerted such an amazing influence on mankind. We have only to remember that it required the best part of a man's life to become acquainted with the dialectics of Aristotle and his commentators; that it was deemed indispensable to education to be master of the philosophy of the schools; that it was linked by a thousand ties to the reigning superstition; that the colossal power of the Roman See was sustained chiefly by the prevalence of this philosophy; and that to doubt the dogmas of that superstition, and of course the philosophy of Aristotle, subjected a man to the horrors of the Inquisition,—and we shall cease to wonder that it so long swayed its sceptre over mankind.

The Reformation had made an incipient aggression on the authority of the Stagyrite, at the same time that the Reformers had defied the thunders of the Vatican. But no mighty genius had yet arisen who was competent to strike an effectual blow at its colossal power. It was reserved for Bacon to put an end forever to the system, and to introduce a method of inquiry which was to annihilate the dominion of Aristotle. At the early age of sixteen, as we have seen, he called in question the correctness of this mode of investigation; and his philosophical life was little more than an effort to rescue the world from the protracted tyranny, and to lay the foundations of a nobler method of inquiry.

It will be recollected that the difference between Aristotle and Bacon related to the *proper mode of investigating truth.* The philosophy of the schools dealt in abstractions. It did not look at facts, but at theories; not at visible and tangible realities, but at fancied essences; not at the world as it is, but at an ideal world; not at things which God had formed, but at the creations of a subtle and refined philosophy, which age after age had laboured to reduce to consistency and to form. The designs and labours of the schoolmen we cannot better present than in the words of Bacon:

"Surely like as many substances in nature which are solid, and do putrify and corrupt worms; so it is the property of good and sound knowledge to putrify, and dissolve into a number of subtle, unwholesome, and (as I might term them) vermiculate questions, which, indeed, have a kind of quickness, and life of spirit, but no soundness of matter, or goodness of quality. This kind of dogmatic learning did chiefly reign among the schoolmen, who having sharp and strong wits, and abundance of leisure, and little variety of reading, but their wits being shut up in the cells of a few authors, (chiefily *Aristotle*, their dictator,) as their persons were shut up in the cells of monasteries and colleges, and knowing little history either of nature or time, did out of no great quantity of matter, and infinite agitation of wit, spin out into those laborious webs of learning which are extant in their books. For the wit and mind of man, if it work upon matter, which is the contemplation of the creatures of God, worketh according to the stuff, and is limited thereby; but if it work upon itself, as the spider worketh his web, then it is endless, and brings forth indeed cobwebs of learning, admirable for the thread and work, but of no substance and profit."—*Advancement of Learning*, vol. ii. p. 428.

Yet, in regard to their talent, Bacon renders the following just acknowledgment.

"Notwithstanding, certain it is, that if the schoolmen, to their great thirst of truth and unwearied travel of wit, had joined variety and universality of reading and contemplation, they had proved excellent lights, to the great advancement of all learning and knowledge; but, as they are, they are great undertakers indeed, and fierce with dark seeking. But as in the inquiry of the divine truth, their pride inclined them to leave the oracle of God's word, and to varnish in the mixture of their own inventions; so in the inquisition of nature, they ever left the oracle of God's works, and adored the deceiving and deformed images, which the unequal mirror of their own minds, or a few received authors or principles did represent unto them."—Vol. ii. p. 429.

One can scarcely help reflecting here, what an amazing advance the unwearied toils of the schoolmen might have made, had their efforts been directed by some such work as the Novum Organum. Had the profound talent of Duns Scotus been employed on the works of nature, or in investigating the properties of mind in any useful way, it is possible that we might never have heard the names of Bacon, Locke, or Newton, or have heard of them only as carrying the discoveries of science far into the regions that are now untrodden by living men, and clothed, to human view, in the shades of profound and "ever-during darkness."

We do not deem it necessary to dwell on the state of science in Europe when Bacon lived. We have not room to do it. Those who wish for detail on this subject—perhaps the most interesting that the history of mind and opinions furnishes—will find it in the works which have, in modern times, attempted to establish just views of mental and moral science. Reid and Stewart have presented this in ample detail.

The grand achievement of Bacon was to break the power of this despotism over mind. To this work no small part of his active life was devoted. In the midst of the toils of office and of law, while seeking for preferment at the feet of his sovereign, (for this was the grand foible of this illustrious man,) and while discharging the duties of a profession which at all times has been deemed enough to occupy the time and energies of the profoundest and most active minds, did this distinguished lawyer lay the foundation of that system on which now rests his fame. He then conceived and digested the plan of his great work on the Advancement of

Learning; and he had so looked over the field of human science; so estimated its defects and its wants; and so contemplated the *objects* at which science should aim, that nothing was needed but a few years of leisure to establish principles which should ultimately change the entire aspect of human science and opinions.

It is to one of those strange and mysterious events which we are perpetually called upon to deplore in the history of man, that we owe the accomplishment of this great design. While making these preparations, Bacon was in the enjoyment of offices and preferments that would have satisfied any man of moderate ambition. But he sought a seat near the *ear* of majesty, and aspired to the highest offices to which a British subject can be elevated. He obtained his wishes; James advanced him to the dignity of lord chancellor; and conferred on him the keeping of the great seal of England. Had his life been spent in the duties of that high office, it is probable that his name would have been known to us, if at all, only in British heraldry, or in the books and records of jurisprudence. But this illustrious man, to use an expression applied by the profligate Horace Walpole to every man, "had his price;" and, in two years, the chancellor of Great Britain was degraded from his office; fined to the amount of fifty thousand pounds; sentenced to be imprisoned at the king's pleasure; and forever excluded from holding any office under the British government. Of the justice of this sentence—which, so far as the fine and imprisonment were concerned, was soon remitted—no one ever entertained a doubt. Of the nature of the offence, and the influence which it should have in forming an estimate of his character, we shall have occasion to speak in the course of this article.

After a fall like this, most men would have abandoned every effort; and, sunk in hopeless despondency, would have blushed to give publicity to their names even by the most splendid discoveries of science. After such a fall most of the ancients would have put a period to their lives. Cato fell by his own hand, unaccused of the crime that dishonours the name of Bacon; and Cassius sought his own death amid misfortunes that, to a sensitive mind, would have been less overwhelming, than was this degradation to the chancellor of England. But it was here, that the nobleness, and, we hope, the religion also, of this illustrious man triumphed. He gave himself not up to despondency. He laid aside the insignia of office, and sought honours beyond what the courts or cabinets of kings could ever bestow.

After his deposition from office, Bacon lived about five years. The closing years of his life he gave entirely to the pursuits of philosophy, and the perfecting and completing of his great works on science. During this period it does not appear that he ever sighed for the honours which he had once so ardently sought, or that he ever wept over the favours of royalty which he had so ignominiously lost. His great mind sought employment in contemplating the advances which science might make, and in laying the foundation for those astonishing improvements which science in all its departments has since made.

The principles of the inductive philosophy, which Bacon reduced to a system, if he did not originate, are easily told and easily understood. To us, therefore, at the present day, it is not very easy to understand why the establishment of such a system should have given to him a celebrity which surpasses all that had before been regarded as great among men. To understand it, it would be necessary to go back to the early periods of science, to watch its slow advances, to look at the mistakes which have been made in all the eras of philosophy. At every step, we should pause and wonder that the obvious principles of the inductive method should not sooner have presented themselves to men. At almost every step we should see philosophy approaching the very principles of the Novum Organum; we should see men half disposed to leave the trammels of *theories*, and to go forth in the manliness of just philosophic inquiry to look at nature as she is; and at every step we should be amazed that men drew back from these obvious paths of inquiry, and retreated into the dark shades and bewildering paths of abstract speculation. This tendency of the human mind to frame theories, rather than to look at facts, to forsake the obvious and plain paths of inquiry for vain and delusive vagaries, we regard both in the scientific and theological world, as one of the most remarkable and melancholy perversities of the human intellect anywhere presented in the history of the race.

There are but two ways of attempting to understand the works of nature, or of ascertaining the relations and properties of things. One is for the philosopher to sit down in his grove or closet, and attempt to frame in his own mind what nature *ought* to be; the other, to become the *interpreter* of nature, and to tell the world what she is. The one attempts, on the basis of a few facts imperfectly ascertained, isolated in their character, and little understood in their connections, to frame a theory that shall account for all the facts in the world, and to construct a bed of Procrustes to reduce all the theories and facts to the same dimensions; the other approaches the works of creation as the Son of God directed his disciples to come to him, with the spirit of little children, and humbly to sit down at his feet. The former course was the most difficult, the least obvious, and was capable of being made to amaze and confound the intellects of men. It would give the longest and most profound employment to the intellect; would most effectually separate philosophers from other men, and introduce what men of philosophic temperament have commonly sought—the honours of *caste*;—an elevation above the millions of humbler mortals beneath their feet. This strange obliquity of the human mind we are compelled to trace, country after country, and age after age, in the history of science. It is constituted alike the teaching of Aristotle, of Pythagoras, of Plato. The only man in antiquity who seems in any measure to have been free from it, was Socrates; and even *his* instructions referred almost solely to morals. We are often led to wonder at the little advances which science made in antiquity. We go to Egypt, the parent of civilization, of learning, and even of art. What has ever been found there, in relation to the sciences, that would entitle her to the very lowest place now in our schools? When we admire the monuments of her power; when we look upon her pyramids, or enter them; or when we wander among the broken columns of Thebes, and are impressed with the proofs of her vast physical power, we are instinctively prompted to pause and ask, where are the monuments of her science? What advances did she ever make in the knowledge of that which could ultimately contribute to the spread of true knowledge among mankind? Of what use was it to the world to construct her pyramids, her obelisks, her sphynxes, or her labyrinths? The playthings of kings, fit monuments of children, or fit tombs of mortals who could seek immortality in them, while the great mass of intellect beneath them grovelled in the most revolting idolatry, and only lived to accomplish what *we* now do much better by the help of the steam-engine.

We are not less struck with the absence of the plainest principles of science even in Greece and Rome. We do not undervalue classic learning, or wish to banish it from the schools. Yet we cannot but be struck with the almost total want in the classic remains of antiquity, of any very valuable explanation of even the more common phenomena. What a conception far, far beyond the loftiest thoughts of antiquity, is presented by the simplest truths of modern astronomy? Though this science among the Chaldeans, the Persians, and the Greeks, was that to which most attention had been paid, and on which they would probably have rested their highest claims to celebrity, yet to what did it amount? To a few theories, involved, unintelligible, and undemonstrated, about the *possible* order in the movements of the heavenly bodies; to the formation, with infinite toil and childish care, of *pictures* of the heavens—arranging the stars into constellations, and giving them outlines, having a fanciful resemblance to some object among animals or reptiles. What was more obvious in the healing art, than to approach the human frame and *examine* it by dissection? Yet this was never done. What more plain than to collect *facts* in regard to diseases, and arrange them by patient induction, and from the science of physiology, and the recorded facts, to attempt to *cure* men? Yet the ancient practice of medicine under Galen, and in the ancient world, was simply to *prevent* disease, and not to *cure* it. By rules of hygiene, and systems of dietetics, they sought to *parry* and ward off the attack, and were strangers to the art of restoration. One of the most obvious and amazing instances of the want of science in antiquity, related to the simplest laws of hydrostatics. The aqueducts of Jerusalem, of Rome, and of Gaul—of all ancient cities and towns, are probably among the most striking monuments on earth, of an entire ignorance of the most simple laws of science, among people so refined and intelligent as they are acknowledged to have been. So amazing has it appeared that one of the simplest laws of hydrostatics should have been unknown to them, that their admirers have sought in vain for some reasons of pride or state, to account for such vast expenditures in supplying their cities with water.

The ancients knew nothing of the present system of arithmetic. The science of *numbers* among them was exceedingly complicated, and never carried beyond what to us are its simplest elements. They knew nothing of algebra, and, of course, nothing of the stupendous calculations to which it has given rise, and nothing of the easy and extended advances which it could give to geometry. They had not learned to simplify profound and laborious calculations by the aid of logarithms, and were utter strangers to fluxions. They had not attained to any just mode of the mensuration of the earth; a matter of so great moment to astronomy, navigation, and commerce. They had not been made acquainted with the mariner's compass; and their navigation was confined to narrow streams, or to the vicinity of the mainland. The laws of gravitation were to them unknown; and, of course, all the science and all the useful arts now dependant on those laws. Nothing can be more complicated or unsatisfactory, than the cycles and epicycles of ancient astronomy, and though in all this, as well as in the labours of Aristotle, we discern proofs of profound talent and indefatigable toil, yet we find also convincing proofs that we are contemplating there what Bacon insists should be called the *infancy*, and not the *antiquity* of the world.

We are struck with the same thing in the mechanic arts. The application of water, for example, to turn a mill—a thing so obvious to us,—is not known to have been accomplished in Greece, and was not attempted at Rome till near the age of Augustus. The propulsion of the saw by any other power than by the hand, was a novelty in England so late as the sixteenth century. Nothing like the *pump*—an instrument so obvious to us—was known to any of the ancient nations.*

These observations might be extended to almost any length. But it is sufficient here to ask of any student of the ancient classics, what valuable fact, or just philosophic theory has he ever found in all the ponderous tomes that have travelled down to us from Greece and Rome? For what single, just

* Webster's Lecture before the Mechanics' Institution.

theory is he indebted to all the master-spirits of the ancient world? We have often been amazed at the slow advances which science made. With all that we admire in the acuteness of their intellect, the richness and splendour of their diction, the profoundness of their moral sayings, the grandeur of their military achievements, and the unrivalled beauty of their specimens of art, we have still seen that there was some mighty spell over all their attempts at science; that there was some spirit of darkness that blasted all their efforts, and withered their energies, and completely stayed their advances in the march to those high attainments which now so dignify and ennoble man. *We* know no reason for this but the dominion which a love of *theory* had gained in all the nations of antiquity. We see there the first movements of that despotism which was destined to reign over Europe for many centuries, and to bury at last in one common grave just mental philosophy, large and liberal views, national freedom, and refinement, as well as to stay all advances in science and the arts.

We might also apply these remarks to other nations, and we should find the same fondness for theory extending itself, and spreading a baleful influence over all the efforts of science and of art. It is customary to acknowledge with gratitude our obligations to Arabia for some of the most important advances in science, particularly the science of chemistry. It is not our wish to lessen this feeling of gratitude. But we cannot withhold the expression of our regret, that the principles of the philosophy of induction were unknown to the Arabians. Even in that land, so remote for a long time from the influence of the Aristotelian philosophy, we discern traces of the same unhappy tendency first to construct a theory, and then to examine nature to establish it. The Arabian *assumed* that all metals might be transmuted into gold. He framed a theory that all metallic substances could be traced to a single basis, and that the purest metals could be produced from the least valuable. Nature was subjected to the torture, to establish this theory; and the discoveries which were actually made, were the result of accident, and made, not because they were sought, but because in the endless investigations which were set on foot, it was *impossible* that they should entirely escape notice. It was *assumed* that there was somewhere an elixir of life, a universal preventive of disease, and prolonger of life. To discover this, was the object of the toil of centuries. It of course failed; but, in the vain and Quixotic effort, many important facts could not but force themselves on the attention of mankind. What would not half the talent and skill expended in these vain and fruitless pursuits, have produced under a happier and wiser system of philosophy? It is needless for us to dwell on the unhappy influence of the philosophy of Aristotle during the Middle Ages. There never has been so long and unbroken a spell over the energies of mankind, as during that dismal period. The human mind has nowhere else exhibited so remarkable a perversity; nor is there anywhere to be found so sad a commentary on the influence of a false philosophy. Age after age was employed in compacting and digesting the dark and terrible system. As it came from the hand of Aristotle, it had much to command admiration. It was, to appearance, a harmless system. Had it remained in Greece, it would not, probably, have greatly fettered the minds of men, or retarded the progress of science. The truth is, that the philosophy of Plato, and Aristotle, and Pythagoras, did not much affect the common mind. It was understood to be adapted only to the Grove and the Lyceum. The great mass of mind was to be unaffected by it; and we do not know that the majority of the Greek population was influenced at all by all the labours of those illustrious men. But during the rise of the papal dominion in Europe, it became indispensable that some system of philosophy should be at the control of the priesthood, that would extend and prolong the shades of darkness as far as the sceptre of the papal power could be made to extend. Some scheme was necessary that should repress investigation; that should convince mankind that all wisdom, as well as power, was located near the Vatican; and that should effectually fetter and bind human faculties, and stay for ages the advance of thought. The grand thing needed to give ascendency and stability to the papacy, was some system that should treat inquiry as constructive heresy, and brand novelty of opinion as dangerous to the purity and power of the church. Had this been left to the *invention* of the friends of the rising spiritual tyranny, we believe that there was not cunning or talent enough among all the adored and canonized fathers of the church, to have devised any effectual scheme. But the work was made ready to their hands, long before even the coming of Christ. The scheme had been framed by one of the profoundest minds that ever approached the topics of human inquiry. Nothing more was wanting effectually to confirm the aspirations of the papacy; to repress inquiry; to chain the mind down to ignorance; to prepare it for all the legends and fooleries of the monastic life, and to fit it to receive all the claims of the papal power, than to give such a direction to the philosophy of the Stagyrite as to adapt it to the common mind, and bestow on it all the tremendous sanctions of religion. This was done. Its reign was secured, and when we see what it was expected to accomplish by it, we cease to wonder that it should call forth the profound talents of such men as Duns Scotus, and even the devoted piety of Thomas Aquinas. When these shades were stretched over the church; when it was understood that this withering philosophy was to attend the dogmas of the papal See, we cease to wonder at its long and gloomy reign. It was sustained by the mightiest talents then on earth; it was urged forward by all the learning that lingered in the monastic cells; by all the achievements of the papal arms; by all the mighty power of religious principle when misdirected; by the energies of a dark and dismal superstition; and, finally, by all the terrors of the Inquisition, and the flames of persecution. Every engine of cruelty in the Spanish dungeons tended to confirm the reign of Aristotle; and every flame kindled in the valleys of Switzerland was designed to confirm and prolong the dark and gloomy domination. It became necessary to fetter and bind *all* the faculties of the soul. Scientific investigations would, at any period, have overthrown the power of the papacy. Large and liberal indulgence given to the cultivation of any single faculty of the mind, would have ultimately set the mind wholly free. The improvement of any single department of science or learning, would have emancipated the human powers, and stayed the desolating reign of the papal supremacy among men. You cannot give enlargement to one of the faculties of the mind, without affecting all. You cannot emancipate man in one department of learning, without ultimately sending a healing and redeeming influence over all that gives rise to inquiry, or that ennobles and purifies man. Hence we see how difficult and slow was the progress of the Reformation. On any effort to emancipate the mind in any department, there rested this superincumbent mass, consolidated for ages. Wherever there was in any department, however obscure, a disposition to inquire, or to doubt, it was the certain precursor of the thunders of the Vatican, and of the terrors of the Inquisition. Every nook and corner of the Roman dominion was searched as with the hundred eyes of Argus; every change of opinion, or advance in science, called to the spot the concentrated vigilance and power of the whole Roman See. Roger Bacon early made advances in science, and was one of the first who acted on the principles of the inductive philosophy, but his improvements died with himself, and for ages his was a solitary name connected with philosophy, in the whole compass of the Roman domination. Jerome of Prague, and Huss, and Wickliffe, dared to think for themselves, and to doubt the infallibility of the prevalent opinions; and the flames of persecution terminated the lives of two of them, and indignity was offered to the bones and the works of the other. Galileo constructed a telescope, exposed to the eye of man the absurdities of the prevailing philosophy, and laid the foundation for the modern discoveries in astronomy; and he was rewarded with a place in the dungeons of the Inquisition. With so keen an eye did the Roman See discern that the slightest advance in science would tend to destroy its far-spread domination, and liberate man from the ignoble and slavish chain. And we may here remark, that the distinguishing features of the papal See in modern times, though varied, are not essentially changed. It is still true, that the philosophy of Aristotle holds *as real* a sway over the Romish Church as ever; and it is true, that it looks with as real a jealousy as ever on the advances which men are disposed to make, and on freedom of opinion, as it did on the opinions of Wickliffe or of Galileo.

The Reformation under Luther broke this mighty power. It was necessary that some tremendous shock should be given to the Roman See, and set the human mind at liberty, and it was done. God raised up men formed for those times, men evidently adapted to make vast changes, and originate stupendous revolutions among men. The papal power once broken; the project of confining all learning to the cells of the monastery being for ever put to an end by the discovery of printing; the terrors of the Inquisition, and the anathemas of the triple crown being ineffectual to prove the telescope to be false; and the superincumbent load of superstition and crimes in the papal dominion being beyond human endurance, the Reformation by one mighty effort threw off the incumbent mass, and man walked forth dignified with the privilege withheld for centuries, of *thinking for himself.* The great truth went forth, never more to be recalled, that man was to be at liberty to frame his own opinions, and that the last successful effort *had* been made effectually to fetter and paralyze the human powers.

It is interesting to the friends of science, to trace the slow advances which were made toward the great truths which now ennoble science. We have already adverted to the labours of Roger Bacon, and the discovery of the telescope by Galileo. We may now remark, that many of the maxims of the inductive philosophy were acted on before they were collected and arranged by Bacon. Thus in the year 1596, John Kepler published his peculiar views on the Harmonies and Analogies of Nature. This was a book constructed wholly on the prevalent system of philosophy, in which he attempts to solve what he calls "the cosmographical mystery of the admirable proportion of the planetary orbits;" and by means of the six regular geometrical solids he endeavours to assign a reason why there *are* six planets, and why the dimensions of their orbits, and the time of their periodical revolutions, were such as Copernicus found them. Perhaps not even in the trifling, but more laborious toils of the schoolmen, could there be found a more melancholy illustration of the prevalent philosophy. A copy of this work was presented by its author to Tycho Brahe, who had been too long versed in the realities of close observation to attach any value to such wild theories. He advised his young friend, "first to lay a solid foundation for his views by actual observation, and then by ascending from these, to strive to reach the causes of things."* On this principle Brahe had long acted, and by the aid of it had reached a distinguished elevation in the philosophical world. On this principle Kepler appears afterwards to have acted,

* Brewster's Life of Newton, p. 120.

and under the guidance of the Baconian philosophy thus compressed into a single paragraph, he abandoned his visionary inquiries, and laid the foundation of that distinguished character for philosophic inquiry which he subsequently obtained. Philosophers were beginning gradually to abandon the long-established maxims of the schools. They began to discover the inutility and barrenness of their speculations. Incidentally, and at intervals, they expressed some great sentiment, which, if followed out, would have freed them from the domination of the prevailing systems. They saw that under the advancing prevalence of the new principles of inquiry, the universe began, to their view, to assume a new aspect; discoveries in science had already characterized the sixteenth century, far more in number and importance than had marked the whole reign of the philosophy of Aristotle, and the way was manifestly opening for some still more splendid advances in science.

At this auspicious period Bacon rose. The world had manifestly worked itself into a form adapted to the moulding of some such mighty mind. Some comprehensive genius was demanded by the circumstances of the age, that could look at once at all the departments of science, ascertain and record all that had been done and that was still defective; point out the errors that had pervaded all the investigations of past generations, expose the causes of the slow progress of science, of its repeated defeats, its little utility, and disclose the true paths of philosophic research. Some single mind of vast native powers and attainments was needed to collect the incipient, though scattered maxims of the true philosophy, and present them in an embodied form; that should trace their *real* influence in the hands of Friar Bacon, of Galileo, of Tycho Brahe, and of Kepler; and that should show in what way the same principles might be applied to all the departments of human investigation. Such a man was Bacon. Nor was there ever a human being so well adapted to occupy this ground as he. He seems to have been fitted by a wise Providence, to stand at the base of the towering and superincumbent system, which had so long held in ignoble bondage all the human powers, and to hasten its decline; and to frame a scheme that should be adapted to all future times, and to set up land-marks along the paths of all the departments of science. Nor do we know that there have ever been put forth more vast and comprehensive views, than those which characterized this illustrious man. The principles of his philosophy are simple, even to the comprehension of a child; and yet vast enough to meet all the investigations of the modern astronomer, to direct all the inquiries of the natural philosopher and chemist, and to give law to all the investigations of mind.

The two great departments of Bacon's work were designed to state what are the proper objects of science, its advances, and its defects; and to submit the outlines of a new method of philosophic inquiry. The first of these he accomplished in his treatise on the Advancement of Learning; the latter in the Novum Organum. The first of these we regard as presenting, even now, by far the best view to be found of the various objects of human pursuit. With a comprehensiveness of mind which shows that he had looked at all the inquiries of the illustrious men of other times, at their successes and their failures, at the true compass of the field of inquiry, and at its actual results, he states what *are* the proper objects of human pursuit; what advances had been made; and what remained yet to be accomplished. It is lamentable, in looking at this work, to see how little had been accomplished by the toils of so many centuries; and no survey could more completely have shown the necessity of some *new* mode of investigation. Men had speculated and framed visionary theories age after age, and yet scarcely a truth in the science of astronomy had been established; and few of the facts of the universe had been subjected to the test of the inductive philosophy. Men had been so bewildered in the pursuit of substantial forms, and real essences; they had been so tossed in vortices, and had listened so anxiously to the imagined music of the spheres; they had so loved the great maxim of the Aristotelian philosophy, that the way to investigate truth is to frame a theory, and construct a syllogism; that science, even down to the time of Bacon, was a vast chaos, and the entire field was to be resurveyed, and subjected to a better and different test.

This test he proposed in the Novum Organum. Never was there a more comprehensive maxim, or one more fitted to revolutionize all the prevalent systems of philosophy—though to us perfectly simple and obvious—than the first sentence of this wonderful work. Never was there an announcement more fitted to arrest the thoughts of a philosophic mind, or to produce a pause in all the inquiries that the world was then making, than when he proclaimed, "Homo, naturæ minister et interpres, tantum facit et intelligit, quantum de naturæ ordine, re vel mente observaverit; nec amplius scit, aut potest." It is not our purpose to attempt an analysis of this vast and comprehensive work. It is, perhaps, of all works, except Butler's Analogy, least capable of abridgment. Our regret is that it is so little known and so little understood by theologians. Its great principles are better understood in all other departments of inquiry than in theology. We were about to add that divinity is almost the only science on which it has not cast a flood of light. Our object in this article will be accomplished, if we can direct the attention of our readers to this great work.

The great principle of the Baconian or inductive philosophy, we have already stated in the advice given by Tycho Brahe to Kepler. It consists in a careful and patient examination of *facts*, or the phenomena of the universe, and deriving from the observation of those facts the principles of a just philosophy, or the laws by which the natural universe is governed. It supposes that God acts on the same principles in the same circumstances, in all places and at all times; and that when we have carefully examined one phenomenon, and have ascertained its cause, we are qualified and authorized to apply the same explanation to all similar facts in the universe. Till then, we are not qualified to frame a theory. Till then, a theory would be visionary, useless, wild, and probably erroneous. On this simple precept the whole of the Baconian philosophy rests, and the wonder to us is, that so much time was necessary in the history of philosophy to bring it out, and that the talents of such a man as Bacon were demanded to establish it on an imperishable foundation. Yet it was long before the world saw its value; and to the mistakes and errors of mankind in regard to this single principle, we are indebted for that stupendous production of the human mind—the Novum Organum.

It was sufficient honour for one man to have laid the foundation of the inductive philosophy; in other words, to have taught the race in what way to approach the works of God with the hope of success. This was the honour reserved for Bacon. Hence we are not to expect that he himself would make great advances in experimental philosophy. His discoveries were few, and many of his experiments incomplete. Yet it is amazing that he subjected so many objects to the test of experiment—that with so incomplete and clumsy an apparatus as could be possessed in his time, he attempted an examination of so many phenomena, and even with so much success.

From the time, however, of the publication of the Novum Organum, the progress of the sciences is well known. As if by the wand of magic, Bacon laid open for correct human investigation all the departments of the material and mental worlds. Galileo had already pointed the telescope to the heavens; and by a single glance had exposed to contempt all the cycles and conjectures of the ancient astronomy. Bacon taught mankind how to look at the stupendous facts which the telescope laid open to view; how to classify and arrange the amazing phenomena which now burst upon the eyes of mankind; how to subject nature to the torture, and how to penetrate into all elements, look at all worlds, and how to listen to the universal voice which the heavens and the earth, the air, the ocean and the land, were ready, with a harmony more grateful than the feeble music of the spheres, to pour on the human ear in relation to science. Europe was prepared to follow her illustrious guide. Centuries had been opening the way for the Novum Organum; and it was impossible but that the boundaries of human science should at once be enlarged, far, far beyond what the world had ever known. A mighty engine was brought to bear on the works of creation; and never before had man been armed with like power in questioning the elements of the universe. We regard the rise of such a man as Newton, who has, by common consent, been placed at the head of the race, as an event which the crisis of the world was just fitted to produce. A peculiar juncture of political affairs has commonly raised up men adapted to their times. Such men as Cæsar and Napoleon, as Hannibal and Scipio, as Leonidas and our own Washington, are formed often by great *crises* in the history of the world. The frame of things makes their existence indispensable; and calls out talent, prowess, and patriotism, which, *but* for such events, would have slumbered unknown.

Newton we regard as indebted to the state of things formed by Wickliffe and Luther; by Galileo, Kepler, Brahe; by John of Salisbury, Roger Bacon, Ludovicus Vives; by Gilbert, who had investigated the laws of magnetic attraction; by Copernicus, who had revived the ancient Pythagorean doctrine of astronomy; by Francis Bacon; and by the prevalence of just principles of philosophy in Europe, for the station which he occupies in fame as at the head of mankind. The development of some such mind, we consider as inevitable in the progress of events, as the formation of the character of Napoleon, fitted to control the whirlwind and direct the storm of revolution in France. And while we wish to concede all honour to his immortal name, we cannot but remark that, under other auspices, Aristotle, or even John Duns Scotus, might have filled the space which Newton's name now fills; and that most certainly some La Place, or Herschell, would have opened the eyes of mankind on the modern astonishing theories of the heavens. In less than half a century from the publication of the Novum Organum, Newton had developed the laws of light, strictly on the principles of the inductive philosophy; had invented the science of fluxions; had discovered and demonstrated the grand principles of the modern astronomy; and by one transcendent effort of intellect, had opened to human view the sublimest scenes which had ever appeared to mortal eyes; and while he *told* us of the amazing distances and magnitudes of the heavenly bodies, seemed almost to annihilate their distances, and made man feel for the first time that he was an inhabitant of the *universe*, and bound by indissoluble ties to distant worlds. It would be easy to extend our remarks to the improvements in chemistry and the kindred sciences. Perhaps in no way would the benefit of the inductive philosophy appear more striking than on a comparison of the labours of Sir Humphrey Davy, with the toils of the alchimists of the dark ages. With the simple, and to us very obvious, principles on which Davy proceeded in the construction of the safety lamp, it is now impossible to conjecture what the Arabian chemists would have produced. We can scarcely help pausing to contemplate what a different destiny *might* have awaited mankind, if those principles had been understood by the Mussulman. The followers of the impostor might then have been put in possession of the amazing mechanical powers and chemical processes which now distinguish and adorn Christian lands. Science would have returned, perhaps, to its native Egypt; have spread over Arabia; have travelled eastward to Persia, to Hindoostan, to China. The magnetic needle might have pointed the ships of Islam to the distant Western World, and established the religion of the prophet here. Our streams might have been navigated, and our lands filled by the Mussulman; and the Tigris, and the Euphrates, and the Ganges, perhaps, might have been the first to open their bosoms to bear the vessel navigated by steam. God designed, doubtless, that these sciences should start up, and receive their form and consummation on Christian soils; and we love to trace the wonderful means by which he has directed man in science and the mechanic arts, as he has in religion; thus showing that the worlds of nature and of grace are under his control. Our limits forbid our following out the bearing of the principles of the inductive philosophy on the arts and sciences. To our mind there is nothing more interesting than to observe the amazing changes which the inductive method has made in the opinions, the philosophy, and the arts of mankind, and in the ultimate effect which we believe those principles will have in sending the gospel around the globe. Hand in hand with the Christian religion, we believe that those arts and scientific results will yet encompass the world. Already we trace their influence in enlarging and liberalizing all the usual modes of thinking among men; in lessening the distances between nations; in rendering it easy to cross seas and plains; in forming *neighbourhoods* of what were remote districts; in producing sympathy and a rapid interchange of feeling between the distant parts of republics and remote kingdoms; and in forming facilities for carrying the gospel around the globe. That these improvements have been made on Christian ground, we regard as proof at once of the large and liberal influence of true Christianity, and at the same time as evidence that it is the *intention* of God that this religion should encompass the world. We do not adduce this as a *proof* that the Christian religion is true; but we cannot but regard it as one of the vast array of circumstances that God has placed everywhere around the Christian scheme, evincing that it is under his benignant care; that all those great advances which tend to exalt and adorn human nature, tend also to the spread of the Christian system; and that such is the economy of things, that no great advance can be made in true science which shall not contribute to strengthen and confirm the evidences of revelation; no facility of communication be opened among mankind—no process of breaking down existing barriers, and annihilating prejudices, and of cementing man and man, of binding nations in one universal brotherhood, which shall not contribute to the spread of the Christian scheme; and no spread of Christianity in its purity which shall not also convey to benighted men letters, science, mechanic arts, and liberty. We discern here, we think, evidence that the scheme has the approbation of God; and in the staid and motionless formality of China, in the corruption of Hindoostan, in the wretchedness of pagan islanders, and Africans, and in the dark features and bloody hands which are everywhere seen under the reign of Islam, we think we discern the frown of God on the schemes of religion which thus fetter and bind down the faculties of man, and which never *have been,* and never *can be,* connected with true science and the mechanic arts.

But one other topic remains, pertaining to the character of Bacon. We refer to his moral and religious character—unhappily the most difficult part of our inquiry. That dark shade which passed over his name toward the close of his life, which hurled him degraded from the office he had so long and so earnestly sought, which led Pope to characterize him as the

> "Wisest, brightest, *meanest* of mankind,"

has rendered it almost impossible to estimate his moral and religious character. To this sad period of Bacon's life, his character, so far as we know, except as a man fond of display, and ambitious, was beyond reproach. In the offices which he held, and in his private deportment, he was never suspected of a want of integrity. Hume declares that he was not only the ornament of his age and nation, but also "beloved for the courteousness and humanity of his behaviour." It is natural for us to seek some palliation for Bacon's great offence; and, happily, there *were* circumstances, which, while they by no means justify his crime, yet serve in some measure to modify its character, and render it much *less* base and ignominious than such an offence would be deemed in our times.

The parliament which was assembled by James in 1621, entered immediately into an investigation of the existing abuses of the nation. Unhappily they found in this, their favourite employment, an ample field of labour. Abuses had crept into the government under James, which this vain monarch either *would* not believe could exist under his wise administration, or which he was unwilling to correct. The necessity of the case, however, compelled him to yield to a determined and inflexible House of Commons. That House, he already saw, was disposed to apply an unsparing hand to all the abuses of the government, and even to most of the royal prerogatives. The necessity of the case compelled him to express his royal gratification with their labours, and to encourage them in their work. "I assure you," said he, "had I before heard these things complained of, I would have done the office of a just king, and out of parliament have punished them, as severely, and peradventure more, than you now intend to do."

Encouraged in this manner, and resolved to strike an effectual blow, they commenced their investigations respecting the character and deeds of the lord chancellor. Unhappily, here also they found an ample field for the work of reform. The result is well known. Charges of extensive bribery were brought against him. It was alleged that he had received money and other presents, to the amount of many thousand pounds, while causes in chancery were depending on his decision. As to these charges, Bacon made a *general* acknowledgement of guilt. With this confession the parliament was wholly unsatisfied. Determined to humble the greatest man of their time, they demanded an explicit confession, in *detail*, of each act of corruption. Power they knew was in their hands. A weak, vain, and silly, though learned monarch, trembled before them. They had commenced a process which *could* terminate only in the fall of the reigning sovereign; and they resolved that the highest man in the realm should feel the weight of their power. Bacon made them an ingenuous, frank, full, and most mortifying confession of guilt, and bowed himself before the representatives of the people. He acknowledged his guilt in *twenty-eight* articles; specified the amount he had received; detailed, as far as was then practicable, the circumstances, and left himself at the mercy of an indignant parliament. "For extenuation," says he, "I will use none concerning the matters themselves; only it may please your lordships, out of your nobleness, to cast your eyes of compassion upon my person and estate. I was never noted for an avaricious man; and the apostle saith that covetousness is the root of all evil. I hope also that your lordships do the rather find me in a state of grace; for that in all these particulars, there are few or none that are not almost two years old; whereas those that are in the habit of corruption do commonly wax worse; so that it hath pleased God to prepare me by precedent degrees of amendment to my present penitency; and for my estate, it is so mean and poor, as my care is now chiefly to satisfy my debts." Being asked by a committee of the House of Lords, whether this was his true and real confession, he used the following noble and touching language, "My lords, it is my act, my hand, my heart; I beseech your lordships to be merciful to a broken reed." The sentence for the crime we have already recorded.

We have no wish to justify these deeply humiliating and disgraceful crimes. We know not an instance in all history where we could weep over human weakness, as over the fall of this great man. It is one of the thousands of instances that everywhere meet us of human depravity; but, if it fixes us in grief, and appals the soul, it shows us man, scarcely "less than an archangel, ruined," and arrests our thoughts, not like the obscuration of a planet, or the withdrawal of the beams of a twinkling star, but with the deep melancholy which is shed over created things, when the sun

"In dim eclipse disastrous twilight sheds
O'er half the nations, and with fear of change
Perplexes monarchs."

The only way in which this offence can be in any manner palliated, is by a detail of the acknowledged circumstances of the case. 1. Bacon was distinguished for want of economy during his whole life. It is clear, as he says, that he was not "an avaricious man," but his great error was a love of office and honour; his great foible, a fondness for display. This fondness had involved him in debts which he was unable to pay. 2. The affairs of his domestic economy, it appears, he intrusted to servants who were regardless of expense, and, probably, unconcerned about the dignity, virtue, or solvency of their master. One article of the charge against him was, that "the lord chancellor hath given way to great exactions by his servants." To this he replies, "I confess it was a great fault of neglect in me, that I looked no better to my servants." 3. It is indisputable that Bacon was not *enriched* by these bribes. 4. It is more than probable, that Bacon only followed a custom which, until that time, had been regarded as no violation of the oath of the lord chancellor. Hume affirms that "it had been usual for former chancellors to take presents." If this was the case, it lessens greatly the enormity of the crime. It also casts much light on the character of the parliament which was thus resolved to make him a victim. 5. It is said that the presents which Bacon received did in no instance influence his decisions. It was never alleged, even by parliament, that he had given an unjust or erroneous sentence. None of his decisions were ever reversed; and it is affirmed that he "had given just decrees against those very persons from whom he had received the wages of iniquity."* It is further to be remarked, that of the twenty-eight charges of corruption against Bacon, but *seven* occurred during the existence of the suit. It remains yet to be demonstrated—a thing which *he* did not acknowledge, and which neither the witnesses in the case, nor the nature of his decisions proved—that even those *presents* influenced in the least his decisions. The more we contemplate the case of Bacon, the more we are disposed to think that injustice has been done to his character. We believe, in relation to the errors and failings of the men of those times—of such men as Calvin, and Cranmer, and Luther, and Bacon,—that men have pronounced sentence with a severity drawn rather from the present views of morals, than from the sober estimate which we *ought* to make, if thrown into the circumstances of their times. This we think particularly true with regard to the

* Hume.

crime of Bacon. While we feel assuredly that crimes such as those with which he was charged deserve the abhorrence of mankind, and go to impair and destroy all justice in the administration of laws, we are still inclined to look upon the errors of that age, and in those circumstances, with less severity than we should be disposed to apply in the more enlightened periods of the world. It is not easy to form an estimate of Bacon's *religious* character. We are favoured with so few and imperfect details of his private habits; we have so little that tells us the true biography of the man—his feelings, his usual deportment, his private modes of action; we are let so little into the interior arrangements of his life, that we cannot easily pronounce on his personal character. Charity would lead us to hope, notwithstanding his fondness for preferment, and the great error of his life, that he may have exemplified in his private life, the principles which he has so ably and so constantly inculcated. On the subject of his religious *opinions* he has left us no room to doubt. There is scarcely to be found in any language or in any writer, so constant a reference to the great religious interests of man, as in the writings of Bacon. There is nowhere to be found a more profound deference to the authority of the Bible. There is, perhaps, nowhere more caution displayed, lest the profoundness, variety, compass, and originality of investigation, should lead the mind astray, than in his investigations. It was one of his recorded sentiments—one of the results of his investigations, which he has expressed without hesitancy or qualification,—"that a little philosophy inclineth a man to atheism; but depth in philosophy bringeth men's minds about to religion; for while the mind of man looketh upon second causes scattered, it may sometimes rest in them and go no farther; but when it beholdeth the chain of them confederate and linked together, it must needs fly to Providence and

Deity."* His belief he has left us in a well-written confession of his faith, embracing the usual articles of the Christian religion. His prayers, which are preserved, breathe a spirit of true devotion, in a style and form which are not surpassed by any compositions of that period, in our language. It would be easy to transcribe page after page of his recorded sentiments; and we might trace, at every step of his life, his profound deference for the theology of the Bible.

We do not believe that the Christian religion depends for its evidences on the suffrage of any one philosopher; or on the bright constellation of names which have expressed their profound regard for the truths of revelation. Still a Christian cannot but look with deep interest on the fact that such men as Bacon, and Boyle, and Newton, bowed their mighty intellects to the authority of revelation; came and brought all the rich and varied treasures of their profound investigations, and laid them at the foot of the Cross; and spent their lives increasingly impressed with the belief that the God of Nature is also the God of the Bible. While we do not claim that on their authority the Scriptures should be accredited as the word of God, we *do* claim that they should be allowed to rebuke the flippancy of youthful and unfledged infidelity; that they should be permitted to summon men to *inquire*, before they *pronounce;* we claim that their authority is sufficient to call on the youthful skeptic to pause, and to suspect that *possibly* he may be wrong. When mighty minds like these have left their recorded assent to the truths of the Christian scheme, it is not too much to ask of minds of far less power to sit down and inquire, at least, whether Christianity may not have come from God. When Newton, after having surveyed world on world, and measured the heavens, and placed himself for profound inquiry at the head of mankind, sat down

* Essays, Civil and Moral.

in the full maturity of his days, and passed the vigor of his life, and the serene evening of his honoured age in the contemplation of the New Testament; when Bacon, after having rescued science from the accumulated darkness and rubbish of two thousand years, after having given lessons to all mankind about the just mode of investigating nature, and after having traversed the circle of the sciences, and gained all that past generations had to teach, and having carried forward the inquiry far into nature, bowed at every step to the authority of the Bible; when Hale, learned in the law, not only believed Christianity to be true, but adorned the Christian profession by a most humble life; when Boerhave, profoundly acquainted with the human frame, and skilled in the healing art, sat with the simplicity of a child at the feet of Jesus Christ; when Locke gave the testimony of his powerful mind to the truth of the Christian religion; when Davy, first of chemists, came on this subject to the same results as the analyzer of light, the inventor of fluxions, and the demonstrator of the theory of gravitation—as the author of the Novum Organum—and the writer of the treatise on the Human Understanding; when each science has thus contributed its founder, its ornament, and its head, as a witness to the truth of the Christian religion, it is not too much to conclude that it may be something different from priestcraft and imposture. When we turn from these lights of men—these broad stars that spread their beams over all the firmament of science, and seek after the wandering and dim luminaries of infidelity; when we make a sober estimate of what the high-priests of unbelief have done for the advancement of science, and the welfare of man, we are struck with the prodigious advance we have made into chilly and tenebrated regions. We have passed amid spirits of another order. We wander in climes as remote almost from science, as from Christianity. We should know where we are as readily by their superficial, but pompous pretensions; by dark, but most confident scientific claims; by erroneous, wandering, but most flippant demands in science, as we do by their infuriated and bitter raging against the claims of the Christian religion. Who are these men? Volney, Diderot, D'Alembert, Voltaire, Paine; Herbert—the best and greatest of them—Shaftesbury, Tindal, Morgan, Bolingbroke, Gibbon, Hume. What have they ever done for science? What advances have they ever made? So far as we know, not one of them has any pretensions to what gives immortality to the names of Boyle, Locke, Newton, Bacon, Hale. What valuable fact have they ever presented in science? What new principle have they originated or illustrated? What department of science have they adorned? Not a man of them has ever trod the regions that constituted the glory of England and of the world—the regions of profound science; of deep and penetrating investigation of the works of nature. In spite of such men, science would still have slumbered in the regions of eternal night; and infidelity, but for Christian men, might have swayed a sceptre, as she desired, over regions of profound and boundless shades of ignorance and crime. We care little for names and authorities in religion. We believe that religion, natural and revealed, accords with the constitution and course of nature. We believe that it is sustained by a force and compass of argument that can be adduced for the truth of no science. On the ground of the independent and impregnable proof of revealed religion, we are Christians. But there *are* men who pride themselves on names. There are those whose only reason for an opinion is, that it was held by some illustrious man. None are really so much under the influence of this feeling as the infidel. That *Hume* was a skeptic; that *Gibbon* was capable of a sneer; that *Paine* was a scoffer; that *Volney* was an atheist, is to them strong as proof of holy writ. Hence they feel that to doubt is the most exalted state of man; that there is argument enough for mortals in a sneer and a jibe; that scoffing becomes a human being; and that to come to the conclusion that man has no Father and no God, that he dies like kindred worms, is the supremacy of felicity, and the perfection of reason. When *such* have been the apostles and high-priests of unbelief—such the hosts which they have mustered—we feel that apart from all *argument* in the case, *we* would rather accord with the sentiments of the great luminaries of mankind in science; and that it is not unworthy of reason and elevated thought to suppose, that *true* religion may be found where we have found every other valuable blessing for mankind; and that the system, attended everywhere with science, refinement, and art, and that has shed light on the intellect, and honour on the names of Locke, and Boyle, and Bacon, is the system with which God *intended to bless men.*

IV.

[CHRISTIAN SPECTATOR, 1833.]

How can the Sinner be made to feel his Guilt. A Discourse prepared at the request of the "Revival Association," Andover.

THE question, "How can the sinner be made to feel his guilt?" is one of the most momentous, in many respects, that can be presented to the human mind. On a correct answer depends the success of the gospel in every nation and in every age. Unless men are made to feel that they are guilty, in vain do we offer them pardon, and in vain is the standard of the cross lifted up in their view. At the present day, especially, this question is invested with a deeper interest, by the revivals of religion with which the church is favoured; and which we have reason to believe will extend from land to land as the great means of ushering in the millennial glory. The reign of Christ on earth must obviously be introduced by great excitement; by profound and anxious inquiry; by a movement throughout all Christendom, and reaching into heathen lands; by the application of some power that shall unclench the grasp of men from the world, alarm their fears, awaken their hopes, and lift their thoughts to GOD. But in any great religious movement, the depth, genuineness, and lasting efficacy of the change produced, must depend on men's views of their guilt, and their need of pardon. As a mere question, then, in the advance of Christianity, the subject before us has an interest commensurate with the value of Christian truth. No preacher can be successful who is not able, with the divine blessing, to lay open the sources and the hiding-places of guilt; to bring the transgressor out to light, and *to hold him there*, while eternal truth, with a full and overpowering blaze, shall do its work, and justice shall shake his frame, and conscience shall make him pale, and mercy shall find out the place of grief, and the memory of crime shall wring tears from eyes unused to weep. The question is often put to ministers, by the awakened sinner, "*How* may I FEEL my guilt, and be brought to repentance?" The inquiry is made with deep emotion; there is some honesty and sincerity about it, though much less than the inquirer supposes; but, we need hardly add, there is nothing holy in the feelings from which it springs. Yet a condition in which a man *will* ask the question, is far more promising than the leaden sleep in which most men lie. It is the business of the ministry to answer this question, and happy will it be if even in a single case, the answer shall give light to a benighted and anxious mind. We shall attempt to do it, by showing what *obstacles* prevent men from feeling their guilt; that Christianity contemplates the *removal* of these obstacles; that it has *power* to demolish them; and that, when they are removed, the gospel is fitted to meet the state of the soul, and to overwhelm it with the consciousness of guilt.

1. The first obstacle to conviction of sin, is the instinctive reluctance which all men feel to the *consciousness* of guilt. The dread of this, indeed, is one of those deep and immovable safeguards which God has laid in human nature itself, for the welfare of society. So painful and terrific is this consciousness of guilt, that many men avoid it by refraining from open transgression, when there is no *better* principle to guard them. The certainty that if they commit iniquity they must yet feel it; that conscience has an ever-goading sting, and a whip of scorpions; that there is an unseen hand to reach a fugitive—a finger that can write his crime on every wall; and a voice of blood that can cry from the earth beneath his feet.

may deter a man from guilt, when no higher principle restrains him.

This same fear, however, may be turned to the most pernicious uses. There may be such a determined purpose of wickedness; such a rush of passion and headlong indulgence; such a propensity to evil that none of the safeguards of virtue will restrain the man. Then, when the crime is committed, it becomes a question how he may avoid the consciousness of it? How he may put back the hand of justice? How silence the voice of blood? How still the thunders of conscience and of law? How go on still in crime, and yet not be harrowed with remorse? Here originates the desire for all those arts of evasion, those subterfuges of guilt, those self-delusions which are made to set in upon the soul, like a mist from the ocean, to shut out the sun of truth, and to elude the eye of justice. Here is the source of all the superstition of misguided men, of all the arts of the pagan and the Jesuit, to ward off the convictions of a man's own guilt; and of all the false systems of morality and theology; and here, too, originates the accelerated love of pleasure and amusement; the plunging into deeper schemes of gain or ambition, that a man may escape from the memory of his crimes, and live at ease, while he violates the laws of man and of God.

Such, too, is the case with a sinner, when God commands him to repent. He fears the consciousness of guilt. He dreads the alarms of conscience. He starts back from the *process* of repentance and of a return to God. That instinctive dread of this consciousness which was one of the safeguards by which God would have deterred him from the commission of crime, he now perverts to a hinderance to his return. He looks upon this return, upon a state of conviction for sin, as a dark and starless way; a condition of gloom and sadness; a course of terror where no light shines on the path but the flashes of the lightning of justice, leaving the darkness deeper and more dreadful. "The spirit of a man," says Solomon, "can sustain *his infirmity; but a wounded spirit*, who can bear?" He anticipates a protracted process in the work of conviction—what he has learned in the books of an older theology, but not in the Sacred Scriptures, to dread as a long and perilous "law-work" on the soul; a dark and dismal journey for weeks, or months, or years, across a barren waste, till he emerges at last in the region of light and peace. The necessity of feeling guilty, even for a few moments, would deter and frighten him. How much more so, when he has been led to suppose that he must go bowed down with this consciousness for months or years, before he can find peace of conscience or reconciliation with God.

Now it is clear that with this apprehension, no man will go through the process of repentance, if he can help it. It is clear, too, that in the workings of human wickedness for six thousand years, more than one way will be found out to avoid it. Hence every man has a shield to throw before himself, to ward off the consciousness of guilt. And hence we are compelled to make our way to the conscience, against this barrier which the sinner has raised; in the face of the mighty determination *not* to be lashed with a whip of scorpions; and to follow the man through a thousand hiding-places, and in a labyrinth of evasion, before the arrows of truth reach the victim, and the quiver is fixed in the panting heart.

One part of the sinner's apprehension is true; the other is not. It *is* true, that we seek and desire to overwhelm him with the consciousness of guilt; and that we wish to inflict pangs in the soul that shall start him from his seat of ease, and teach the tear of penitence to flow down the cheek of guilt. But it is *not* true, that religion seeks to throw him into a land of storms, and gloom, for weeks and years. Religion comes with pardons in her hand and peace in her train. The sunshine of mercy beams through the storm, and even while the tempest pours, and the thunder rolls, it has already, though unseen, painted the bow of hope in the distant sky. The idea that men *must* suffer pangs and gloom for years; that they *must* go through the tremendous and protracted process of what, in old theology, is called "the law-work," is what a false philosophy has added to the Sacred Scriptures. Nothing there forbids the thought, that they may at once exercise repentance and be pardoned. One emotion of genuine sorrow for sin; one act of faith in the Lord Jesus Christ, will secure pardon and eternal life. Nor will the soul be better fitted for the change by long rebellion in a state of anxiety and gloom; by stern and stubborn resistance when sinners *know* their duty; by a war against the Holy Ghost protracted for months and years, than by a frank and ingenuous acknowledgment of guilt at once, and a rushing to the arms of Christ's outstretched mercy. We speak much of the *improvements* of theology in modern times. Perhaps the greatest practical advance consists in removing this cumbersome burden from the gospel of Christ; and in the grand truth, now beginning to be felt, that the gospel may convey the balm of consolation to a wounded spirit *at once;* and that the Great Physician of souls needs not that the gangrene of sin should prey on the vitals for years; that the leprosy should spread and rage, and torment the soul, through many dark and gloomy months, before the healing hand *can* be stretched out to restore. The sinner may be relieved at once. The first terrific view of guilt may be followed by the tender voice of pardon, and the sight of a merciful Redeemer speaking peace.

2. Closely allied to this, is the second obstacle which I shall mention, viz., An unwillingness to *avow* and *confess* guilt, even when the mind is conscious of it. This also is an instinctive feeling, and is another of the safeguards thrown around the human heart, but capable also of great perversion. The fact

that guilt must be avowed if felt, that others must know it, and that the condition of the world is such as to extort the confession of it, is one of the many means which God has employed to prevent its commission. Every man knows that if he is guilty and is conscious of it, it must be revealed. The burning cheek, even when he wishes to drive the blood to the heart, will betray him. The eye, when he would have it fixed and calm, will be distracted and turn away. The brow that he would have smooth and calm, will be clouded. The thoughts, which he would "drive down into the soul," will start up with living power, and shed a trembling influence over the whole frame. He will be betrayed. God has guarded this matter too well to suffer him to escape. Society is organized to bring him out. Laws, and jurors, and judges; the injured man or society, become spies upon his movements, and have an *interest* in bringing guilt from its hiding-place; and all the array of witnesses, and all the terrors of conscience, and the processes of judgment, and justice, are *pressing* upon the man to make him confess his crimes.

Yet there is nothing which a man is less willing to do. And hence arise all the evasions in court, and in common life, to suppress the evidence of crime; all the arts of dishonest trade, and no small part of the wiles of policy, and ambition, and of the perverted codes of morals and religion among men. Hence, too, the efforts of guilty men to obliterate the marks of a guilty conscience which God has fixed in the eye, and on the cheek, and in the tremblings of the frame, to proclaim a man's own guilt. Thus guilty youth *must* proclaim *its* crime, but hardened villany shall have learned to fix the eye, and command the nerves, and fortify the cheek against the rush of blood at the consciousness of guilt. And the most hardened villain may sometimes go through society, or rise to posts of honour, accredited as a man of virtue, until his crimes shall be too much for the earth to bear, and an unexpected array of circumstances shall engulf his soul, and his name, in the depths of infamy.

All this operates with tremendous power in religion. There is no man on earth who more dreads an ingenuous avowal of guilt; who is more reluctant to admit the full charge of God against himself, than the immoral, or the *moral* man. To admit that he is guilty and lost; that all God has said of the *worst* of men, and nothing worse could be said, is true of *him;* to admit that his heart has been proud, selfish, ungrateful, unsubdued; that he has violated all laws; despised all "entreaties;" held in contempt prophets, martyrs, and the Son of God; and that the eternal home of the drunkard, the adulterer, and the pirate whom he would not admit into his presence, would be the abode *fit* for him:—all this is too humbling, and before a man will come to this, he will flee to every hiding-place of guilt; adopt any system of religion, however absurd; or associate with any society, however much he may despise it. Hence one class of men pray us to prophecy to them smooth things. Another become angry at faithful dealing. Another run away from the sanctuary, and seek smoother preachers. Another devote the Sabbath to gain, or study, or reading novels, or newspapers, or books that lie along the borders of religion, that they may not wholly fall out with their consciences for violating the Sabbath. Another seek refuge in a *form* of godliness; and another in those places where the Saviour is denied, and they are told there is no danger that "these shall go away into everlasting punishment."

Yet in a return to God, it is indispensable that there should be a full and frank *confession* of guilt. The very idea of repentance involves it, and the man *must* be the herald of his own guilt, as far as the knowledge of his penitence may go. It must be made in the face of companions who will regard him as weak and superstitious; before even parents who may despise religion and its God; in view of elevated and refined society amid which the penitent has moved; before associates, partners in crime or amusement; in the face of thoughtless and deriding men; and before the wide world. Nay, more, it must be made before the universe, with a willingness that every created intelligence may mark the flowing tear of shame and grief; every eye witness the heavings of the guilty bosom; and every ear hear the sigh of the soul contrite for sin. God himself, the great Being who surveys all hearts, and against whom the soul has long sinned, is also to witness the subdued and humble tread of the haughty man, as with bending head and a face bathed with tears, and with faltering steps, he approaches the throne of grace, confessing that God is right, and he is wrong, even when he has no assurance yet of his favour, or that he may not *frown* him into hell.

Now it is clear that against this avowal of guilt, there will stand opposed all the hatefulness of shame; all the pride of rank and wealth; all the influence of miserable self-valuation; all the flattery of friends and of men's own hearts; all the pride of station and office; all the incense offered to splendid talents and attainments; all the aspirings of ambition; and all the allurements of pleasure. Where is the man that would not rather climb the steeps of praise with incense burning around him, and the multitude rendering homage at his feet, than be found pleading for mercy with bitter tears, or weeping in the prayer-meeting, or in his office, or counting-room? Where is the man that would not rather recline on his bed of down, and seek enjoyment in his splendid abode, than weep with Jesus Christ in the garden or on the mountains? Where is the daughter of gayety that would not rather seek for pleasure in the theatre, or be the admiration of the splendid circle, than like Mary bathe the feet of Jesus with tears?

3. A third obstacle to conviction of sin, is the influence

of false philosophy and unscriptural opinions. These I shall just enumerate. 1. The ancient Pharisee had his system of self-righteousness reduced to statute, and intrenched with subtle arguments, to oppose the claims of God. The modern man of self-righteousness has a system just like his, and one equally insurmountable by human means. 2. The apostles found the world organized into sects, and names of philosophy all standing in array against the command to repent. The Stoic held that all things were ordered by the Fates over which he had no control; and, of course, he had no consciousness of crime. The Epicureans held that pleasure is the *summum bonum*, and the common interpretation was, that *all* pleasure was to be enjoyed, and, of course, he felt no guilt for sensuality and gross indulgence. The gods of the Greeks were represented to be as bad as any man could wish to be; and as the standards of morals among all men will be formed from the character of the gods, they felt no obligation to repent until they reached a point which they were sure not to reach—a descent to the same level of depravity as their gods. Thus Augustine says that "the Gentile gods are most unclean spirits, desiring under the shapes of some earthly creatures, to be accounted gods, and, in their proud impurity, taking pleasure in those obscenities, as in divine honours. Hence arose those routs of gods, and others of other nations as well as those we are now in hand with, *the senate of selected gods—selected not for virtue, but for villany.*"* The same thing is to be encountered in all pagan lands; and hence one of the *peculiar* difficulties of the missionary is to make the heathen feel their guilt. 3. The same thing is true of the false systems of civilized lands. Systems of morals are so framed as to evade the conviction of guilt. This is eminently true of most of the forms of infidelity. An absolute and decided

City of God. Book vii. chap. 33.

fatalism has found its way commonly into the scheme of the Deist. If he has admitted the existence of guilt at all, it has been only of those enormous crimes which a proper regard to the opinions of men would not allow him to deny. The tendency of the scheme has been to obliterate the memory of crime, and to leave men to the indulgence of all mad and ferocious passions. Hence France, under the reign of this terrible system, was drenched in blood, and men were taught to feel that carnage and lust were not offensive in the eyes of heaven. Hence Hobbes held that all property should be common, and that a man had a right to it wherever he could find it—the same doctrine that we have had among us; and hence Hume left it as his recorded opinion, that adultery should be practiced if men would obtain the chief benefit of life, and that suicide is lawful. With such views of laws and morals, repentance was out of the question. When a man by his very system was allowed the indulgence of every passion, for what was he to be grieved at the close of life? 4. Men often adopt systems of *physical* philosophy whose tendency is to destroy all sense of obligation to repentance. One man believes the soul to be *material*, and, of course, that he is under no obligation to seek any moral change. Another supposes disease of the mind to be like that of the body; a misfortune indeed, but not truly criminal. A man of science will often run his views of materialism through the subjects of morals. Thought is but some motion in the brain or nervous system. Passion, or emotion, is but a movement of animal spirits. Reason, fancy, conscience, are but some comformations of matter, and in these certainly no man is bound to make a change. Another holds that depravity is the very *nature* of man. That he is born with it as an original propensity of the same kind as that of the tiger or adder. He holds that no human power *can* reach that;—that it must be counteracted by the infusion of some principle equally independent of the will, of a contrary tendency ; and that all his efforts would be like attempting to aid the Almighty in propelling the planets. With such views we call on him in vain to exercise repentance towards God. 5. A fifth perversion respects the doctrine of ability. The man avers that he *cannot* repent, and while this stands in the way, there is an end of the matter. It would be in vain to call on a man to remove a mountain, or to raise the dead. We might as well proceed to the tombs, and summon their lifeless tenants to come forth. And especially is this true when the plea of inability is one which the man has not made up for himself, but has learned from others in places of spiritual power, and can defend by the endless dogmas of the church, and find in the almost infinite tomes of theology. No man would *dare* to invent such a plea for himself; nor *could* he keep himself long in countenance with such a pretence, if he were left alone. It is so obviously a reflection on the goodness and justice of God; such a manifest violation of all his own views of right, and of all the dictates of his own conscience; so plainly in the face of the Bible, that a man would be compelled to forsake it if he had not the countenance of some of the better class of Christians. I verily believe, indeed, that Satan never furnished to sinners a more obvious, useful, and unanswerable defence of impenitence, than has thus been furnished by the ministry of the gospel. Tell a man that he cannot repent, or love God, or obey him, and your work will be done. The effect of one such dogma will go through life; will shed a baleful influence on large regions of Christian truth; and, like the tree of Upas, or the Siroc of the desert, will shed a desolation all around the moral feelings of a man in regard to his duties towards God. 6. Men pervert the doctrine of election and decrees, and either with mistaken views of the doctrine, or by design, bar up all access to their souls against truth adapted to produce the conviction of guilt.

4. A fourth reason why men do not feel their guilt, is

found in the fact, that they have different views of sin from those of God. *He* commands repentance on the ground of what *He* believes to be the human character, and repentance naturally results from the sinner's entertaining the same views. When *our* feelings coincide with those of God, it is impossible but that men should repent. Yet on no subject do men differ more from their Maker, than on this. He has declared *His* view in every possible form. No man can mistake what God thinks of him, if he will give credit to his declarations. He has expressed views of every man, which no human law, and no poetic description, has ever expressed of the worst of men. To charge a man with being a *hater* of God, is to sum up all crimes in one; and beyond that charge you cannot go. Yet God has charged this on man. He has done it not as an abstract and cold proceeding; not as a matter of poetry, romance, or declamation; not merely to produce terror, but as the result of his profound knowledge of the human heart, and of the secret deeds of every man. He has done it, too, in the most solemn and tender manner. In the midst of judgments, in his threatenings, in his promises, and in the dying groans and agonies of his own Son.

We might ask of sinners, have you ever sympathized with God in his views of sin, as expressed in the cross of Jesus Christ? Have you never practically felt that God was misguided and deceived in supposing that your sins demanded such a sacrifice? Have you ever looked on the dying sufferings of the Son of God, bleeding between murderers; cursed by men; rejected by his nation; subjected to the malignant devices of the enemy of God; and forsaken by his Father,—and felt that your sins deserved woes like these? Have you ever felt that it would be right that God should subject *you* to woes like those of Gethsemane—prolonged through revolving ages in eternity; that it would be right in him to waken his "thunder red with uncommon wrath," and summon the universe to witness your sufferings for sin; that it would be right to forsake you, and to pour into your own soul the deep sorrows of abandonment, as he did into the bosom of his Son on the cross? Have you ever felt that it was right in God to annex eternal woes to crime committed in this world, and that your sins deserved the endless damnation of hell? Have you ever gone and cast an anxious eye into the world of wo, and realized that infinite despair and gloom were the proper recompense of unbelief and sin in this life? We should not need to pause for a reply. Every impenitent sinner knows that he has never felt this. On this whole matter he has differed from his Maker. The sentiment of his *heart* is that God is severe, arbitrary, and cruel in dooming the soul to penal and inextinguishable fires. Had he the views of sin which Jesus Christ had when he bled on the cross, he would repent. Had he the views which the eternal Father had when he appointed endless woes as a recompense, he would weep that God is laid under a necessity, if I may so speak, to defile and mar the beauty of his universe with the smoke of an eternal hell. With those views he has commanded men to repent. And it is needless to add, that while they differ from their Maker, "far as from the centre thrice to the utmost pole;" while they regard sin as a trifle; hell as an arbitrary appointment, a place of holy martyrdom in the cause of injured innocence; and the scenes of Calvary as a pompous show, an unmeaning display, and a gorgeous parade, they will not repent. This *single* reason would account for the fact that men *will* not repent of their sins.

5. A fifth cause is found in absorption in the things of this world. How can a man repent whose mind is wholly occupied with the business of gain? It fills all his time; engages all his energies; taxes all his powers. The world addresses him a thousand times where the gospel does once, and with prodigious advantage. It is with him in his family; amid his

friends; in his counting-room; in the sanctuary; in solitude; on the Sabbath; and in all the periods when other men find leisure for reading or devotion. How can a man repent whose soul is engrossed with the wily policy of ambition; who seeks office, fame, applause; on whose favours flatterers hang, and around whose steps thousands are offering the incense of adulation; whose very business is a species of evading the right road of honesty, and travelling in just such a devious path as the sinner loves to tread? How will the man repent who is wholly engrossed with the toils of professional life? Every moment calls him from the great work of the soul, and demands his time in the business of his calling. How will she repent who gives her life to amusement? Will she enter the theatre, or the gay circle, with the tear of penitence on her cheek, or her eyes red with grief for sin? Will she seek her closet, and her Saviour, and bedew his feet with tears, as a preparation for the scenes of gayety, and of song? And when such scenes engross the soul, we wonder not that the command of God is unheeded, and the ways of impenitence still loved; we wonder not that repentance is postponed from youth to manhood—from manhood to old age—and again in old age is still deferred to some future time. Now is the time for innocent pleasure, is the language of the young, and not the time of sorrow—forgetting that there *is* no innocence but in the love of God, and no true enjoyment but in the hopes of religion. Now is the time to attend to my great affairs of life, says the man in middle life—forgetting that there is no affair of life so *great* as that of religion, and that to provide for future years may be to lay up gold for some thankless heir, a wretch, ruined by this very gold, when he is in the grave, and when to him gold may be valueless. Now is the time, we hear even from the faltering lips of old age, for me to enjoy the results of a life of industry, and to find repose in my declining years—when he *has* no repose, and every thing in his circumstances admonishes him to prepare to die.

We repeat, we wonder not that men do not repent. And we add, that all this is so absorbing, so well arranged, so interwoven with all the business of this life, so adapted to every passion, to every age, to every employment, that it bears indubitable marks of being under the guidance of some presiding spirit of evil. It is part of one great plan, bearing the impress of one master-mind of wickedness, and arraying all the mighty passions of men, and all the offices and employments of life, in one gigantic enterprise against God. See how these things meet a man on every hand, oppose all our appeals, stand alike to resist the impression when the law speaks out its thunders, and when "the gospel, in strains as sweet as angels use, whispers peace." These temptations arise from all that is winning and attractive in the eyes of men. In moments of seriousness, when the mind is disposed to thought, and half resolved to repent, some new form of vanity, or some new scheme of gain, with gaudy colours, will burst upon the view, and, at once, all serious thought is banished. In times of deep anxiety, some friend invites the sinner to a scene of amusement; or derides his thoughtfulness; or calls him a Methodist or a Puritan; and, ashamed of religion, he snaps the silken cord that was drawing him to God; thrusts back the hand that was dissolving the chains of the world; puts out the sun that began to shed its beams on his path; and covers with a frown the countenance of God which had begun to beam benignantly on his return. All these temptations come under the influence of the tenderest earthly friends. The authority of a father may recall him from the place of prayer, and demand his continuance in the ways of sin. The example and entreaties of a brother, or a sister, or the loved or tender voice of a mother, often check all seriousness; and her hand, awful abuse of a mother's power, opens new sources of pleasure, and demands the presence of a daughter, while, even in advancing years, *she* seeks the insipid and senseless joys of a gay and misguided world.

6. A sixth reason why men do not feel their guilt, is found in the ascendency and power of some plan of unfinished crime; in some scheme of known and deliberate wickedness that requires months or years for its completion. To repent *now* would demand that the man should break off that plan, arrest his gains, or stifle his ambition. He is now engaged in a successful scheme of gain or gratification. Some passion he fully resolves to indulge, even at the expense of virtue and his soul. Some scheme of vengeance he intends to fill up and accomplish, even should he die in the attempt. Some work of supplanting a rival, and of humbling a foe, he intends to effect—though by the toil of years, and at the peril of his soul. Thus the man engaged in the slave-trade; in the traffic of ardent spirits; in unlawful speculation; in unjust gains in merchandise; in a career of licentious pleasure; in the hall of gambling; in the business of rapine, murder, and blood, intends to *complete* his scheme; and in vain does conscience now lift its voice, and the heavy thunders of justice echo from heaven; or even damnation roll its terrors along his path. *Now* there is no voice of tenderness or of justice—no appeal to his conscience, his fears, or his hopes—that can reach his heart.

Yet nothing is further from this man's feelings than an intention never to repent. No man has more good designs; none more pious purposes; none more heavenly resolves. Good intentions are made every day, renewed each periodical season of his life, with the solemnity and regularity of the mile-stone that moves not, but will tell you how far you have gone, and how near you are to your journey's end. There he stands filled with good resolves; fired with noble purposes *always* for future years, and, if intentions constitute goodness, one of the best of men. Little do we wonder that God grants to so few men repentance unto life. In all the catalogue of crimes of which mortal men stand accused, we deem *this* state of mind *least* to be envied, and lying least near the fountains of mercy. We love an honest man—we were about to say honest even in sin. But who can love a man whose purpose *now* is to rebel against God; to devote his strength and talent to the business of setting aside the plain demands of conscience and of duty, with a cold, unfeeling resolve—a biting sarcasm on the claims of the Almighty—to abuse his patience as long as he can, and then give to him the tears of the crocodile for doing what he always *meant to do;* and the whimpering grief of enfeebled age, when the hands are no longer strong enough for purposes of evil, and the palsied tongue can no longer calumniate his name.

The work of evading the demands of the gospel is, therefore, one of time, and toil, and skill. The obstructions which the gospel meets every time it is preached, are the accumulations of centuries, and the result of no small part of the plans of men. It is the profoundest scheme in this world of sin, the most gigantic enterprise that men ever formed, to go through this world, committing sin every day, and yet evading remorse of conscience; indulging in guilty passions, and yet escaping the thunders of the law; gaining as much of the world as a man pleases, and yet not harrowed in his solitary moments by the accusings of conscience; passing amid the blightings of God's indignation, and yet not terrified; and hearing all the time the appeals of mercy, and yet not moved. Never was there so vast a scheme of wickedness, so complicated, elaborate, and compacted on any other subject. Philosophy here has lent its aid; poetry its charms; eloquence its appeals; false theology its alliance; learning its skill; age its experience; and youth its ardour, in forming plans to oppose the obvious claim of the gospel. And it is complete. While this influence governs the sinner, what cares he for the groans of Jesus Christ; or the offers of mercy; or the judgment-seat of God; or the glories of heaven; or the pains of hell? What cares he that we appeal to him by every thing that is sacred in heaven, and terrible in despair; that is tender in love, and bleeding in mercy, or that is infinite in the interests of his own soul, or terrible in the future scenes of wo? To all these appeals he is indifferent. His Protean scheme meets all this. He has heard it a thousand times; and a thousand times been practicing the art of hearing it with unconcern. He has learned to meet God at every point; to parry the gospel at every turn; and to go from the sanctuary as coolly as if he had listened to an address to sepulchral monuments. In this unholy work men pass their lives; and some of their last efforts in sinking to the grave, are to frame excuses for not repenting and turning to God. We marvel not, that no man was ever renewed to repentance but by the Spirit of God; and we love to leave our ministry there, and to feel that there is *one* power that can crush the excuses of the sinner at once, and bend him, weeping, at the feet of mercy. It is a work worthy of God. And, assuredly, if there is any doctrine whose necessity is laid in the wickedness of man, it is that the Holy Ghost alone will ever renew the sinner's soul.

Such are the obstacles which prevent men from feeling their guilt. These must be taken away, and we proceed to show how this may be done. The ministers of religion must be qualified not merely to declaim, but convince; not only to weep and plead, but to stand up against philosophic men and convince them that they are wrong; to show that the fatalism of the Stoic, and of the better kind of Deists; the sensuality of Epicureans, and of the mass of infidels; and the dogmas of a theology founded on ancient and false philosophy, are as much in the face of true science as they are of the Bible

If in this pursuit we are drawn into the regions of metaphysics, the fault is not ours but that of those who led us there. If the sinner, like hunted game, will flee to dens and hiding-places, we must follow him; and he should be the last to complain that we preach to him metaphysics. It must be *proved* to men that they *are* wrong. The time has gone by when declamation can be substituted for argument. Dark dogmas, however pompous, statuary, and solemn, will not supply the place of evidence in an age of light. Men will think and reason, and draw their own conclusions; and this must be fully understood by the ministry. Man must be made to feel that God's view of sin is just; that what *he* has expressed is the true measure of human guilt; that the dying agonies of the Redeemer were but a fair expression of the guilt of men; that God has a right to affix the penalty to crime; and to declare that these shall go away into *everlasting* punishment. Men must be *roused*, and severed—however rudely—from earthly things; and hurried onward, and thrown into the deep solemnities of a universe where the God of justice reigns; where every thing is full of God; and where voices from earth and heaven and hell mingle and fall on his ear, and tell him to hasten away from his delusions, and be prepared to die. Man must be brought to a willingness to arrest his plans of wickedness where they are; to abandon the unfinished scheme; to stop in his career of pleasure; to relinquish a plan of gain, however flattering, and a scheme of ambition, however imposing, and pause, and turn to the living God. The purpose must be one that shall be executed *now*. Like an honest man, he who has been meeting God with the ironical and sarcastic purpose to repent at some future time, must resolve to do it *now*, and just as he is: resolve to forsake every sin, and devote himself to the serious work of repentance.

This is the work to be done. We admit that if done it will

not be by mere human power, but by the Spirit of God. Still it is done under the influence of a system of truth *adapted* in the highest degree to remove the obstacles, and to find its way to the soul of man. That truth, it is the business of the ministry to wield. Under that truth, these obstacles are to be taken away; and he is the most skilful preacher who so understands the human heart and the power of the gospel, as to adapt the message to the varying forms of iniquity, and make the sinner tremble and weep before God in view of sin. Our next object is to show what the state of the soul is, if these obstacles be removed; or what *capacities* or *susceptibilities* it has, on which the call to repentance may be made to act. Here we must be brief. And it is not needful at great length to present this part of our subject. We remark, then,

1. That a man is endowed with *reason*. Reason coincides with the doctrines of God when fairly presented; and when reason is convinced, and its suffrage is secured in favour of truth, no small advance is made in the work of the gospel. When a man is convinced of what you say; when he sees all the arguments which in other minds have produced conviction, and when *his* understanding accords with yours, the way is prepared for any impression which the truth is fitted to produce. When you have convinced the man of pleasure that he will waste his estate or health; a young man that he is in danger of intemperance or ruin; or a magistrate that the cause you plead is one of justice or of law; or a man of property that you are poor and unfortunate, and that your helpless wife and children are perishing with want; when you have convinced a man's sober judgment that his country calls him to the field of blood, you are prepared to make any thrilling appeal, and to excite all that is tender and philanthropic in his bosom. Thus the gospel addresses men, and it expects that those who proclaim its truths shall be able to *convince* men that the Bible is a revelation from Heaven. It expects

that they will go forth conscious that they are called to preach a system which *supposes* that men are *rational*, and that the system is one that will bear the test of the science of all ages; of all the arts of criticism; all the advances in the knowledge of the human mind; all enlarged views of physical researches and refinement, in all coming ages of the world. The ministry are expected, therefore, to be men not fitted merely to declaim, but to sit down coolly and convince men:—to sit down with them at any department of investigation, and to show them that this and that science leads to no fair results that do not coincide with the oracles of God; and to show to infidelity that it arrays itself as much against the fair deductions of science as against the Bible. It is needless to add, that if *this* be the case, the danger is not that the ministry will be too thoroughly imbued with sound learning; and that the kind of learning wanted, is *the bearing of the existing state of science on the evidences and doctrines of revelation.*

2. A second power of the mind to which the system of divine truth adapts itself is that of *conscience.* Its province is not to communicate truth, but to coincide with it and press it with convicting power on the mind. It seems almost to be an independent agent, which God has fitted up for the special designs of moral government—answering the purposes of an ever-present Divinity:—using the language which God himself would use; and performing the office which the divinity would perform, if he attended us every moment, spoke in our listening ears in solitude, or when allured by the world, or when under the influence of mighty and infatuating passions. It performs to men the office which Socrates fabled to be performed by his attending genius. There is no more striking proof of God's power and wisdom, than in placing this tremendous witness in any part of his moral government; and in making the guilty mind to be its own tormentor and executioner. Its power—its full power—has not yet been known.

Intimations of its terrible inflictions have been given in this world, just enough to tell us what it *may* be in hell. We have only to see its power in heathen lands, where man at bloody altars will offer his first-born son and his dearest objects of affection to obtain peace; we have only to follow a convicted sinner through the gloom of many weeks and years in that starless night when he is professedly inquiring the way to God; we have only to look upon the pale face, and trembling limbs, and retreating eye of the murderer, who, though the crime was long since committed, finds that the blood of innocence will still be in his path, and the stains, to *his* eye, WILL NOT be wiped out, and who at last yields himself to justice and flees to the grave as if this reprover would not follow him there,—to see what the power of conscience *may be*, if rightly used, as a means of leading the sinner back to God. Its whole testimony coincides with the appeals of the gospel. Never do we preach a sermon, however severe and cutting its truths, that does not find the concurrence of conscience. And the gospel comes to avail itself of this power, and to excite and direct it, till the man *cannot* but feel his guilt and tremble. It seems almost as if in the constitution of man—before his fall—there was laid the foundation for his recovery; and that God deposited there, in innocence, an ever-abiding principle, which, *while* man was innocent, might be innocuous or consoling, but which was fitted also for terrible inflictions in the days of guilt; as beneath a city he may lay sulphur, and pent-up gases, and nitre, innocent or useful while the city is innocent; but terrible when some sinful Lisbon or Calabria shall demand that God shall kindle the elements and whelm guilty men in ruin.

3. Man is a creature of *emotions*, of hopes, and fears, and love; susceptible of pain, and joy; of anxiety, or sorrow; seeking peace here, and capable of immortal joys in another world. The gospel addresses itself to all these; and it is the

gospel alone which meets them fully. The utmost power of *fear* may be felt when man looks at an eternal hell. The farthest limit of *hope* may be met when he looks at an eternal heaven. All the desires of sympathy, friendship, love, may be gratified in the prospect of an eternal heaven. The utmost intensity of love may be exhausted in the effort to love God. And all the mightiest powers of the soul may be summoned in an effort to *understand* the works and word of God, and to do his will. Man is in ruins—but the ruins are mighty, and are grand, and tell us what *he* was, as broken arches and columns tell us what once Thebes was. And ruined as he is, there is no object in this world that satisfies the original susceptibilities of the mind. After men have sought the world, gained its wealth, run its round of pleasure, and climbed its steeps of ambition, still they sit down in the evening of life, and the big tear steals down the cheek when they reflect that not one single propensity of the mind has been met and gratified. Wealth had no such happiness to bestow as it promised; and the theatre and assembly-room never met and *filled up* the desire of joy; the toils of professional life have not filled the measure of the soul; the country's call to the field of liberty and victory has not satisfied the desires of the immortal mind. And there sits the man great in the ruins of sin, and even of age, still showing desires of something unreached and untasted, and still as restless, and unsatisfied as he was in all the aspirings of youthful ambition. There he sits wailing, as it were, on the shore of a boundless and unpassed ocean, for some *new* bark to bear him to climes he has never trod, and to an Elysium he has not yet found. How do the heavings of his bosom, and the last kindlings of his eye, and the last sighs of ambition, show that he has never found what was adapted to ALL the original propensities of men. *That* is the gospel of the blessed God—the voice of pardon—the hope of immortality. There the mind reposes, and is at ease. There like the weary traveller at the end of his journey, not among strangers, but at last *at home*, it finds that which *meets* his demands; nor is there a desire of happiness, or peace; a susceptibility of hope, of fancy, of friendship, of love, of boundless wishes, that is not fully met by the gospel of God, and the looking forward to immortality. When man feels this, he weeps over the sins which so long shut it from his view, and repents and turns to God. He reclines his head on his Redeemer's bosom, and every desire is satisfied, and he calmly waits his change.

On a soul thus endowed with reason, conscience, and the strongest susceptibilities, the gospel is *fitted* to act. To the soul thus endowed, it brings its appeal, that man may feel his guilt, and turn to God by repentance. Our last inquiry, then, is, what does the gospel bring *adapted* to produce repentance in such a state of mind. Here we remark,

1. That the gospel comes to men under the full benefit of a *concession* to its demand. The man knows, sees, admits that he *ought* to repent. He feels that it is *right* to weep at guilt, and turn from it. He knows he ought to be humbled before God, and seek pardon for his sins. Here we have an advantage that is felt scarcely anywhere else but in religion. We may urge the duty on sinners as ingenuous men who have conceded all we ask of them, and who are pressed with all the considerations drawn from heaven, earth, and hell, to repent and turn to God. On a man's own *admission* of guilt, we may press upon him a return by every thing sacred in religion, tender in the love of God, and momentous in the eternal destiny of the soul.

2. The gospel comes with all the terrors and the demands of law. The thunders of Sinai were preliminary to the designs of the gospel. They denounce, for the purpose of arousing men to seek for mercy. The law was a schoolmaster to lead us to Christ. It is designed to affect the hearts of men

with a consciousness of guilt, that they may be led to seek for pardon. Men are called upon to repent by all the evils of violated law; by all its solemn and awful claims; by the beauty and order which obeyed law would confer on the universe. That law, if obeyed, would have diffused peace and happiness in all worlds. That law, broken, has been the source of all our woes, and is now the great terrifier of men in view of future calamities. Man may be made to feel that this law is right. His reason, his conscience, his fears may all be roused, and his eye be fixed on the terrors of justice, and the pains of hell, till he trembles, turns pale, and his heart sinks within him, at the remembrance of his sins. Yet we do not mean that the preaching of terror is the only, or the happiest way of bringing men to see their guilt. It is not simply to terrify that the claims of law are urged. It is that men may *see* and feel, that that sin which has broken in upon the order of the universe, is an evil of amazing magnitude; and while the sinner looks upon the tide of woes which is rolling onward here; and the broad, and deep, and turbid tide of guilt and despair, that is hour by hour, and day by day, and age by age, pouring by a measureless cataract into eternity, that the eye may weep, and the heart relent. We do not believe that great good results to the cause of religion from a very frequent use of vivid pictures of future misery; still less that these should be used to round or point a period, or to supply materials for an awful or imposing declamation. God never used them with such an intention. He never held them up to view merely to frighten men. In his word they have a meaning. They are full of significancy to the entire measure of the language; and they seem to be drawn from his bosom, and uttered with a suppressed aud solemn voice, when the benevolent God *must* speak of the endless wretchedness of his creatures. So they should be used by us—with the deep conviction that *we* deserve all that they convey, and that in using them of others, we are expressing the measure of our *own* guilt. Yet that men should hear those truths, and see that law, and be fixed in contemplation of them, is indispensable, in order that they may see their guilt. And we come to men with this advantage—presenting a law which conscience approves, and whose penalty has been fixed by the unerring decision of the wisest mind in the universe. When a man sees that he has injured a friend or a benefactor, he will weep. When a child is made conscious that he has violated the law of a parent, and that that law is good, he will weep. When a felon feels that he has injured his country; that he has aimed a blow at its interests; that, in violating law, he has aimed a stab at all which gives to his fellow-men security of property, reputation, or life; when a man can be made to see that, you have found the way to bring him to repentance. And, when to all this you add the higher laws of the universe, you have completed the pressure on the man's conscience, and the mighty sinner *must* bow before God and bewail his crimes.

And here we may remark, that the gospel owes much of its success in modern times, to the doctrine of the *immediate obligation* of man to obey that law. In the preaching of the most successful ministers, and in the revivals of religion which have characterized this age and land, this doctrine has more prominently than any other been kept before the view. Nor is it known that any marked success has attended any other preaching than that which is based on this doctrine. This we regard as the cardinal point; the limit which separates schools of divinity; and draws the boundaries around the places where God eminently blesses the ministry. Let a man honestly and fully press *this* point, and on other subjects of practical preaching he will not be likely to go wrong. It was this which was connected with the prototype and grand exemplar of all true revivals of religion on the day of Pentecost. Acts ii. 37, 38. And the reason of this fact is easily understood.

Leave a man with the impression that it is *not* his *duty* NOW to repent and believe, but that it *may be* at some future time, or under some more favourable influence from heaven, and you send a paralysis through his whole moral frame. No man will feel it, and no man will care about future duty. No man will tremble or be alarmed unless he feels that he is guilty *now*, and now bound to obey. What cares the sinner for that *future?* At that time he will attend to it. *Now* he is too busy, or too thoughtless, or he feels that the time has not come, and he will concern himself in the affairs of his merchandise or farm. Wo to the ministry which, by indolence, or false doctrine, or the fear of man, makes an impression like this! That cold, abstract, and formal doctrine, which directs men only to the future; that miserable perversion of the doctrine of the Spirit's influence which directs the eye onward and permits him to wait; diffuses the chills of Greenland over the soul, and the long death of the tomb over a congregation. Glad would be any assassin or murderer; glad would be any drunkard or gambler who may now be lashed and scourged by the stings of remorse, to find such a preacher, who would tell him *not* to feel or be disturbed now, but to wait God's time in this matter. A more consoling minister of peace you could not send into any prison, or den of wickedness; into any band of highwaymen, or pirates, or into a slave-ship, than would be these. But, oh! let not the Christian ministry be charged with folly and guilt like this. On a sinner's soul there is NOW pressing all the elements of obligation that can sink it down in any future scenes. Duty relates not to the future. It presses NOW; and that amazing pressure the sinner must be made to feel, or must jeopard the eternal interests of his soul.

3. We approach men with all the proofs of the truth of revelation; and the end of those proofs is to teach men to feel their guilt. The argument from miracles and prophecy is not

a speculative inquiry, like the cold and formal steps of mathematical science, or the researches of philosophy. Each argument is a part of the vast array of proof, to show that the declarations which affirm the lost condition of men are confirmed by demonstration. It is an array of evidence to prove that the account given of *their* guilt is really the judgment of Almighty God; that the declaration that men hate God is one that has been breathed from his lips, and has come from *his* profound view of all human hearts; that such was his view of *their* guilt that there was *no way* of expressing it but by the very scenes which the *infinite* love of Christ, and the retributions of eternity laid open. Language could not do it. Human speech faltered; and the poetic fancy of the singers of Israel, the dark and awful flights of prophetic description, and the eloquent tongue of apostles could not do it. There was a mode. God's infinite Son could become incarnate. And it was by giving a living demonstration in the groans of Gethsemane, and when the dead were rising in that ill-fated city where the Saviour died, that he could tell the sinner what *his* sins deserved; and point him to those scenes, and say, in that garden and on that cross you may *see* what your sins deserved. There was one more mode. It was possible that men should suffer forever—and the infinite God has told us that such are *his* views of human guilt, that nothing *but that* will be a fair expression of that evil to other worlds. Now every time we press the evidences of religion it is with reference to just this result. And this was the use the apostles made of it; and this is the way in which *they* convinced men of their guilt. They urged the proofs of the resurrection of the Saviour; and, on the ground of that, they pressed the guilt of man who had crucified him. And the result was that thousands of his murderers trembled, and asked with deep solicitude what they should do.

4. We come to men with all the evidence drawn from the

history of the world, that they are guilty, and that the guilty must suffer. All this analogy belongs properly to the province of religion. God has left his views of sin in no measured or doubtful form in the history of devils and of man. The sinner himself is ruined, and he feels it and knows it. His alarms of conscience; his humbling anticipations; his calamities, his sickness, and bereavements; his wasting frame, and his approaching death,—all admonish him of it. Man is a sinner, and the earth, arched with the graves of the dead; and the plague, the pestilence, and war, prove it. Man is a sinner, and each ruined capital, each desolated city, each town reeling beneath the upheaving earth, or falling by its own crimes, proves it. The broken columns and mighty fragments of arches in ancient towns, are monuments to preserve the memory of the guilt which caused their ruin, and are emblematic of the broken and prostrate character of man. To each vice God has affixed its own marks of crime. The drunkard proclaims everywhere in his face and frame, that *God* thinks him to be an evil man, and hates his crime. And so each gambler, pirate, murderer, becomes everywhere the herald of his own sin. The entire history of man lies before the ministry, as constituting materials of the proof of guilt. In every age, every nation, God has written with his own finger his view of the guilt of men; he has uttered it in every language; and we come to men with the demonstration drawn from the experience of six thousand years, to press this mighty argument on their minds, to show that God esteems them to be sinners, and that except they repent, they shall all likewise perish.

5. The gospel, in the sufferings and death of Jesus Christ, has exhausted all the appeals which can be made to men's sensibilities to make them feel their guilt. It comes in at the end of law; and when all the other topics of persuasion have been found to be ineffectual. For four thousand years, in pagan

and Jewish lands, law had uttered its denunciations almost in vain. God had exhausted the forms of those appeals in the terrors of Sinai; the inflictions of a guilty conscience; and the threatenings of hell. Men were guilty—they felt it—knew it. They mocked him with vain oblations; sprinkled impure altars with the blood of innocence offered by unholy hands, and then returned to their pollution. It became needful that some *other* plan should be tried to see whether men could be made so effectually to perceive their guilt, and ill-desert, as to hate it, and abandon it. That plan is what was expressed in the cross of Christ. The essence of that plan consists in man's being made to see an innocent Being suffering unutterable agonies in his stead, and as the proper expression of his crime.

Now the value of that plan may be seen by supposing, that human law had some such device. One thing strikes every man on going into a court of justice. It is that the criminal, who knows his guilt, and who may expect to die, is so unmoved by the scene, and the danger; and especially that he seems to have so little sense of the evil of the crime for which he is to die. One reason is, that there is little in the law that will make him feel; and less in the proceedings. His mind is taken off from his guilt, by the technicalities of the law; by the contests of advocates; by the discrepancies of witnesses; often by the coldness and want of feeling in the judge, the jury, and hardened spectators. But suppose there could be placed in full view, where the man alone could see it, some *innocent being* voluntarily suffering what *his* crime deserved —*illustrating* on the rack, or amid flames—just what he *ought* to suffer, and bearing this so patiently, so mildly, as he sank into the arms of death, as to be the highest expression of pure friendship. Suppose this was the brother, or the father of the man he had slain, and that the dying man should tell him that he bore this to show the importance of maintaining violated law, and that *but* for these sufferings the guilty wretch *could* not be saved from death, and how much more affecting would be this, than the mere dryness of statutes, and the pleadings of counsel, and the charge of the judge. You may find here, perhaps, a slight illustration of the principle on which the gospel acts. Law had tried its power in vain, and the only effectual scheme is to place before the sinner the innocent Lamb of God, bleeding for his sins. Thus it was said of him, "He shall be set for the fall and rising again of many in Israel, and for a sign to be spoken against, that thereby the thoughts of many hearts may be revealed." And thus also it was prophesied: "They shall look upon him whom they have pierced, and shall mourn." Hence the apostles met with such success; whose preaching was a little more than a simple statement of the truth that Jesus died, and rose. And, however it is to be accounted for, it is this which has in all ages been attended with the convictions of guilt among men. Gosner, the celebrated Bavarian Catholic priest, at present a Protestant clergyman in Berlin, who has probably been the means of the immediate conversion of more souls than any man living, is said seldom to vary in his manner of preaching. The love of Christ is almost his constant theme, and his preaching is almost a constant pouring out of the warm effusions of the heart in the love of God, the preciousness of the Saviour, and the desirableness of heaven.* The affecting experience of the Moravian missionaries in Greenland is well known. For many years they endeavoured to teach the benighted pagans the existence and attributes of God, and the doctrines of retribution. Never was work more unsuccessful than this. The heart of the Greenlander, cold as his own snows, was unmoved, and the missionaries appeared to toil in vain. On one occasion it happened that one of them read in

---

Biblical Repository, vol. iii. pp. 535, 536.

the hearing of a savage, the account of the Saviour's sufferings in the garden and on the cross. "How is this?" said one of the savages. "Tell me it once more, for I would be saved"—and laid his hand on his mouth and wept. Here was learned, almost by accident, the great secret of their success in the world. Here was illustrated anew the principle of the gospel, adapted to all ages and people, that the account of a suffering Redeemer is to be the grand means of teaching sinners everywhere their guilt; and of drawing forth tears of repentance from eyes that, but for this, would never weep. Our own experience in the ministry has been short. But we may, perhaps, be allowed to say, that the only revival of religion in which we, as a pastor, have been permitted to engage, began in the progress of a series of sermons on the work of Christ; and that the effect of that truth was visible through the series, till almost the entire congregation bowed at once before the cross, and a deep and awful solemnity pervaded all ranks in the community. Nor do we doubt that *this* is the way in which men must be taught to feel their guilt, as the gospel spreads over the world. If you wish to make men feel the evil of sin, go and tell them that its magnitude is so great that none but God's own Son could undertake the task of bearing the burden of the world's atonement. Go and remember that angelic might was not equal to this; that all on high but God was incapable to breast the tide of human sins; that so great were the plans of gigantic and all-spreading evil, that it was needful that God should become incarnate, and in our nature meet the evils of sin, aimed at his head and his heart. Go and look on embodied holiness—the august blending of all virtues in the person of the Son of God, moving a present deity through the scenes of earth; and himself the only innocent being that had blessed our world with his presence. Then go and see innocence itself in torture, and ask, why was this? Is this the fair expression of the desert of our sin? Did God judge aright when he deemed that woes like these should tell *how much* man ought to endure? If so, then bitter sorrows should come over our souls at the remembrance of all these sufferings, and of the sins that caused the death of this stranger-friend that came to seek out the guilty, and to die.

6. One other mode consists in bringing before a man, so that he *must see it,* the tremendous scenes of the judgment. We must diminish the apparent journey which he has to tread, and place him amid the scenes of the judgment day. This help religion furnishes to bring guilty men to repentance. It assures us that we shall be there; and that that tribunal is a place where the sinner *must* feel. You perhaps have marked in a court of justice some guilty man, who, at the beginning of his trial, assumed the Stoic, and was bold, and, apparently, unconcerned. Yet you have marked the change in the man when the witnesses have been called; when one circumstance after another has *pointed* at his guilt; when an argument to condemn him might already have been made out. And you may have marked the cloud on his brow, and the paleness on his cheek, when he sees some witness advance deliberately, who, he knows, is acquainted with his guilt, who he hoped or believed would not have been there, and who now solemnly swears to declare the whole truth. His last refuge has failed, and he must die. So the sinner must be made to draw near to the judgment. His delusions and evasions must be swept away. He must be borne onward, and must look at those scenes. Time, and friends, and pleasures, and honours, must be made to leave him,—and he must be shut up and encompassed in the still, solemn scenes, where conscience shall no more be silent; where the eye of the all-seeing Judge shall be witness enough of guilt; and where he must stand riveted by that eye, quailing beneath its piercings, horror-stricken at an opening hell; and amid that vast multitude, trembling by himself—surrounded by numberless millions, yet weeping

apart. All this power the gospel wields; and, with this it intends to *press* on the soul till the haughty man is bowed down; and the hardened man melts into tears, and the profligate man trembles in view of judgment and of hell.

The gospel is, therefore, a simple device, though mighty, *adapted* to the state of man. It was originated by him who knew what was in man; and who knew the way to the human heart. It is founded on the manifest guilt of men; it meets the susceptibilities of men; enlists on its side all that is tender and thrilling, and awful in the human bosom; and has devised a plan calling in from three worlds, all that can move, excite, win, or awe. Could this plan have been invented by men? Is it like any thing that men ever have invented?

The work of the ministry is one of great difficulty, and demanding great skill. It is no light work to wield that which is designed to effect great changes in the human bosom, and to revolutionize the world. It is no unimportant task to be engaged in applying that which has called forth all the wisdom of God, and which *must* affect forever the destinies of men. But this is not the only difficulty. It is a work of laying open human guilt; bringing out secret offences; revealing crime; attempting to excite the energies of conscience; to inflict the pangs of remorse on men; and to bring them to the posture of grief, and the bitterness of penitence. It is not to be wondered at if we are regarded as ministers of gloom, and "suspected of taking a pleasure in attempting to overwhelm the soul in dark and melancholy forebodings." Nor are we to be disappointed if one man thinks we are close, or personal, or severe; or another would like smoother prophesyings; and another be uneasy that his repose is disturbed; and another attempt to suppress his ill-concealed feelings; and another find quietude in some place where the mighty and pungent doctrines of the cross are concealed, or men are taught not to be afraid of the declaration that God is a consuming fire.

We see here what makes death so terrible to a sinner. The mask is then off. The world recedes and appears as it is. Its delusions have vanished. The mist is gone, and the naked soul, the conscience, the feelings, the apprehensions, are laid bare to the insufferable blaze of truth, and the piercings of the eye of God. The tossed sinner cannot help himself, then. There is no delusion; no new mist; no cavern there; no far projecting rock; no way to silence the voice, or turn away the eye of God. There it is everywhere. The sinner dying, may roll and toss, but the eye of God is there—everywhere—just as bright, as keen, as riving—as justice and indignation can make it—and as it will be in an eternal hell. And there, too, is a finger mysteriously moving on the wall,—nor can he turn from that,—and writing his damnation. The man is afraid to live and afraid to die. Verily it is a fearful thing to die a sinner, and to lie on such a death-bed as that. God grant that no such struggling spirit of any of our readers may go to the judgment-seat of the eternal God!

V.

[CHRISTIAN SPECTATOR, 1834.]

Episcopacy tested by Scripture. By the Right Reverend HENRY U. ONDERDONK, D.D., Assistant Bishop of the Protestant Episcopal Church, in the Commonwealth of Pennsylvania. New York: published by the Protestant Episcopal Tract Society. pp. 46.

THE history of this tract is this. It was first published as an essay, in the "Protestant Episcopalian," for November and December, 1830. It was then issued in a pamphlet form, without the name of the author. It was next requested for publication by the "Trustees of the New York Protestant Episcopal Press;" and, after being amended by the author, with an addition of several notes, it was printed in the form of a tract, and as such has had an extensive circulation.

The tract is one which has strong claims on the attention of those who are not Episcopalians. The name and standing of the author will give it extensive publicity. The fact that it comes from the "Press" of the Episcopal Church in this country; that it is issued as one of their standing publications, and that it will, therefore, be circulated with all the zeal which usually characterizes associations organized for defending the exclusive views of any religious body; and, most of all, the character of the tract itself, and the ground assumed by it, give it a title to our attention, which can be claimed by hardly any *single* tract of the kind ever published in our country. Our views of it may be expressed in one word. It is the best written, the most manly, elaborate, judicious, and candid discussion, in the form of a tract, which we have seen on this subject. Our Episcopalian friends regard it as unanswerable. They have provided amply for its circulation, and rely on its making converts wherever it is perused; and, in a tone which cannot be misunderstood, they are exulting in the fact that, to this day, it has been left entirely unnoticed by the opponents of prelacy.* And *we* wonder, too, that it has not been noticed. There are men among us who seem to consider the external defence of the church as intrusted to their peculiar care; who delight to be seen with the accoutrements of the ecclesiastical military order, patrolling the walls of Zion; who parade with much self-complacency, as sentinels in front of the temple of God; who are quick to detect the movements of external enemies; and who are admirably adapted to this species of warfare. They seem to have little heart for the interior operations of the church, and seldom notice them, except to suggest doubts of the expediency of some new measure proposed, or to promote discord and strife, by laying down rules for the conduct of those who are labouring in the direct work of saving souls. Much do we marvel that these men have suffered this tract to lie so long unnoticed.

We have never regarded the Episcopal controversy with any very special interest. Our feelings lead us to dwell on subjects more directly connected with the salvation of the soul. We have no taste for the species of warfare which is often waged in guarding the outposts of religion. Christianity, we have supposed, is designed to act directly on the *hearts* of men; and we regard it as a matter of very little moment in what particular church the spirit is prepared for its eternal rest, provided the great object be accomplished of bringing it fairly under the influence of the gospel.

---

* "Has the tract 'Episcopacy tested by Scripture,' been answered? This, we believe, is neither the first time of asking, nor the second, nor the third."—*Protestant Episcopalian.*

But, we propose, for the reasons already suggested, to examine the arguments of this tract. We do it with the highest respect for the author; with a full conviction that he has done ample justice to his cause; that he has urged on his side of the question all that can be advanced; and we enter on the task with sincere pleasure at meeting an argument conducted with entire candour, without misrepresentation, and with a manifest love of truth. Our wish is to reciprocate this candour; and our highest desire is to imitate the chastened spirit, the sober argumentation, and the Christian temper evinced in this tract. It is firm in its principles, but not illiberal; decided in its views, but not censorious; settled in its aims, but not resorting to sophism, or ridicule, to carry its points. There is, evidently, in the author's mind too clear a conviction of the truth of what he advances, to justify a resort to the mere *art* of the logician; too manifest a love of the cause in which he is engaged, to expose himself to the retort which might arise from lofty declamation, or the expression of angry passions towards his opponents.

One object which we have in view, in noticing this tract, is to express our gratification that the controversy is, at last, put where it should have been at first—on *an appeal to the Bible alone.* Never have we been more digusted than at the mode in which the Episcopal controversy has usually been conducted. By common consent, almost, the writers, on both sides, have turned from the New Testament, where the controversy might have been brought to a speedy issue, to listen to the decisions of the Fathers; and, as might have been expected, have

"Found no end, in wandering mazes lost."

It was the policy of the friends of prelacy to do so; and it was the folly of their opponents to suffer them to choose the field of debate, and to weary themselves in an effort to fix the meaning, to secure the consistency, and obtain the suffrages of the Fathers. Full well was it known, we believe, by the friends of Episcopacy in other times, that the New Testament could furnish a most slender support for their claims. In the times of the Papacy, it had always been defended by an appeal to the Fathers. The system had risen, sustained, not even *professedly*, by the authority of the Bible, but by the traditions of the elders. The ranks and orders of the papal priesthood could be defended only by the authority of a church which claimed infallibility, and which might dispense, therefore, with the New Testament. The Reformers came forth from the bosom of the Papacy with much of this feeling. They approached this subject with high reverence for the opinions of past times; with a deference for the Fathers, nourished by all the forms of their education, by all existing institutions, and by the reluctance of the human mind to break away from the established customs of ages. On the one hand, the advocates of Episcopacy found their proofs in the *common law* of the church, the institutions which had existed "time whereof the memory of man runneth not to the contrary;" and, on the other hand, the opponents of prelacy were equally anxious to show that *they* had not departed from the customs of the fathers, and that the defence of their institutions might be found in times far remote, and in records which received the veneration, and commanded the confidence, of the Christian world. Into this abyss both parties plunged. In this immense chaos of opinions and interpretations; into these moving, disorganized, jostling elements, where, as in the first chaos, light struggled with darkness and confusion reigned, they threw themselves, to endeavour severally to find the support of their opinions. "Whatsoever time, or the heedless hand of blind chance," says Milton, "hath drawn down from of old to this present, in her huge drag-net, whether fish or seaweed, shells or shrubs, unpicked, unchosen, those are the

Fathers." With those who, according to Mosheim,* deemed it not only lawful, but commendable, to deceive and lie for the sake of truth and piety, it would be singular if *any* point could be settled that involved controversy. With men who held to every strange and ridiculous opinion; to every vagary that the human mind can conceive;† it would be remarkable if *both* sides in this controversy did not find enough that had the appearance of demonstration, to perplex and embarrass an opponent *ad libitum*. In examining the controversy, as it was conducted in former times, we have been often amused, and edified, at the perfect complacency with which a passage from one of the Fathers is adduced in defence of either side of the question, and the perfect ease with which, by a new translation, or by introducing a few words of the context, or more frequently by an appeal to some other part of the same author, not studious himself of consistency, and probably having no settled principles, the passage is shown to mean just the contrary; and then, again, a new version, or yet another quotation, shall give it a new aspect, and restore it to its former honours.‡ Thus the Fathers became a mere foot-ball between the contending parties; and thus in this controversy the weary searcher for truth finds no solid ground. Eminently, here, "he which is *first* in his cause seemeth just; but his neighbour cometh and searcheth him." Prov. xviii. 17. To this wearisome and unsatisfactory toil he is doomed who will read all the older controversies on Episcopacy. There he,

> "O'er bog or steep, through strait, rough, dense or rare,
> With head, hands, wings, or feet, pursues his way,
> And swims, or sinks, or wades, or creeps or flies."

Were we to adduce the most striking instance of the plastic

---

* Murdock's Mosheim, vol. i. p. 159.

† See Tillemont's Ecclesiastical History, *passim*.

‡ See the Letters of Dr. Miller, and Dr. Bowden, on Episcopacy, *passim*.

nature of this kind of proof, we should refer to the epistles of Ignatius. To our eyes they seem to be a plain, straightforward account of the existence of Presbyterianism in his time. They are substantially such a description as a man would give, writing in the inflated and exaggerated manner in which the Orientals wrote, of Presbyterianism as it exists in the United States. Yet it is well known that, with the utmost pertinacity those letters have been adduced as proving the doctrine of Episcopacy. And so confident have been the assertions on the subject, that not a few non-Episcopalians have given them up as unmanageable, and have stoutly contended, what may be very true, that no inconsiderable part of them are forgeries.

Any man can see what a hopeless task is before him, if he endeavours to settle this controversy by the authority of the Fathers. The waste of time, and talent, and learning, on this subject, is fitted deeply to humble the heart. And even yet the passion has not ceased. Even now, men high in office and in rank, leave the New Testament and appeal to the Fathers. Episcopacy is discarded, not principally because the New Testament is a stranger to it, but because Jerome was not a prelatist; it is rejected, not because it cannot be made out from the Bible, but because it is a matter of debate, whether the Fathers teach it or not.

From this unprofitable and endless litigation, we are glad to turn to the true merits of the case. We rejoice sincerely that one man can be found who is willing to bring to this subject the great principle of the Protestant Reformation, that *all* religious opinions are to be tested by the Scriptures. And we especially rejoice to see this principle so decisively advanced by a man of the talents and official rank of Dr. Onderdonk; and that it is so prominently avowed by sending forth from the "Protestant Episcopal Press," a tract in its defence. It indicates a healthy state of things in the Episcopal Church in this country. It will save endless disputes about words, and much useless toil in endeavouring to give consistency and sense to the Fathers. This mode of reasoning, too, will soon decide the controversy. Long have we wished to see this matter brought to so obvious and so just an issue; and long have we expected that when this should be the case, the matter would be soon decided. Hereafter let it be held up as a great principle, from which, neither in spirit nor in form, we are ever to depart, that if the peculiar doctrines of Episcopacy are not found in the Scriptures, they are to be honestly abandoned, or held, as Cranmer held them, as matters of mere expediency. Let this truth go forth, never to be recalled; and let every man who attempts to defend the claims of bishops, appeal to the Bible alone. On this appeal, with confidence, we rest the issue of this case.

The great principle on which the argument in this tract is conducted, is indicated in its title; it is further stated at length in the tract itself. Thus, in the opening sentence, "The claim of Episcopacy to be of divine institution, and, therefore, obligatory on the church, rests fundamentally on the one question,—" Has it the authority of Scripture? If it has not, it is not necessarily binding." Again, on the same page, "No argument is worth taking into the account, that has not a palpable bearing on the clear and naked topic—the scriptural evidence of Episcopacy." Having stated this principle, the writer proceeds to remark, that "the argument is obstructed with many extraneous and irrelevant difficulties, which, instead of aiding the mind in reaching the truth on that great subject, tend only to divert it and occupy it with questions not affecting the main issue." The first object of the "essay" is then stated to be, "to point out some of these extraneous questions and difficulties, and expose either their fallacy or their irrelevancy." "The next object will be, to state the scriptural argument.'

In pursuing this plan, the writer introduces and discusses, as one of these extraneous difficulties, the objection that Episcopacy is inimical to a free government. He next notices, as "another of these extraneous considerations, the comparative standing in *piety* as evinced by the usual tokens of moral and spiritual character, of the members respectively of the Episcopal and non-Episcopal churches." A third "suggestion" noticed is, "that the *external* arrangements of religion are but of inferior importance, and that, therefore, all scruple concerning the subject before us may be dispensed with." p. 5. A fourth, "apparently formidable, yet extraneous difficulty, often raised, is, that Episcopal claims unchurch all non-Episcopal denominations." p. 6. This consequence, the author of the tract says is not by him allowed. "But granting it to the fullest extent," it is asked, "what bearing has it on the truth of the single proposition than Episcopacy is of divine ordinance?" A fifth among these extraneous points, is, "the practice of adducing the authority of individuals, who, although eminent in learning and piety, seem at last to have contradicted themselves on their public standards on the subject of Episcopacy." p. 7. The last objection noticed, as not affecting the ultimate decision of the controversy, is, "that though the examples recorded in Scripture should be allowed to favour Episcopacy, still that regimen is not there explicitly commanded." p. 9.

To most of the observations under these several heads, we give our hearty assent. And it will be perceived, that the controversy is thus reduced to very narrow limits; and that, if these principles are correct, numberless tomes which have been written on both sides of the question are totally useless. We are glad that all this extraneous matter is struck off, and should rejoice if every consideration of this kind were hereafter to be laid out of view.

In discussing the second topic proposed, "the *scriptural*

evidence relating to this controversy," (p. 11,) the first object of Dr. Onderdonk is to state the precise point in debate. It is then observed, that "parity declares that there is but one *order* of men authorized to minister in sacred things, all of this order being of equal grade, and having inherently equal spiritual rights. Episcopacy declares that the Christian ministry was established in *three orders*, called ever since the apostolic age, bishops, presbyters or elders, and deacons; of which the highest only has a right to ordain and confirm, that of general supervision in a diocese, etc." p. 11. The main question is then stated, correctly, to be, that "concerning the superiority of bishops;" and the object of the essay is to prove that, according to the New Testament, *such* an order existed, and was clothed with such peculiar powers. p. 11. Let it not be forgotten that this is the main point in the case; and that if this is not made out, so as to be binding on the church *everywhere*, the claims of Episcopacy fall to the ground.

In endeavouring to establish this point, the author maintains, "that the apostles ordained," and denies that elders (presbyters) ever did. p. 14. In supporting this position, the plan of argument is to show, that "the apostles and elders had *not* equal power and rights. p. 14. An attempt is, therefore, made to prove that the difference between the two orders is, that the former had the power of ordination, the latter not. In pursuing the reasoning, (p. 16,) the writer endeavours to show, that "there is no scriptural evidence that mere elders (presbyters) ordained." Under this branch of the argument, he examines the texts which have usually been adduced in favour of Presbyterian ordination. Having shown, as he supposes, that these passages do *not* prove that they did thus ordain, Dr. Onderdonk next proceeds to the last branch of the subject, viz., that "this distinction between elders and a grade superior to them, in regard especially to the power of ordaining, was so persevered in, as to indicate that it was a *permanent* arrangement, and not designed to be but temporary." p. 23.

This is the outline of the argument. It manifestly embraces the essential points of the case. And if these positions cannot be maintained, Episcopacy has no binding obligation on men, and such a claim should be at once abandoned. This argument we propose, with great respect, but with entire freedom, to examine. And we expect to show, that the point is *not* made out, that the New Testament has designated a superior rank of church officers, intrusted with the sole power of ordination, and general superintendence of the church.

In entering on this discussion, we shall first endeavour to ascertain the *real* point of the controversy, and to show that the Scripture authorities appealed to, do *not* establish the point maintained by Episcopalians. In pursuance of this, we remark, that the burden of proof lies wholly on the friends of Episcopacy. They set up a claim,—which they affirm to be binding on all the churches of every age. It is a claim which is specific, and which must be made out, or their whole pretensions fall. In what predicament it may leave other churches, is not the question. It would not prove Episcopacy to be of divine origin, could its friends show that Presbyterianism is unfounded in the Scriptures; or that Congregationalism has no claims to support; or that Independency is unauthorized; or even that lay-ordination is destitute of direct support. The question, after all, might be, whether it was the design of the apostles to establish *any* particular form of church government, any more than to establish a fixed mode of civil administration? This question we do not intend to examine now, neither do we design to express any opinion on it. We affirm only that it is a question on which much may be said, and which should not be considered as settled in this controversy. The specific point to be made out is, that there is scriptural authority for that which is claimed for the bishops. And we may remark, further, that this is not a claim which can be defended by any doubtful passages of Scripture, or by any very circuitous mode of argumentation. As it is expected to affect the whole organization of the church; to constitute, in fact, the peculiarity of its organization; and to determine, to a great extent at least, the validity of all its ordinances, and its ministry; we have a right to demand that the proof should not be of a doubtful character, or of a nature which is not easily apprehended by the ordinary readers of the New Testament.

We repeat, now, as of essential importance in this controversy, that the burden of proof lies on the friends of Episcopacy. It is theirs to make out this specific claim. To decide whether they can do so, is the object of this inquiry.

The first question, then, is, What *is* the claim; or, what is the essential point which is to be made out in the defence of Episcopacy? This claim is stated in the following words: (p. 11:) "Episcopacy declares, that the Christian ministry was established in *three orders*, called, ever since the apostolic age, bishops, presbyters or elders, [if so, why do they *now* call the second order *priests?*] and deacons; of which the highest only has the right to ordain and confirm, that of the chief administration in a diocese, and that of the chief administration of spiritual discipline, besides enjoying all the powers of the other grades." The main question, as thus stated, relates to the authority of bishops; and the writer adds, "If we cannot authenticate the claims of the Episcopal office, (the office of bishops,) we will surrender those of our deacons, and let all power be confined to the one office of presbyters." The same view of the main point of the controversy is given by Hooker, in his Ecclesiastical Polity." b. vii. § 2.

It will be seen that *several* claims are here set up in behalf of bishops. One is, the right of ordination; a second, that of confirmation; a third, that of general supervision; a fourth, that of the general administration of discipline. These are separate points to be made out; and a distinct argument might be entered into, to show that *neither* of them is founded on the authority of the Scriptures. To enter on this discussion, would require more time and space than we can now spare. Nor is it necessary, for we presume the Episcopalian would be willing to stake the whole cause on his being able to make out the authority of *ordination* to lie solely in the bishop. For, obviously, if *that* cannot be made out, all the other pretensions are good for nothing; and, as the writer of this tract limits *his* inquiries to this single point, we shall confine our remarks to that also.

The question, then, is, Has a bishop the sole power of ordaining? Is setting apart to a sacred office,—to the office of preaching and administering the sacraments, confined in the New Testament exclusively to this order of ministers? The Episcopalian claims that it is. We deny it, and ask him for the explicit proof of a point so simple as this, and one which we have a right to expect he will make out, with very great clearness, from the Sacred Scriptures.

The first proof adduced by the author is, that the apostles had the sole power of ordaining. This is a highly important point in the discussion, or rather, as already remarked, the very hinge of the controversy. We cannot, therefore, but express our surprise that a writer who can see the value and bearing of an argument so clearly as Dr. Onderdonk, should not have thought himself called upon to devote more than *two* pages to its direct defence; and that, without adducing any explicit passages of the New Testament. The argument stated in these two pages, or these parts of *three* pages, (14, 15, 16,) rests on the assumption, that the apostles *ordained*. "That the apostles ordained, all agree." Now, if this means any thing to the purpose, it means that they ordained *as apostles;* or that they were set apart to the apostolic office for the *purpose* of ordaining. But this we shall take the liberty to deny, and to prove to be an unfounded claim. Having made this assumption, the writer adds, that a *distinction* is observed in the New Testament between "the apostles *and* elders," the apostles *and* elders, *and* brethren." He next attempts to show, that this distinction was not made because they were appointed by Christ personally," nor because "they had seen our Lord after his resurrection;" nor "because of this power of working miracles:" and then the writer adds, "It follows, therefore, or *will not at least be questioned,*—a qualification which, by the way, seems to look as if the writer had himself no great confidence in the consecutiveness of the demonstration,—"that the apostles were distinguished from the elders, because they were *superior* to them in ministerial power and rights." p. 15. This is the argument; and this is the whole of it. On the making out of this point, depends the stupendous fabric of Episcopacy. Here is the corner-stone on which rest the claims of bishops; this the foundation on which the imposing and mighty superstructure has been reared. Our readers will join with us in our amazement, that this point has not been made out with a clearer deduction of arguments, than such as were fitted to lead to the ambiguous conclusion, "it follows, therefore, *or*—."

Now, the only way of ascertaining whether this claim be well-founded, is to appeal at once to the New Testament. The question, then, which we propose to settle now, is, Whether the apostles were chosen for the *distinctive* and *peculiar* work of ordaining to sacred offices? This the Episcopalian affirms. This we take the liberty of calling in question.

The Evangelists have given three separate and full accounts of the appointment of the apostles. One is recorded by Matthew, ch. x.; another by Mark, iii. 12, etc; the third by Luke, ch. vi. They were selected from the other disciples, and set apart to their work with great solemnity. Luke vi. The act was performed in the presence of a great multitude, and after the Saviour had passed the night in prayer to God. Luke vi. 12. The instructions given to them on the occasion occupy, in one part of the record, (Matt.) the entire chapter of forty-two verses. The directions are given with very great particularity, embracing a great variety of topics, evidently intended to guide them in all their ministry, and to furnish them with ample instruction as to the nature of their office. They refer to times which should follow the death of the Lord Jesus, and were designed to include the whole of their peculiar work. Matt. x. 17–23.

Now, on the supposition of the Episcopalian, that the peculiarity of their work was to *ordain*, or that "they were distinguished from the elders because they were *superior* to them in ministerial powers and rights," (p. 15,) we cannot but regard it as unaccountable, that we find not one word of this here. There is not the slightest allusion to any such distinguishing "power and rights." There is nothing which can be *tortured* into any such claim. This is the more remarkable, as on another occasion he sent forth seventy disciples at one time, (Luke x. 1–16,) usually regarded by Episcopalians as the foundation of the *second* order of their ministers; (see "The Scholar Armed;") and there is not the slightest intimation given, that *they* were to be inferior to the apostles in the power of ordaining, or superintending the churches. We do not know what explanation the Episcopalian will give of this remarkable omission in the instructions of the primitive bishops.

This omission is not the less remarkable in the instructions which the Lord Jesus gave to these same apostles, after his resurrection from the dead. At *that* time, we should, assuredly, have expected an intimation of the existence of some such peculiar power. But, not the slighest hint occurs of any such peculiar authority and superintendence. Matthew, (xxviii. 18–20,) Mark, (xvi. 15–18,) and Luke, (xxiv. 47–49,) have each recorded these parting instructions. They have told us that he directed them to remain in Jerusalem (Luke) until they were endued with power from on high, and then to go forth, and preach the gospel to every creature: but not a solitary syllable about any *exclusive power of ordination;* about their being a peculiar order of ministers; about their *transmitting* the peculiarity of the apostolic office to others. We should have been glad to see some explanation of this fact. We wish to be apprised of the reason, if any exists, why, if the peculiarity of their office consisted in "*superiority* of ministerial powers and rights," neither at their election and ordination, nor in the departing charge of the Saviour, nor in any intermediate time, we ever hear of it; that even the advocates for the powers of the bishop never *pretend* to adduce a solitary expression that can be construed into a reference to any such distinction.

We proceed now to observe, that there is *not anywhere else, in the New Testament,* a statement that this was the peculiarity of their apostolic office. Of this any man may be satisfied, who will examine the New Testament. Or, he may find the proof in a less laborious way, by simply looking at the fact, that neither Dr. Onderdonk, nor any of the advocates of Episcopacy, pretend to adduce any such declaration. The apostles often speak of themselves; the historian of their doings (Luke) often mentions them; but the place remains yet to be designated, after this controversy has been carried on by keen-sighted disputants for several hundred years, which speaks of any such peculiarity of their office.

This point, then, we shall consider as settled, and shall feel at liberty to make as much of it as we possibly can in the argument. And we might here insist on the strong *presumption* thus furnished, that this settles the case. We should be very apt to regard it as decisive in any other case. If two men go from a government to a foreign court, and one of them claims to be a plenipotentiary, and affirms that the other is a mere private secretary, or a consul, we expect that the claimant will sustain his pretensions by an appeal to his commission or instructions. If he maintains that this is the *peculiarity* of his office, though he may "enjoy all the powers of the other grades," (p. 11,) we expect to find this clearly proved in the documents which he brings. If he is mentioned by no *name* that designates his office,—as the Episcopalian admits the bishop is not,—(pp. 12, 13,) if his commission contains no such appointment, and if we should learn that *specific* instructions were given to him at his appointment, and again repeated in a solemn manner when he left his native shores; we should at least look with strong suspicions on these remarkable claims. Would not any foreign court decide at once that such pretensions, under such circumstances, were utterly unfounded?

We proceed now to inquire whether it is possible to ascertain the *peculiarity* of the apostolic office? for it must be conceded that there was *something* to distinguish the apostles from the other ministers of the New Testament. Here, happily, we are in no way left in the dark. The Saviour, and the apostles and sacred writers themselves, have given an account which cannot be easily mistaken; and our amazement is, that the writer of this tract has not adverted to it. The first account which we adduce is from the lips of the Saviour himself. In those solemn moments when he was about to leave the world; when the work of atonement was finished; and when he gave the apostles their final commission, he indicated the nature of their labours, and the peculiarity of their office, in these words: (Luke xxiv. 48:) "*And ye are* WITNESSES *of these things.* And, behold, I send the promise of my Father upon you," etc. The object of their special appointment, which he here specifies, was, that they should be WITNESSES to all nations. (Comp. v. 47, and Matt. xxviii. 18, 19.) The "things" of which they were to bear witness, he specifies in the preceding verse. They were *his sufferings in accordance with the predictions of the prophets:* "thus it is written, and thus it behooved Christ to suffer;" *and his resurrection from the dead:* "and to rise from the dead the third day." These were the points to bear "witness" to which they had been selected; and these were the points on which they, in fact, insisted in their ministry. See the Acts of the Apostles, *passim*.

We would next remark, that this is *expressly declared* to be the "peculiarity" of the apostolic office. It was done so at the election of an apostle to fill up the vacated place of Judas. Here, if the *peculiar* design had been to confer "superiority in ministerial rights and powers," we should expect to be favoured with some account of it. It was the very time when we should expect them to give an account of the reason why they filled up the vacancy in the college of apostles, and when they actually did make such a statement. Their words are these: (Acts i. 21, 22:) "Wherefore, of these men which have companied with us, all the time that the Lord Jesus went in and out among us, beginning from the baptism of John, unto that same day when he was taken up from us, *must one be ordained to be a* WITNESS WITH US *of his resurrection*." This passage we consider to be absolutely decisive on the point before us. It shows, first, for what purpose they ordained *him;* and, second, that *they* were ordained for the *same* purpose. Why do we hear nothing on this occasion of their "superiority of ministerial rights and powers?" why nothing of their peculiar prerogative to ordain? why nothing of their "general superintendence" of the church? Plainly, because they had conceived of nothing of this kind as entering into their original commission and peculiar design. For this purpose of bearing *testimony* to the world of the fact of the resurrection of the Messiah, they had been originally selected. For this they had been prepared by a long, intimate acquaintance with the Saviour. They had seen him; had been with him in various scenes, fitted to instruct them more fully in his designs and character; had enjoyed an intimate personal friendship with him, (1 John i. 1,) and were thus qualified to go forth as "witnesses" of what they had seen and heard—to confirm the great doctrine that the Messiah had come, had died, and had risen, according to the predictions of the prophets. We just add here, that these truths were of sufficient importance to demand the appointment of twelve honest men to give them confirmation. It has been shown, over and over again, that there was a consummate wisdom in the appointment of witnesses *enough* to satisfy any reasonable mind, and yet not so many as to give it the appearance of tumult or popular excitement. The truth of the whole scheme of Christianity rested on making out the fact that the Lord Jesus had risen from the dead: and the importance of that religion to the welfare of mankind demanded that this should be substantiated to the conviction of the world. Hence the anxiety of the eleven to complete the number of the original witnesses selected by the Saviour, and that the person chosen should have the same acquaintance with the facts that they had themselves.

It is worthy, also, of remark, that in the account which the historian gives of their labours, *this* is the main idea which is presented. Acts ii. 32. "This Jesus hath God raised up, whereof *we are witnesses*." v. 32. "And we are *witnesses* of these things." x. 30–41. "And we are *witnesses* of all things which he did, both in the land of the Jews and in Jerusalem, whom they slew and hanged on a tree." "Him God raised up the third day, and showed him openly *not unto all the people, but unto* WITNESSES *chosen before of God, even unto us,*" etc. In this place we meet with another declaration that this was the object of their original appointment. They were "chosen" for this, and set apart in the holy presence of God to this work. Why do we not hear any thing of their superiority in ministerial rights and powers?" Why not an intimation of the power of confirming, and of general superintendence? We repeat, that it is not possible to answer these questions, except on the supposition that they did not regard any such powers as at all entering into the peculiarity of their commission.

Having disposed of *all* that is said in the New Testament, so far as we know, of the original design of the appointment to the apostolic office, we proceed to another and somewhat independent source of evidence. The original number of the apostles was twelve. The design of their selection we have seen. For important purposes, however, it pleased God to add to their number, one, who had *not* been a personal attendant on the ministry of the Saviour, and who was called to the apostleship four years after the crucifixion and resurrection of Christ. Now this is a case, evidently, which must throw very important light on our inquiries. It is independent of the others. And as he was not a personal observer of the life and death of Jesus; as he was not an original "witness" in the case, we may expect in the record of *his* appointment, a full account of his "superiority in ministerial rights and powers." If such superiority entered into the peculiarity of the apostolic office, this was the very case where we expect to find it. His conversion was *subsequent to* the resurrection. He was to be employed extensively in founding and organizing churches. He was to have intrusted to him almost the entire pagan world. Comp. Rom. xv. 16. His very business seemed to call for some specific account of "superiority in ministerial rights," if any such rights were involved in the apostolic office. How natural to expect a statement of such rights, and an account of the "general superintendence" intrusted to him as an apostle! Let us look, therefore, and see how the case stands. We have three distinct accounts of his conversion and appointment to the apostleship, in each of which the *design* of his appointment is stated. Acts xxii. 14, 15. In his discourse before the Jews, he repeats the charge given to him by Ananias, at Damascus: "The God of our fathers hath chosen thee, etc. For thou shalt be his WITNESS *unto all men of what thou hast seen and heard.*" Again, (Acts xxvi. 16,) in his speech before Agrippa, Paul repeats the words addressed to him by the Lord Jesus in his original commission: "I have appeared unto thee *for this purpose,* to make thee a minister and a WITNESS of those things," etc. Again, (Acts xxiii. 11,) in the account which is given of his past and future work, it is said: "As thou hast *testified* of me in Jerusalem, so must thou bear *witness* also at Rome."

This is the account which is given of the call of Saul of Tarsus to the apostolic office. But where is there a single syllable of any "superiority in ministerial powers and rights," as constituting the peculiarity of his office? We respectfully ask the writer of this tract, and all other advocates of Episcopacy, to point to us a "a light or shadow" of any such Episcopal investment. We think their argument demands it. And if there *is* no such account, neither in the original choice of the twelve, nor in the appointment of Matthias, nor in the selection of the apostle to the Gentiles; we take the liberty to insist with firmness on a satisfactory explanation of the causes which operated to produce the omission of the very essence of their office, according to Episcopacy. We insist on being told of *some* reasons, prudential or otherwise, which made it proper to pass over the very vitality of the original commission.

But we have not done with the apostle Paul. He is too important a "witness" for us, as well as for the purpose for which he was appointed, to be dismissed without further attention. It has been remarked already that he was not a personal follower of Jesus of Nazareth, and was not present at his death and ascension. It may be asked, then, how could he be a witness, in the sense, and for the purposes already described? Let us see how this was provided for. We transcribe the account from his own statement of the address made to him by Ananias. Acts xxii. 14. "The God of our fathers hath chosen thee, that thou shouldst know his will, *and* SEE *that Just One, and shouldst hear the words of his mouth.*" That he *had* thus seen him, it is not necessary to prove. See 1 Cor. xv. 8; Acts ix. 5, 17. The inference which we here draw is, that he was permitted to *see* the Lord Jesus in an extraordinary manner, for the express purpose of qualifying him to be invested with the *peculiarity of the apostleship*. This inference, sufficiently clear from the very statement, we shall now proceed to put beyond the possibility of doubt.

We turn, then, to another account which Paul has given of his call to the apostleship, 1 Cor. ix. 1, 2: "Am I not an apostle? Am I not free? Have I not seen Jesus Christ our Lord?" We adduce this passage as proof that *to have seen Jesus Christ*, was considered as an indispensable qualification for the apostleship. So Paul regarded it in his own case. We adduce it also for another purpose, viz., to strengthen our main position, that the apostles was designated to their office specifically as *witnesses* to the character and resurrection of Christ. If this was *not* the design, we ask, why does Paul appeal to the fact that he had *seen* the Saviour, as proof that he was *qualified* to be an apostle? And we further ask, with emphasis, if the apostles, as Episcopalians pretend, did, in virtue of their office, possess "superiority in ministerial powers and rights," why did not Paul once *hint* at the fact in this passage? His express object was to vindicate his claim to the apostleship.

In doing this, he appeals to that which *we* maintain to have constituted the peculiarity of the office, his being "*witness*" to the Saviour. In this instance we have a circumstance, of which Paley would make much in an argument, if it fell in with the design of the "Horæ Paulinæ." We claim the privilege of making *as* much of it, upon the question whether the peculiarity of the apostolic office was "*superiority* of ministerial powers and rights."

We have now examined all the passages of Scripture which state the design of the apostleship. And we have shown, if we mistake not, that the ground of the distinction between the "apostles *and* elders," "the apostles *and* elders, *and* brethren," was not that the former had superiority of "ministerial powers and rights." We might leave the argument here; for if the Episcopalians cannot make out *this* point to entire satisfaction, all that is said about *successors* in the apostolic office, and about perpetuating apostleship, must be nugatory and vain. But we have an independent topic of remark here; and one which bears on the subject, therefore, with all the force of a cumulative argument. To the consideration of this we are led by the next position of Dr. Onderdonk. This is stated in the following words: that "there was *continued*, as had begun in the apostles, an order of ministers *superior* to the elders." p. 16. This he attempts to prove, on the ground that "there is no scriptural evidence that mere elders (presbyters) ordained." pp. 16–23. And that "the above distinction between elders and a grade superior to them, in regard especially to the power of ordaining, was so persevered in as to indicate that it was a *permanent* arrangement, and not designed to be but temporary." pp. 23–29. We shall reverse the order of this argument.

In the inquiry, then, whether this distinction was *continued* or persevered in, we might insist on what has been already shown, as decisive. If the original distinction was what we have proved it to be, it could *not* be persevered in, without (as in the case of Paul) a personal, direct manifestation of the ascended Saviour, to qualify every future incumbent for the apostleship. 1 Cor. ix. 1. No modern "bishop," we presume, will lay claim to this. The very supposition that any such revelation was necessary, would dethrone every prelate, and prostrate every mitre in Christendom.

But we have, as before remarked, an independent train of arguments on this point. It is evident that the whole burden of proof here lies on the Episcopalian. He maintains that such an original distinction existed, and that it was perpetuated. Both these positions we deny. The first we have shown to be unfounded, and have thus virtually destroyed the other. We proceed, however, to the comparatively needless task of showing that Dr. Onderdonk's *second* position is equally unfounded. His evidence we shall examine as we find it scattered throughout the tract before us.

The first argument is, that "some are named apostles in Scripture, who were not thus appointed, (*i. e.* by the Saviour himself,) as Matthias, Barnabas, and probably James, the brother of our Lord, all ordained by merely human ordainers. Silvanus also, and Timothy, are called 'apostles;' and, besides Andronicus and Junia, others could be added to the list." p. 15.

The argument here is, that the *name* "apostle" is given to them, and that they held, therefore, the peculiar *office* in question. But the mere circumstance that they had this *name*, would not of itself establish this point. It is not necessary, we presume, to apprize our readers, that the word *apostle* means *one who is sent*, and may be applied to any person employed to deliver a message; and in a general sense, to any ministers of religion, or to any one *sent* to proclaim the message of life. Thus in John xiii. 16, it is applied to *any* messenger, sustaining the same relation to one who sends him, that the servant does to his master. "The servant is not greater than his lord, [master,] neither he that is sent, *ἀπόστολος*, greater than he that sent him." Thus it is applied (Phil. ii. 25) to Epaphroditus, not as an apostle, in the specific sense of the term, but as *a messenger*, sent by the church at Philippi, to supply the wants of Paul. (Comp. Phil. iv. 18.) "Epaphroditus, my brother and companion in labour, but *your messenger*," *ὑμῶν δὲ ἀπόστολον*, your *apostle*. Thus also in 2 Cor. viii. 23, it is applied to the "brethren," "the messengers of the churches;" "our brethren are *the messengers of the churhes*," *ἀπόστολοι ἐκκλησιῶν*. These passages show beyond a question, that the name is often used in the New Testament in its *generic* signification, and consequently the mere fact that it is applied to an individual, is not proof that he was an apostle in its specific sense,—the only sense which would be of value in the argument of the Episcopalian. The *connections*, the circumstances, are to determine its meaning. We make this remark, in accordance with the judicious observation of Dr. Onderdonk, p. 13: "*A little reflection and practice will enable any of our readers to look in Scripture for the several sacred* OFFICES, *independently of the* NAMES *there or elsewhere given to them.*"

The question then is, Whether the name *apostle* is so given to the persons here designated, as to show that it is used in its strict, specific sense?

The first case is that of "Matthias." The *reason* why the name was given to him, we have already shown. He was an apostle in the *strict, proper* sense, because he was chosen to be a "witness" of the resurrection of the Saviour. Acts i. 22.

The second is that of Barnabas. He is once called an apostle. Acts xiv. 14. That he was not an apostle in the strict, proper sense, Dr. Onderdonk has himself most laboriously and satisfactorily proved. In his argument against Presbyterian ordinances, (pp. 16, 17,) he has taken much pains to show that Barnabas was set apart (Acts xiii. 1–3) "to a special missionary work;" "was merely set apart to a particular field of duty;" that is, was sent as a messenger of the church to perform a particular piece of work. It is observable that before this, Barnabas is called merely "a prophet and teacher;" (Acts xiii. 1–11;) that he is called an *apostle* in immediate connection with this designation, and nowhere else. Acts xiv. 14. How Dr. Onderdonk, after having shown so conclusively, as we think, that the transaction at Antioch was not a Presbyterian ordination; that it was a mere *designation to a particular field of labour*, should persist in maintaining that Barnabas was an apostle, in the strict sense, as having a "superiority of ministerial rights and powers," we profess our inability to conceive. We shall thus dismiss the case of Matthias and Barnabas.

The next case is "*probably* James, the brother of our Lord." The use of the word probably, here, shows a wish to *press* cases into the service, which we regret to see in a tract making strong pretensions to strict demonstration, (comp. pp. 3, 11, 16, 23, etc.;) but it evinces a *deficiency* of strong, palpable instances, which betrays the conscious feebleness of the argument. "James, the Lord's brother," is *once* mentioned as an apostle. Gal. i. 19. But it could not have escaped the recollection of Dr. Onderdonk, that there were *two* of the name of *James* among the apostles in the specific sense of the term; viz., James the brother of John, and son of Zebedee, and *James the son of Alpheus*. Matt. x. 3; Luke vi. 15. Nor can it be unknown to him, that the word *brother* was used by the Hebrews to denote a relative more remote than that which is designated by the ordinary use of the word among us; and that *Alpheus* was probably a connection of the family of our Lord. What proof, then, is there, that he was not referred to in the passage before us? As this case is alleged to have only a *probability* in its favour, we consider it disposed of.

Silvanus and Timothy are the next mentioned. As their claim to be considered *apostles* rests on the same foundation, so far as the *name* is any evidence, we shall dispose of these cases by considering that of Timothy at length in a subsequent part of the argument.

The remaining cases are those of Andronicus and Junia. The foundation for their claim to be enrolled as apostles, is the following mention of them by Paul: (Rom. xvi. 7:) "Salute Andronicus and Junia, my kinsmen, *who are of note among the apostles,*" ὅιτινές εἰσιν ἐπίσημοι ἐν τοῖς ἀποστόλοις. On this claim we remark: (1.) Admitting that they are here *called* apostles, the name, as we have proved, does not imply that they had any "superiority of ministerial rights and powers." They might have been distinguished as messengers, or labourers, like Epaphroditus. (2.) It is clear, that the apostle did not *mean* to give them the name of *apostles* at all. If he had designed it, the phraseology would have been different. Comp. Rom. i. 1; 1 Cor. i. 1; 2 Cor. i. 1; Phil. i. 1. (3.) All that the expression *fairly* implies, is, that they, having been early converted, (Rom. xvi. 7,) and being acquainted with the apostles at Jerusalem, were held *in high esteem by them;* the apostles regarded them with confidence and affection. We consider this case, therefore, as disposed of.*

The next point of proof in the tract before us, "that the distinction between elders and a grade superior to them, in regard especially to the power of ordaining, was so persevered in as to indicate that it was a *permanent* arrangement," is drawn from the charge given by the Apostle Paul to the elders of Ephesus, Acts xx. 28–35. The point of this evidence, as we understand it, is this. Paul charges the elders at Ephesus

* Dr. Onderdonk says that Calvin, in his Institutes, "allows Andronicus and Junia to have been apostles;" but he ought to have added that Calvin, in his Commentary on the passage, written at a later period, denies that they were apostles in the *specific* sense of the term.

to "take heed to themselves,"—"to take heed to all the flock over which the Holy Ghost had made them overseers,—to feed the church of God,—to watch against the grievous wolves that would assail the flock," etc. In all this, we are told, there is not a word respecting the power of ordaining, nor any thing which shows that they had the power of clerical discipline. "No power is intimated to depose from office one of their own number, or an unsound minister coming among them." They are to "tend" or "rule" the flock as shepherds; "for shepherds do not tend and rule shepherds." pp. 23, 24.

This is affirmed to be the sole power of these elders. In connection with this, we are asked to read the Epistles to Timothy,—the power there given "personally to Timothy *at Ephesus*," (p. 23,) or as it is elsewhere expressed, "Compare now with this sum-total of power assigned to mere elders, or presbyters, that of *Timothy* at Ephesus, the very city and region in which those addressed by Paul, in Acts xx., resided and ministered." p. 25. In those epistles it is said, that the "right of governing the clergy, and ordaining, is ascribed to him personally;" and numerous undisputed passages are then adduced, to show that Timothy is addressed as having this power. 1 Tim. i. 18; iii. 14, 15; iv. 6; 1 Tim. i. 3; v. 19–21, etc. etc.

Now this argument proceeds on the following *assumptions*, viz.: 1. That Timothy was called an apostle; was invested with the same powers as the apostles, and was one of their *successors* in the office. 2. That he was, at the time when Paul gave his charge to the elders at Miletus, bishop of Ephesus. 3. That the "elders" summoned to Miletus, were ministers of the gospel of the second order, or as they are now termed, usually, *priests*, in contradistinction from bishops and deacons. If these points are not made out from the New Testament, or if any one of them fails, this argument for

"Episcopacy tested by Scripture," will be of no value. We shall take them up and dispose of them in their order.

The first claim is, that Timothy is called an "apostle," and was, therefore, clothed with apostolic powers. This claim is advanced on p. 15: "Silvanus, also, and Timothy, are called 'apostles,'" and the claim is implied in the whole argument, and is essential to its validity. The *proof* on which this claim is made to rest is contained in 1 Thess. i. 1, compared with 1 Thess. ii. 6. Paul, Silvanus, and Timothy, are joined together in the commencement of the epistle, as writing it to the church at Thessalonica; and, in ch. ii. 6, the following expression occurs: "Nor of man sought we glory, when we might have been burdensome as the *apostles* of Christ." This is the sole proof of the *apostleship* of Timothy,—of which so much is made in the Episcopal controversy, and which is usually appealed to as itself sufficient to settle the question.

Now, without insisting on the point which we have made out, that the apostolic office was conferred not to impart "superiority of ministerial rights and powers," but to establish everywhere the great doctrine of the truth of Christianity, and that consequently *if* Timothy is called an apostle, it is only in the generic sense of the word, to which we have adverted, and that Paul might also on this occasion speak of himself, as joined with Timothy and Silvanus, as *a messenger* of the churches; (comp. Acts xiii. 2; xiv. 14; Rom. xvi. 25; 2 Cor. viii. 23;) not to insist on this position, we shall dispose of this claim by the following considerations: 1. The passage does not fairly imply that Timothy was even called an apostle. For it is admitted in the tract, (p. 15,) that "it is not unusual for St. Paul to use the plural number of himself only." It is argued, indeed, that the words "apostles" and "our own souls," (v. 8,) being inapplicable to the singular use of the plural number, hence the "three whose names are at the head of the epistle, are here spoken of jointly." But if Paul used the plural number as applicable to himself, would it not be natural for him to continue its use, and to employ the adjectives, etc., connected with it in the same number? Besides, there is conclusive evidence that Paul did *not* intend to include the "three" named at the head of the epistle, in this expression in v. 6. For, in the verses immediately preceding, mention is made that "*we* had suffered before, and were shamefully treated, as ye know, at Philippi," etc. Now it is capable of demonstration that *Timothy* was *not* present at that time, and was not engaged in those labours, or subjected to those sufferings at Philippi. Acts xvi. 12, 19; xviii. 1–4. It follows, therefore, that Paul did *not* intend, here, to imply that "the three named at the head of the epistle" were apostles; and, that he either intended to speak of himself alone, in v. 6, or what is more probable, that he spoke of himself as one of the apostles, and of what the apostles *might* do in virtue of their office; that is, that they might be burdensome, or might "use authority," as in the margin.

Our next proof that Timothy was not an apostle, is, that he is *expressly distinguished* from Paul, as an apostle; that is, in the same verse, Paul is careful to speak for *himself* as an apostle, and of *Timothy* as *not* an apostle. Thus, 2 Cor. i. 1, "Paul an *apostle* of Jesus Christ, *and Timothy our brother*." Again, Col. i. 1, "Paul an *apostle* of Jesus Christ, and Timothy *our brother*." Now our argument is this, that if Paul regarded Timothy as an apostle, it is remarkable that he should be so careful to make this distinction, when *his own name* is mentioned as an apostle. Why did he not also make the same honorable mention of *Timothy?*—Will some of our Episcopal friends be kind enough to state *why* this distinction is made?—The distinction is the more remarkable, from the next consideration to be adduced, which is, that Paul is so cautious on this point—so resolved *not* to call Timothy an apostle, that when their names *are* joined together, as in any sense claiming the same appellation, it is not *as apostles*, but *as servants*. Phil. i. 1: "Paul and Timotheus *the servants* of Jesus Christ." See also 1 Thess. i. 1; 2 Thess. i. 1. These considerations put it beyond debate, in our view, that Timothy is *not* called an apostle in the New Testament. This, it will be perceived, is an important advance in our argument.

The second claim for Timothy is, that he was bishop of Ephesus. This claim is essential to the argument of Dr. Onderdonk, and is everywhere implied in what he says of Timothy. See pp. 23–25. Proof is not, indeed, attempted; but it is assumed as a conceded point. Now this point should have been made out, for it is not one of those which we are disposed by any means to concede. It is to be remembered, too, that it is a point which is to be made out from the *New Testament*, for our inquiry is, whether Episcopacy can be defended "by Scripture." Let us see how this matter stands.

It may be proper here to remark, that the subscription at the close of the second Epistle to Timothy, "ordained first bishop of the church of the Ephesians," etc., is admitted on all hands not to be inspired, and, therefore, is of no authority in this argument. Assuredly Paul would not close a letter in this way, by seriously informing Timothy that he wrote a second epistle to him, etc., and by *appending* this to the letter. By whom these subscriptions to the epistles were added is unknown. Some of them are manifestly false; and none of them, though true, are of any authority. The subscription here belongs, we believe, to the former class.

Now, how does the case stand in the New Testament, with respect to Timothy? What testimony does it afford as to his being "bishop of Ephesus?" A few observations will save further debate, we trust, on this subject.

1. It is admitted that he was *not* at Ephesus at the time when Paul made his address to the elders at Miletus. Thus,

p. 25, "Ephesus was without a bishop when Paul addressed the elders, Timothy not having been placed over that church till some time afterward." Here, then, was a *diocese*, or one collection of churches, which is admitted to have been constituted *without* a bishop. The presumption is, that all others were organized in the same way.

2. The charge which Paul gives to the elders *proves* that Timothy was not there; and proves further, that they, at that time, *had* no bishops, and that they previously had none. They are charged to take heed to themselves, and to all the flock, "to feed" or "to rule" the flock, etc. But not one word is to be found of their having then any prelatical bishops; not one word of Timothy as their episcopal leader. Not an exhortation is given to be subject to any prelate; not an intimation that they would ever be called on to recognise any such bishops. Not one word of lamentation or condolence is expressed, that they were not fully supplied with all proper episcopal authority. All of which is inexplicable, on the supposition that they were then destitute, and that they would be supplied with an officer "superior in ministerial rights and powers." Nay, they are *themselves* expressly called bishops, without the slightest intimation that there were any *higher*, or more honourable prelates than themselves, (Acts xx. 28:) "Take heed, therefore, to yourselves, and to all the flock over the which the Holy Ghost hath made you *bishops*," ἐπισκόπους.

3. It is admitted by us, that Timothy subsequently *was* at Ephesus, and that he was left there for an important purpose, by the Apostle Paul. This was when Paul went to Macedonia. 1 Tim. i. 3. This is the *only* intimation that we know of in the New Testament, that Timothy was ever at Ephesus at all. It is important, then, to ascertain whether he was left there as a *permanent bishop*. Now, in settling this, we remark, it is nowhere intimated in the New Testament, that he was

such a bishop. The passage before us, 1 Tim. i. 3, states, that when they were travelling together, Paul left him there, while he himself should go over into Macedonia. The *object* for which he left him is explicitly stated, and that object was not that he should be a permanent bishop. It is said to be "to charge some that they teach no other doctrine, neither to give heed to endless genealogies," etc.; that is, manifestly to perform a *temporary* office of regulating certain disorders in the church; of silencing certain false teachers of Jewish extraction; of producing, in one word, what the personal influence of the apostle himself might have produced, but for a sudden and unexpected call to Macedonia. Acts xx. 1. Hence it is perfectly clear that the apostle *designed* this as a temporary appointment for a specific object, and *that* object was not to be *prelate* of the church. Thus he says, 1 Tim. iv. 13, "*Till I come*, give attention to reading," etc.: implying that his temporary office was then to cease. Thus, too, referring to the same purpose to return and join Timothy, he says, 1 Tim. iii. 14, 15, "These things I write unto thee, hoping to come unto thee shortly; but *if I tarry long*, that thou mightest know how thou oughtest to behave thyself in the house of God," etc.; implying that these directions were particularly to serve him during his appointment to the *specific* business of regulating some disordered affairs produced by false teachers, and which might require the discipline of even some of the *bishops* and deacons of the church. ch. v. vi. These directions, involving *general* principles, indeed, and of value to regulate his whole life, yet had, nevertheless, a manifest *special* reference to the cases which might occur there, in putting a period to the promulgation of erroneous doctrines by Jewish teachers. 1 Tim. i. 3.

4. It has been shown by the late Dr. Wilson, of Philadelphia, from the New Testament itself, that Timothy was not the bishop of the church at Ephesus. To this argument,

which is too long to be inserted here, and which cannot be abridged, we can only refer.*

5. The claim that Timothy was bishop of Ephesus, is one that must be made out by Episcopalians from the New Testament. But this claim has *not* been made out, nor can it ever be.

6. The Epistle to the Ephesians shows further, that at the time of writing that, there was no such bishop at Ephesus. Though the apostle herein gives the church various instructions about the relations which existed, there is not the slightest hint that Timothy was there; nor is there the least intimation that any such officer ever had been, or ever would be, set over them.

Now, if it cannot be made out that Timothy was bishop of Ephesus, if the point is not established beyond a doubt, then in reading Paul's charge to the elders at Miletus, we are to regard *them* as intrusted with the care of the church at Ephesus. It is not necessary to *our* argument to inquire whether they were ruling elders, or presbyters ordained to preach as well as to rule. All that is incumbent on us, is to show that the New Testament does not warrant the assumption that they were subject to a diocesan bishop. We affirm, therefore, simply, that Paul addressed them as intrusted with the spiritual instruction and government of the church at Ephesus, without any reference whatever to any person, either then or afterward placed over them, as superior in ministerial rights and powers. And this point is conclusively established by two additional considerations; first, that *they* are expressly called *bishops*, ἐπισκόπους, themselves—a most remarkable appellation, if the apostle meant to have them understand that they were to be under the administration of *another* bishop of superior ministerial powers and rights; and, secondly, that they are

* The Primitive Government of the Christian Churches, pp. 251–262.

expressly intrusted with the whole spiritual charge of the church, ποιμαίνειν τὴν ἐκκλησίαν, κ. τ. λ. But every thing in this case is fully met by the supposition that they were invested with the simple power of *ruling*. Dr. Onderdonk himself admits that the word translated "feed," ποιμαίνειν, may be rendered to "rule." p. 37. And if this point be conceded, the idea that they were *elders* in the Presbyterian sense, is all that can be proved from the passage. It is *essential* to the argument of Episcopalians, that they should be able to make out that these *elders* not only *ruled*, but also preached the gospel, and performed the other functions of their "second order" of clergy.

Let us now gather the results of our investigation, and dispose of the case of Timothy. We have shown that he was not an apostle. We have further shown that he was not bishop of Ephesus. We have thus destroyed the claim of the *permanency* of the apostolic office, so far as Timothy is concerned. And we now insist that the readers of the New Testament, they who wish to defend Episcopacy by "Scripture," should read the two Epistles to Timothy, without the vain and illusory supposition that he was bishop of Ephesus. Agreeing with Dr. Onderdonk that this point must be settled by the New Testament, and that "*no argument is worth taking into the account which has not a palpable bearing on the clear and naked topic—the scriptural evidence of Episcopacy*," (p. 3,) we now insist that these Epistles should be read without being interpreted by the unsupported position that Timothy was the permanent bishop of Ephesus. We insist, moreover, that *that* supposition shall not be admitted to influence the interpretation. With this matter clear before us, how stands the case in these two Epistles? We answer, thus:—

(1.) Timothy was sent to Ephesus for a *special* purpose—to allay contentions, and prevent the spreading of false doctrine. 1 Tim. i. 3. (2.) This was to be *temporary*. 1 Tim. i. 3. Comp. iii. 14, 15; iv. 13. (3.) He was intrusted with the right of ordination, as all ministers of the gospel are, and with the authority of government. 1 Tim. i. 3; v. 19–21; v. 22; 2 Tim. ii. 2. (4.) Laying out of view the gratuitous supposition that he was bishop of Ephesus, the charge given to Timothy was just such a one as would be given to any minister of the gospel authorized to preach, to ordain, to administer the ordinances of the church and its discipline. It is just such as is given now to men who hold to the doctrine of ministerial parity. The "charges" which are given to Presbyterian and Congregational ministers at ordination, are almost uniformly couched in the same language which is used by Paul, in addressing Timothy; nor is there any thing in those Epistles which may not be, and which is not, in fact, often addressed to ministers on such occasions. With just as much propriety might some antiquarian hereafter—some future advocate for Episcopacy—collect together the *charges* now given to ministers, and appeal to them as proof that the churches in New England, and among Presbyterians, were *Episcopal*, as to appeal now to the Epistles to Timothy, to prove his office as a prelate. (5.) The Epistles themselves contain evidence of the falsehood of the supposition, that there was an order of men superior to the presbyters in "ministerial powers and rights." There are but *two* orders of ministers spoken of, or alluded to in the Epistles—*bishops* and *deacons*. There is not the slightest allusion to any other order. We call the attention of our readers here to an emphatic remark of Dr. Onderdonk, p. 12: "ALL that we read in the New Testament concerning 'bishops,' is to be regarded as pertaining to the 'middle grade:' *i.e.* nothing in these epistles or elsewhere, where this term is used, has any reference to a rank of ministers superior 'in ministerial powers and rights.'" The case here, then, by the supposition of the

Episcopalians, is this:—Two epistles are addressed by an apostle to a successor of the apostles, designated as such, to retain and perpetuate the same rank and powers. Those epistles are designed to instruct him in the organization and government of the churches. They contain ample information, and somewhat protracted discussions on the following topics: The office of a presbyter. The qualifications for that office. The office of the deacons. The qualifications for that office. The qualifications of deacon's *wives.* 1 Tim. iii. The proper discipline of an elder. The qualifications of those who were to be admitted to the office of *deaconesses.* 1 Tim. v. The duties of masters and servants. 1 Tim. vi. The duties of *laymen.* 1 Tim. ii. 8. And of Christian females. 1 Tim. ii. 9–11. Nay, they contain directions about the apostle's *cloak,* and his *parchments,* (2 Tim. iv. 13;) but from the beginning to the end, not one single syllable respecting the existence of a grade of officers in the church superior "in ministerial rights and powers;" not a word about their qualifications, of the mode of ordaining or consecrating them, or of Timothy's fraternal intercourse with his brother prelates; nothing about the subjection of the priesthood to them, or of their peculiar functions of confirmation and superintendence. In one word, taking these Epistles by themselves, no man would dream that there were any such officers in existence. We ask now, whether any candid reader of the New Testament can believe that there *were* any such officers; and that two epistles could have been written in these circumstances, without the *slightest* allusion to their existence or powers? "*Credat Judæus Apella.*" We ask whether there can be found *now* among *all* the charges which Episcopal bishops have given to their clergy, any two in which there shall not also be found *some* allusion to the "primitive and apostolic order" of bishops in the churches? It remains for our eyes to be blessed with the sight of *one Episcopal charge,* reminding us, in this respect, of the charges of Paul to Timothy.

We now take our leave of the case of Timothy. The case of Titus, the next in order, (pp. 26, 27,) we must despatch in fewer words. The argument of Dr. Onderdonk, in defence of the claim respecting Titus, does not vary materially from that used in reference to Timothy, p. 26. It is, that he was left in Crete to ordain elders in every city, and that the powers of "ordination, admonition, and rejection, are all committed to Titus personally." Titus i. 6–9; iii. 10. The only point here which requires a moment's examination, in addition to what we have said on the case of Timothy, is the purpose for which he was left at Crete. Titus i. 5. The claim of the Episcopalians here is, that this indicates such a *perseverance* in the "distinction between elders and a grade superior to them," as to prove that it was "to be a *permanent* arrangement." p. 23. In other words, Titus was to be a *permanent* bishop of Crete, superior to the elders "in ministerial rights and powers." This claim it is necessary for them to establish from the New Testament. If there are any intimations that it was *not* designed to be *permanent*, they will be fatal to the argument. We affirm, then, in opposition to this claim, that the case is fully met by the supposition that Titus was an extraordinary officer, like Timothy, at Ephesus, appointed for a specific purpose. 1. The appointment itself looks as if this was the design. Paul had himself commenced a work there, which, from some cause, he was unable to complete. That work he left to Titus to finish. As it cannot be pretended that *Paul* had any purpose of becoming the permanent bishop of Crete; so it cannot be pretended that Titus's being left to *complete* what Paul had begun, is proof that Paul expected that Titus would be *permanent* bishop. An appointment to *complete* a work which is begun by another, when the original designer did not contemplate a permanent employment, cannot surely be adduced in proof of a permanent office. If I am employed to complete an edifice which is commenced, it does not suppose that I am to labour at it all my life; still less, that I am to have successors in the undertaking. We presume that this passage, to most unbiassed minds, would imply that Paul expected that Titus, after having *completed* what he had left him to do, would leave the island of Crete, and accompany him in his travels. 2. That this *was* the fact; that he had no expectation that Titus would be a *permanent* bishop of Crete, superior in "ministerial rights and powers," is perfectly apparent from the direction in this same Epistle, (ch. iii. 12:) "When I shall send Artemas unto thee, or Tychicus, *be diligent to come unto me at Nicopolis.*" Here we find conclusive proof, that the arrangement respecting Titus in Crete was temporary. To suppose the contrary, is to maintain a position in the very face of the directions of the apostle. Every thing in the case shows, that he was an extraordinary officer, appointed for a specific purpose; and that when that work was effected, which the apostle supposed *would be* soon, he was to resume his station as the travelling companion and fellow-labourer of the apostle. 3. That this was the *general* character of Titus; that he was so regarded by Paul, as his companion, and very valuable to him in his work, is further apparent from 2 Cor. ii. 12, 13; vii. 6–13. In the former passage he says, that he expected to meet him at *Troas*, and intimates that his presence and help were very necessary for him. "I had no rest in my spirit, because I found not Titus my brother." In the latter place, (2 Cor. vii. 6–13,) we find him the companion of the Apostle Paul, in Philippi. Again, (2 Cor. xii. 18,) we find him employed on a special embassy to the church in Corinth, in respect to the collection for the poor saints at Jerusalem. Comp. Rom. xv. 26. And again we find him on a mission to *Dalmatia*, 2 Tim. iv. 10. Assuredly these various migrations and employments do not appear as if he was designed by the apostle as the permanent bishop of Crete. 4. It is to be presumed that Titus regarded the apostolic mandate, (Titus iii. 12;) that he *left* Crete in accordance with Paul's request; and, as there is no intimation that he returned, as the New Testament throws no light on that point, as indeed there is not the slightest proof anywhere that he died there, we come to the conclusion that he was employed for a temporary purpose, and that having accomplished it, he resumed his situation as the companion of Paul. Comp. Gal. ii. 1. It must be admitted, on all hands, that the Episcopalian cannot *prove* the contrary. Since, moreover, our supposition meets *all* the circumstances of the case as well as his, and we are able to show that this was the general character of the labours of Titus, we shall dismiss his case also.

The last argument of Dr. Onderdonk is derived from the epistle to the seven churches of Asia. Rev. ii. iii. This argument is embodied in the following position: "Each of those churches is addressed, not through its clergy at large, but through its 'angel,' or chief officer; this alone is a very strong argument against parity in favour of Episcopacy." "One of those churches is Ephesus; and when we read concerning its angel, '*thou* hast tried them which say they are apostles, and are not, and hast found them liars,' do we require further evidence that what Timothy, the chief officer there, was in the year 65, in regard to the supreme right of discipline over the clergy, the same was its chief officer when this book was written, in 96?" The singular number, it is added, is used emphatically in the address to each of the angels, and "the individual called 'the angel,' is, in each case, identified with his church, and his church with him." pp. 27, 28.

This is the argument; and this is the whole of it. We have sought diligently to see its bearing; but our labour, in doing it, has not been crowned with very flattering success. We can see, indeed, that those churches were addressed through their ministers, or pastors, called "angels;" but it requires more penetration than we profess to have, to discover how this bears on the precise point, that there is an order of men superior to others "in ministerial rights and powers." Such an argument can be founded only on the following assumptions: 1. That there was an *inferior* body of clergymen, called here "clergy at large." *Assuming* this point, it would not be difficult to make out an argument from the address "to the angel." But this is a point *to be proved*, not to be assumed. We would respectfully ask the writer of this tract, where he finds an intimation of the existence of an order of "*clergy at large*," in these churches. In the Epistles themselves there is not the slightest *hint* of the existence of any such personages distinct from "the angels." Nay, the very stylè of address is strong presumption that there were not any such inferior clergymen. The only mention which occurs, is of *the angel* and *the church*. We hear nothing of an intermediate order; nothing of any supremacy of "the angel" over "the clergy at large;" not the least intimation of any duty to be performed by the supposed prelatical "angel," toward the inferior presbyters. Why is a reference to them omitted, if they had any existence? Is it customary in addressing "bishops" *now*, to omit all reference to their duties over the inferior "clergy at large?" This is a point of too much consequence to be left now so unguarded; and, accordingly, the rights and duties of the order, superior "in ministerial rights and powers," are sedulously marked out and inculcated.* 2. It must be *assumed*, in this argument, that there were in

---

* We, of course, lay out of view, here, the case of the "elders at Ephesus," as being already disposed of; and as not being relevant to Dr. Onderdonk's argument, since that they were "clergy at large," is to be *proved*, not *assumed*.

each of those cities more churches than one; that there was a circle, or confederation of churches that would answer to the modern notion of a diocese, over which "the clergy at large" of *inferior* "ministerial rights and powers," might exercise a modified jurisdiction. If this is not assumed, the argument has no force; since if there were but *one* church in each of those cities, the "angel" was *not* a bishop in the Episcopal sense, but a pastor in the ordinary acceptation. Now this is a point which, in an argument like this, should not be *assumed.* It should be *proved,* or at least rendered highly probable from the New Testament. But there is not the slightest hint of any such divided and scattered diocesan organization. In each instance, the church is addressed as one, and undivided. "The angel of *the church*"—not the churches—of "Ephesus." Rev. ii. 1. "The angel of *the church* in Smyrna," (ii. 8;) "the angel of *the church* at Thyatira," (ii. 18;) "the angel of *the church* in Sardis," (iii. 1,) etc. In every instance the address is the same. The point of inquiry now is, whether in this address the Saviour meant to intimate that there was a *plurality* of churches, an ecclesiastical, diocesan organization? This is a point for Episcopalians to *prove,* not to assume. Light may be thrown on it by comparing it with other places where a church is spoken of. The presumption is directly *against* the Episcopalian. It is, that the apostles would not organize separate churches in a single city; and that, if it were done, they would be specified as *the churches.* Accordingly, we learn that the apostle organized "a church" at Corinth. 1 Cor. i. 1, 2. Thus, also, at Antioch. Acts xiii. 1. Thus, also, at Laodicea. Col. iv. 16. And in the Epistle to one of the very churches under consideration, that at Ephesus, it is mentioned not as *the churches* of Ephesus, but as *the church.* Acts xx. 28. When Paul addressed this same church in an epistle, it was directed, not to *the churches,* but to *the saints* at Ephesus. Eph. i. 1. But where there were *distinct* churches organized, there is a *specific* mention of the fact of the plurality. They are mentioned as being many. Thus, Acts xv. 41: "Paul went through Syria confirming (*i.e.* strengthening, establishing) *the churches.*" Rom. xvi. 4: "the *churches* of the Gentiles." 1 Cor. xvi. 1: "the *churches* of Galatia." 19: "the *churches* of Asia." 2 Cor. viii. 1: "the *churches* in Macedonia." See also 2 Cor. viii. 19, 23; xi. 8; Gal. i. 22; Rev. i. 4. Now if it is neither proved that there was a body of "clergy at large," nor that there were separate churches in each of those cities, we ask, What is the force of the argument of Dr. Onderdonk from this case? How does it bear on the point at issue? What has it to do with the subject?

With one or two additional remarks, we shall dismiss this point. The first is, that it cannot be argued from the term *angel,* given to those ministers, that they were Episcopal bishops. That term, as is well known, has no such exclusive applicability to a prelate. It is nowhere else applied to the ministers of religion; and its original signification, "a messenger," or its usual application to celestial spirits, has no special adaptedness to an Episcopal bishop. An ordinary pastor—a messenger sent from God; a spiritual guide and friend of the church, will as fully express its sense, as the application to a prelate. Without invidiousness, we may observe, that prelates have not usually evinced any such extraordinary sanctity as to appropriate this title to themselves alone by prescriptive right. Our other remark is, that the supposition that these *angels* were *pastors* of the churches—presbyters on a parity with each other, and with all others—will fully meet every thing which is said of them in the book of Revelation. This supposition, too, will meet the addresses made to them, better than the assumption that they were prelates. Their union, as Dr. Onderdonk remarks, to the church is intimate. "The angel is in each case identified with his church, and his church with him." Now to which does this remark best apply? to the tender, intimate, endearing relation of a pastor with his people; to the blending of their feelings, interests, and destiny, when he is with them continually; when he meets them each week in the sanctuary; when he administers to them the bread of life; goes into their abode when they are afflicted, and attends their kindred to the grave?—or does it best apply to the union subsisting between the people of an extended *diocese*—to the formal, unfrequent, and, in many instances, stately and pompous visitations of a diocesan bishop; to the *kind* of connection formed between a people scattered into many churches, who are visited at intervals of a year, or more, by one claiming "a superiority in ministerial rights and powers," robed in lawn, and perhaps with the crosier and mitre, as emblematical of office, state, and power; who must be a stranger to the ten thousand tender ties of endearment which bind as one the hearts of a pastor and his people? To our minds, it seems clear that the account which Dr. Onderdonk has given of the "identity" of the angel and the church applies to the former, and not to the latter. It speaks the sentiments of our heart, as respects the union of a pastor and people. And, while we would not allow ourselves to speak with disrespect of the episcopal office, we still feel that the language of the Saviour, by the mild and gentle John, to the churches of Asia, breathes far more of the endearing "identity" of the pastoral relation, than it does of the comparatively cold and distant functions of one, who, in all other lands but this, has been invested with his office by the imposing ceremony of *enthroning*, and who has borne, less as badges of affection than of authority, the crosier and the mitre.

We have now gone entirely through with the argument of Dr. Onderdonk, in proof that there is an order of men superior "in ministerial rank and powers." We have intended to do justice to his proofs, and we have presented the whole of them.

Our readers have *all* that Episcopalians rely on from the Scriptures in vindication of the existence of such an order of men. It will be remembered that the burden of proof lies on *them*. They advance a claim which is indispensable to the existence of their ecclesiastical polity. These are the arguments on which they rely. Whether their arguments justify the language of assumption which we sometimes hear; whether they are such as to render appropriate the description of all people but the members of Episcopal churches, as left to "the uncovenanted mercies of God;"* whether they are such as to prompt, legitimately, to a very frequent reference to "the primitive and apostolic order" of the ministry; or to the modest use of the term "the church," with an exclusive reference *to themselves*, must now be left to the judgment of our readers.

It was our intention, originally, to have gone somewhat at length into a defence of the Scripture doctrine of ministerial parity. But the unexpected length of our article admonishes us to close. We are the less dissatisfied with this admonition, because we conceive the point already made out. If Episcopalians cannot make good *their* claims in reference to their bishop, it follows of course that ministers are on an equality.

* We do not charge Dr. Onderdonk with having any such views and feelings. We have great pleasure in recording his dissent from the use of such language, and from such consequences. p. 6. "An apparently formidable, yet extraneous difficulty, often raised, is, that Episcopal claims *unchurch* all non-Episcopal denominations. *By the present writer this consequence is not allowed.*" We simply state this with high gratification. We are happy also that we are not called upon to *reconcile* the admission with the claim set up in this tract, that "the authority of Episcopacy is permanent, down to the present age of the world," (p. 40;) that the obligation of Christians to support bishops—*i. e.* to conform to Episcopacy—is not ended, (p. 40;) that of "any two ministries now existing, the former (Episcopacy) is obligatory, to the *exclusion* of the latter," (parity, p. 39;) and that "the position cannot be evaded, that Episcopacy is permanently *binding* 'even to the end of the world.'"

The whole argument is concentrated in *their* claim. We take our stand here. It is admitted on all hands, that there is somewhere in the church a right to ordain. Episcopalians, with singular boldness, in not a few instances with *professed*, and in all with *real* exclusiveness, maintain that this power lies *only* in the *bishop*. They advance a claim to certain rights and powers; and if that claim is not made out, the argument is at an end. The power of ordination must remain with those over whom they have set up the power of jurisdiction and control. This claim, as we have seen, is not made out. If, from the authority of the New Testament, they cannot succeed in dividing the ministers of religion into various ranks and orders, it follows that the clergy remain on an equality.

On this point, also, they are compelled, as we conceive, to admit the whole of our argument. So manifest is it, that the sacred writers knew of no such distinction; that they regarded all ministers of the gospel as on a level; that they used the same name in describing the functions of all; that they addressed all as having the same episcopal, or pastoral supervision, that the Episcopalians, after no small reluctance, are compelled at last to admit it. They are driven to the conclusion that the term *bishop*, in the New Testament, does not *in a single instance*, designate any such officer as now claims exclusively that title. Thus Dr. Onderdonk says, that "*that name* (bishop) *is there*, (*i.e.* in the New Testament) *given to the middle order, or presbyters; and* ALL *that we read in the New Testament concerning 'bishops,' (including of course the words 'overseers' and 'oversight,' which have the same derivation,) is to be regarded as pertaining to that middle grade.* It was *after* the apostolic age that the name 'bishop' was taken from the second order, and appropriated to the first." p. 12. This admission we regard as of inestimable value. So we believe; and so we teach. We insist, therefore, that the name *bishop* should be restored to its primitive standing. If men lay claim to a higher rank than is properly expressed in the New Testament by this word, we insist that they should assume the name *apostles.* As they regard themselves as the successors of the apostles; as they claim that Timothy, Titus, Andronicus, Junia were called *apostles,* why should not the same be retained? The Christian community could then better appreciate the force of their claims, and understand the nature of the argument. We venture to say, that if the name "apostles" were assumed by those who claim that they are their successors, Episcopacy would be soon "shorn of its beams," and that the Christian world would disabuse itself of the belief in the scriptural authority of any such class of men. We admit that if "the *thing* sought" (p. 12) were to be found in the Scriptures, we would not engage in a controversy about the mere name. But we maintain that the fact here conceded is strong presumptive proof that "the thing sought" is *not* there. The *name,* therefore, is to be given up; that is, it is conceded by Episcopalians, that the name bishop does not anywhere in the New Testament designate any such class of men as are now clothed with the episcopal office.

We remark now, that *the thing itself* is practically abandoned by Episcopalians themselves. If other denominations can be *true churches,* (see the remark on p. 6, that the Episcopal claims do not "*unchurch* all non-Episcopal denominations,") then their ministers can be true ministers, and their ordinances valid ordinances. Their minister may be ordained *without* the imposition of the hands of "a bishop;" and thus the whole claim is abandoned. For what constitutes "non-Episcopal denominations" churches, unless they have a valid ministry, and valid ordinances? Still further: It is probably known to our readers, that even ordination is never performed in the Episcopal Church by the bishop alone. In the "Form and manner of Ordering Priests," the following direction is given: "The bishop, *with the priests* [presbyters] *present*, shall lay their hands severally upon the head of every one that receiveth the order of priesthood; the receivers humbly kneeling, and the bishop saying: Receive the Holy Ghost, for the office and work of a priest in the church of God, now committed unto thee by the imposition of OUR *hands*," etc. We know that there is among them a difference of opinion about the *reason* why this is done. One portion regard the *bishop* as the only source of authority.* The other suppose that the presence and act of the presbyters express the assent and confidence of the churches, and that it is essential to a valid ordination. But, whichever opinion is maintained, it is, *in fact*, a Presbyterian ordination. If not, it is an unmeaning and idle ceremony; and the presence of the presbyters is mere pageantry and pomp.

We have now passed through the argument. Could we enter farther into it, we could prove, we think, *positively*, that there were no ministers in the apostolic churches superior to presbyters "in ministerial powers and rights;" and that a presbytery did actually engage in an ordination, and even in the case of Timothy.† But our argument does not require it, nor have we room. We have examined the whole of the claims of Episcopalians, derived from the New Testament. Our readers will now judge of the validity of those claims. We close, as Dr. Onderdonk began, by saying, that if the claim is not made out, on *scriptural authority*, it has no force, or binding obligation on mankind.

Who can resist the impression, that if the New Testament had been the only authority appealed to in other times, Episcopacy would long since have ceased to urge its claims, and have sunk away with other dynasties and dominations, from the notice of mankind? On the basis which we have now

---

* Hooker's Eccl. Pol., book vii. § 6.

† 1 Tim. iv. 14.

examined, this vast superstructure; this system which has in other ages spread over the entire Christian world; this system which, in *some* periods at least, has advanced most arrogant claims, has been reared. The world, for ages, has been called to submit to various modifications of the episcopal power. The world, with the single exception of the Waldenses and Albigenses, *did* for ages submit to its authority. The prelatical domination rose on the ruins of the liberties of cities, states, and nations, till all the power of the Christian world was concentrated in the hands of one man—"*the servant of the servants of God!*" The exercise of that power in his hands is well known. Equally arrogant have been its claims, in other modifications. The authority has been deemed necessary for the suppression of divisions and heresies. "The prelates," says Milton, "as they would have it thought, *are the only mauls of* schism." That power was felt in the days when Puritan piety rose to bless mankind, and to advance just notions of civil and religious liberty. Streams of blood have flowed, and tears of anguish have been shed, and thousands of holy men have been doomed to poverty and want, and imprisonment, and tears, as the result of those claims to supremacy and validity in the church of God. It may surprise our readers to learn, that *all* the authority from the Bible which could be adduced in favour of these enormous claims has now been submitted to their observation. And we cannot repress the melancholy emotions of our hearts, at the thought that *such* power has been claimed, and *such* domination exercised by man, on so slender authority as this.

We have little love for controversy;—we have none for denunciation. We have no war to wage with Episcopacy. We know, we deeply feel, that much may be said in favour of it, apart from the claim which has been set up for its authority from the New Testament. Its past history, in some respects, makes us weep; in some others, it is the source of sincere rejoicing and praise. We cannot forget, indeed, its assumptions of power, or hide from our eyes the days of the Papacy, when it clothed in sackcloth the Christian world. We cannot forget the days, not few or unimportant, in its history, when even as a part of the Protestant religion, it has brought "a numb and chill stupidity of soul, an inactive blindness of mind upon the people, by its leaden doctrine;" we cannot forget "the frozen captivity" of the church, "in the bondage of prelates;"* nor can we remove from our remembrance the sufferings of the Puritans and the bloody scenes in Scotland. But we do not charge this on the Episcopacy of our times. We do not believe that it is essential to its existence. We do not believe that it is its inevitable tendency. With more grateful feelings we recall other events of its history. We associate it with the brightest and happiest days of religion, and liberty, and literature, and law. We remember that it was under the Episcopacy that the church in England took its firm stand against the Papacy; and that this was its form when Zion rose to light and splendour from the dark night of ages. We remember the name of Cranmer,—Cranmer first, in many respects, among the reformers; that it was by his steady and unerring hand that, under God, the pure church of the Saviour was conducted through the agitating and distressing times of Henry VIII. We remember that God watched over that wonderful man; that he gave this distinguished prelate access to the heart of one of the most capricious, cruel, inexorable, bloodthirsty, and licentious monarchs that has disgraced the world; that God, for the sake of Cranmer and his church, conducted Henry, as "by a hook in the nose," and made him faithful to the Archbishop of Canterbury, when faithful to none else; so that, perhaps, the only redeeming trait in the character of Henry is his fidelity to this first British prelate under the

* Milton.

Reformation.* The world will not soon forget the names of Latimer, and Ridley, and Rogers, and Bradford; names associated in the feelings of Christians, with the long list of ancient confessors "of whom the world was not worthy," and who did honour to entire ages of mankind, by sealing their attachment to the Son of God, on the rack or amid the flames. Nor can we forget that we owe to Episcopacy that which fills our minds with gratitude and praise, when we look for examples of consecrated talent, and elegant literature, and humble, devoted piety. While men honour elevated Christian feeling; while they revere sound learning; while they render tribute to clear and profound reasoning, they will not forget the names of Barrow and Taylor, of Tillotson, and Hooker, and Butler; —and when they think of humble, pure, sweet, heavenly piety, their minds will recur instinctively to the name of Leighton. Such names, with a host of others, do honour to the world. When we think of them, we have it not in our hearts to utter one word against a church which has thus done honour to our race, and to our common Christianity.

Such we wish Episcopacy still to be. We have always thought that there are Christian minds and hearts that would find more edification in the forms of worship in that church, than in any other. We regard it as adapted to call forth Christian energy that might otherwise be dormant. We do not grieve that the church is divided into different denominations. To all who hold essential truth we bid God-speed;

---

* It may be proper here to remark, that Cranmer by no means entertained the modern views of the scriptural authority of bishops. He would not have coincided with the claims of the tract which is now passing under our review. He maintained "that the appointment to spiritual offices belongs indifferently to bishops, to princes, or to the people, according to the pressure of existing circumstances. He affirmed *the original identity of bishops and presbyters;* and contended that nothing more than mere election, or appointment, is essential to the sacerdotal office, without consecration or any other solemnity."—*Le Bas's Life of Cranmer*, vol. i. p. 197.

and for all such we lift our humble supplications to the God of all mercy, that he will make them the means of spreading the gospel around the globe. We ourselves could live and labour in friendliness and love in the bosom of the Episcopal Church. While we have an honest preference for another department of the great field of Christian action; while providential circumstances, and the suggestions of our own hearts and minds, have conducted us to a different field of labour, we have never doubted that many of the purest flames of devotion that rise from the earth, ascend from the altars of the Episcopal Church, and that many of the purest spirits that the earth contains minister at those altars, or breathe forth their prayers and praises in language consecrated by the use of piety for centuries.

We have but one wish in regard to Episcopacy. We wish her not to assume arrogant claims. We wish her not to utter the language of denunciation. We wish her to follow the guidance of the distinguished minister of her church, whose book we are reviewing, in not attempting to "unchurch" other denominations. We wish her to fall in with, or to go in advance of others, in the spirit of the age. Our desire is that she may become throughout—as we rejoice she is increasingly becoming—the warm, devoted friend of revivals and missionary operations. She is consolidated; well marshalled; under an efficient system of laws; and pre-eminently fitted for powerful action in the field of Christian warfare. We desire to see her what the Macedonian phalanx was in the ancient army; with her dense, solid organization, with her unity of movement, with her power of maintaining the position which she takes; and with her eminent ability to advance the cause of sacred learning, and the love of order and of law, attending or leading all other churches in the conquests of redemption in an alienated world. We would even rejoice to see her who was first in the field at the Reformation in England, first, also, in the field when the Son of God shall come to take to himself his great power; and, whatever positions may be assigned to *other* denominations, we have no doubt that the Episcopal Church is destined yet to be, throughout, the warm friend of revivals, and to consecrate her wealth and power to the work of making a perpetual aggression on the territories of sin and of death.

VI.—Scriptural Argument on the Episcopal Controversy.

[CHRISTIAN SPECTATOR, 1835.]

Answer to a Review (in the Quarterly Christian Spectator) of "Episcopacy tested by Scripture:" first published in the Protestant Episcopalian, for May, 1834. Philadelphia: Jesper Harding; 1834. pp. 19.

When the review of the tract, "Episcopacy tested by Scripture," was prepared,* it was not our design to engage in a controversy on the subject there discussed. We well knew how unprofitable and how endless such a controversy might become; and we felt that we had more important business to engage our attention, than that of endeavouring to defend the external order of the church. The subject attracted our notice, because, on two different occasions, the tract which was the subject of the review, had been sent to us, in one instance accompanied with a polite request—evidently from an Episcopalian—to give to it our particular attention; because, too, the tract had been published at the "Episcopal Press," and it was known that it would be extensively circulated; because it has been the subject of no small self-gratulation among the Episcopalians, and had been suffered, notwithstanding the manifest complacency with which they regarded it, to lie unanswered; *mainly*, because it made an appeal at once to the Bible, and professed a willingness that the question should be settled by the authority of the Scriptures alone. This appeared to us to be placing the subject on a new ground. The first emotion

---

* Christian Spectator, vol. vi.

produced by the title of the tract was one of surprise. We had been so accustomed to regard this controversy as one that was to be settled solely by the authority of the Fathers; we had been so disheartened and sickened by the unprofitable nature, the interminable duration, and the want of fixed bounds and principles, in that investigation; we had seen so little reference made to the Bible, on either side of the question, that it excited in us no small degree of surprise to learn that a bishop of the Episcopal Church should be willing to make a direct, decisive, and unqualified appeal to the New Testament. It was so unusual; it gave so new a direction to the controversy; it promised so speedy an issue, and one so little auspicious to the cause which the bishop was engaged in defending, that we were not unwilling to turn aside from our usual engagements, and to examine the proofs adduced in this somewhat novel mode of the Episcopal controversy.

Shortly after our review was published, an "Answer" to the article appeared in the "Protestant Episcopalian," understood to come from the author of the tract. With a copy of this the writer of the review was politely furnished by Dr. Onderdonk. The "Answer" is marked with the same general characteristics as the tract itself. It evinces, in general, the same spirit of Christian feeling and of candid inquiry; the same calm, collected, and manly style of argument; the same familiarity with the subject; and the same habit—by no means as common as is desirable—of applying the principles of the inductive philosophy to moral subjects. To this *general* statement, perhaps, should be made a slight exception. A candid observer possibly would discern in the "Answer," some marks of haste, and some indications of disturbed repose—possibly of a slight *sensation* in perceiving that the *material point* of the argument in the tract had not been as strongly fortified as was indispensable. As instances of this sensation, we might notice the train of remarks in pp. 8, 9, and especially in the following expressions: "The reasonings throughout his article (the reviewer's) are much the same as those usually brought against Episcopacy; and where they are not the same, they are so much *minus* the former ground," etc. "No one, for three years, brought these old reasonings against the tract,—no one till the reviewer fancied he had discovered a weak spot in it, and might, therefore, reproduce some of them with effect." "The present is only a start in its slumber." And again, on p. 15, the author of the reply speaks of the reviewer, as one whom he suspects "to be a *new comer* into this field of controversy," if not with the intention, at least with the *appearance*, of designing to disparage the force of the arguments which the reviewer had urged. Now, it is unnecessary for us to remind Dr. Onderdonk, that the inquiry is not, whether the arguments are old or new, but whether they are pertinent and valid. Nor is the question, whether one is a "new comer" into this controversy. Arguments may not be the less cogent and unanswerable, for being urged by one who has not before entered the lists; nor will arguments from the Bible be satisfactorily met by an affirmation that they are urged by one unknown in the field of debate. It may be proper, however, for us to observe, in self-vindication, that the arguments which we urged were drawn from no other book than the Bible. The "Tract" and the New Testament were the only books before us in the preparation of the article. The course of argument suggested was that only which was produced by the investigation of the Scriptures. Whether we have fallen into any train of thinking which has been before urged by writers on this subject, we do not even now know, nor are we likely to know; as it is our fixed purpose not to travel out of the record before us—the inspired account of the matter in the sacred Scriptures. If, however, the arguments which we have urged be "the same as those usually brought against Episcopacy," (p. 8,) it furnishes a case of coincidence of results, in investigating the New Testament, which is itself some evidence that the objections to Episcopacy are such as obviously occur to different minds engaged in independent investigation.

When the reply appeared, it became a question with us, whether the controversy should be prolonged. A perusal of the "Answer" did not suggest any necessity for departing from our original intention, *not* to engage in such a controversy. It did not appear to furnish any new argument which seemed to call for notice, or to invalidate any of the positions defended in the review. Almost the whole of the "Answer" appeared to be simply an *expansion* of a note in the tract, (p. 12, note *z*,) which, when the review was prepared, seemed not to furnish an argument that required particular attention. The fact, too, that *then* the argument was expressed in a *note*, in small type, and at the bottom of the page, was an indication that it was not of much magnitude in the eye of the author of the tract himself. Why it is now *expanded*, so as to constitute the very body and essence of the reply, is to us proof that the subject, on the *Episcopal* side, is exhausted. This fact is of such a nature, as to impress the mind strongly with the belief that, henceforth, nothing remains to be added, in the effort to "Test Episcopacy by Scripture."

In departing from our original purpose, it is our wish to reciprocate the kind feeling and candour of the author of the "Tract" and of the "Answer." Truth, not victory, is our object. We have but one wish on this subject. It is, that the principles upon which God designed to establish and govern his holy church, may be developed and understood. We resume the subject with profound and undiminished respect for the talents, the piety, and the learning of the author of the Tract and Answer, and with a purpose that this shall be *final*, on our part, unless something new, and vital to the subject, shall be added. In this, as well as in all other things, our desire is not to write one line, which, dying,—or in heaven,—

"We would wish to blot."

Still, this desire, so deeply cherished, does not forbid a full and free examination of arguments. Our conscientious belief is, that the *superiority* "in ministerial power and rights," (Tract, p. 15,) claimed by Episcopal bishops, is a superiority known in the Episcopal churches only, and not in the New Testament; and this we purpose to show.

In entering upon our examination of the "Answer," we may remark, that the scriptural argument for Episcopacy is now fairly and entirely before the world. On the Episcopal side, nothing material to be said can remain. The *whole* argument is in the Tract and in the Answer. If Episcopacy is not established in these, we may infer that it is not in the Bible. If not in the Bible, it is not "necessarily binding." (Tract, p. 3.) To this conclusion—that the whole of the material part of the scriptural argument is before the world in these pamphlets—we are conducted by the fact, that neither talent, learning, zeal, nor time, have been wanting in order to present it; that their author entered on the discussion, manifestly acquainted with *all* that was to be said; that the subject has now been before the public more than four years, (see advertisement to the Tract;) and that, during that time, it is to be presumed, if there had been any more *material* statements to be presented from the Bible, they would have appeared in the "Answer." There is much advantage in examining an argument with the conviction that nothing more remains to be said; and that we may, therefore, contemplate it as an unbroken and unimprovable whole, without the possibility of any addition to the number of arguments, or increase of their strength. On this vantage-ground we now stand, to contemplate the argument in support of the stupendous fabric of Episcopacy in the Christian church.

In entering upon this examination, we are struck with—what we had indeed anticipated—a very strong inclination, on the part of the author of the tract, to appeal again to certain "extraneous" authorities, of which we heard nothing in the tract itself, except to disclaim them. The tract commenced with the bold and startling announcement, that if Episcopacy has not the authority of Scripture, it is not "necessarily binding," p. 3. "No argument," the tract goes on to say, "is *worth taking into the account*, that has not a palpable bearing on the clear and naked topic—the scriptural evidence of Episcopacy," p. 3. We have italicised part of this quotation, to call the attention of our readers particularly to it. The affirmation, so unusual in the mouth of an Episcopalian, is, that no argument is WORTH TAKING INTO THE ACCOUNT, that does not bear on the scriptural proof. Now we anticipated that, if a reply was made to our review, from any quarter, we should find a qualification of this statement, and a much more complacent regard shown to the Fathers, and to other "*extraneous considerations*," (Tract, p. 4,) than would be consistent with this unqualified disclaimer in the tract. The truth is, that the Fathers are regarded as too material witnesses to be so readily abandoned. The "tradition of the elders" has been too long pressed into the service of Episcopacy; there has been too conscious a sense of the weakness of scriptural proof, to renounce heartily, entirely, and forever, all reliance on other proof than the New Testament. The "Answer" would have lacked a very material feature which we expected to find in it, if there had been no inclination manifested to plunge into this abyss of traditional history, where light and darkness struggle together, and no wish to recall the testimony of uninspired antiquity to the service of prelacy. Accordingly, we were prepared for the following declaration, which we quote entire, from pp. 3 and 4 of the Answer:—

"Because the author of the tract rested the claims of Episcopacy finally on Scripture,—because he fills a high office in the church,—and because the tract is issued by so prominent an Episcopal institution as the 'Press,' the reviewer seems to think that Episcopalians are now to abandon all arguments not drawn directly from the Holy Volume. Not at all. The author of the tract, in his sermon at the consecration of the four bishops, in October, 1832, advocated Episcopacy, besides on other grounds, on that of there being several grades of office in the priesthoods of all religions, false as well as true, and in all civil magistracies and other official structures,—and, in his late Charge, he adverted to the evidence in its favour contained in the Fathers. And the 'Press,' at the time it issued the tract, issued also with it, in the 'Works on Episcopacy,' those of Dr. Bowden and Dr. Cooke, which embrace the argument at large. There is no reason, therefore, for thinking that, however a single writer may use selected arguments in a single publication, either he or other Episcopalians will (or should) narrow the ground they have usually occupied. The Fathers are consulted on this subject, because the fabric of the ministry which they describe forms an historical basis for interpreting Scripture. And general practice, in regard to distinct grades among officers, throws a heavier burden of disproof on those whose interpretations are adverse to Episcopacy: this latter topic we shall again notice before we close."

This passage, so far from insisting, as the Tract had done, that no argument *was worth taking into the account,* except the scriptural proof, refers distinctly to the following points, which we beg leave to call "*extraneous considerations,*" as proof of Episcopacy. (1.) The fact that there "are several grades of office in the priesthood of all religions;" (2.) That the same thing occurs "in all civil magistracies and other official structures;" (3.) The evidence of the Fathers; and, (4.) "Other grounds," which the author informs us he had insisted on, in an ordination sermon, in 1832. And in this very passage, he makes the following remarkable statement, which we propose soon to notice further: "The fathers are consulted on the subject, because the fabric of the ministry which they describe, forms an historical basis for interpreting Scripture."

Slight circumstances often show strong inclinations and habits of mind. How strong a hold this reference to other "considerations" than the Scriptures, has taken upon the mind of the author of the Tract, and how reluctant he was to part with the "extraneous" argument from the Fathers, is shown by the fact, that he again recurs to it in the "Answer," and presents it at much greater length. Thus on pp. 18, 19, at the very close of the Answer, we are presented with the following recurrence to the argument from other considerations than the Scriptures:

"One word more concerning the 'burden of proof,' as contrasted with the 'presumptive argument.' The tract claimed no presumption in its favour, in seeking for the scriptural proofs of Episcopacy. We do—a presumption founded on *common sense*, as indicated by common practice. Set aside parity and Episcopacy, and then look at *other systems of office*, both religious and civil, and you find *several grades* of officers. In the Patriarchal church, there was the distinction of 'high-priest' and 'priest.' In the Jewish church, (common sense being, in this case unquestionably, divinely approved,) there were the high-priest, priests, and levites. Among the Pagans and Mohammedans, there are various grades in the office deemed sacred. Civil governments have usually governors, a president, princes, a king, an emperor, etc., as the heads of the general, or state, or provincial magistracies. In armies and navies there is always a chief. If the reviewer should claim exceptions, we reply they are exceptions only, and very few in number. The *general rule* is with us. That general rule, next to universal, is, that, among officers, there is a *difference* of power, of rights, of rank, of grade, call it what you will. And this general rule gives a *presumption* that such will also be the case in the Christian church. We go to Scripture, then, with the presumptive argument fully against parity. If we should find in Scripture neither imparity nor parity, still *common sense* decides for the former. If we find the tone of Scripture doubtful, on this point, imparity has the advantage, common sense turning the scale. If we find there intimations, less than positive injunctions, in favour of imparity, common sense, besides the respect due to Scripture, decides for our interpretation of them. And if any thing in Scripture is supposed to prove or to justify parity, it must be very explicit, to overturn the suggestion of common sense. The 'presumptive argument,' then, is clearly with *us*, and the 'burden of proof' lies on parity. Let the reviewer peruse the tract again, bearing in mind the principles laid down in this paragraph, and he will, we trust, think better of it."

These observations, it will be remembered, are made by the same writer, and in connection with the same subject as the declaration, that "NO ARGUMENT IS WORTH TAKING INTO THE ACCOUNT, *that has not a palpable bearing on the clear and naked topic,—the scriptural evidence of Episcopacy.*"

Now, against the principles of interpretation here stated, and which the Tract led us to suppose were abandoned, we enter our decided and solemn protest. The question—the only question in the case—is, Whether Episcopacy "has the authority of Scripture?" (Tract, p. 3.) The affirmation is, that if it has not, "it is not necessarily binding," (p. 3.) The principle of interpretation, which in the Answer is introduced to guide us in this inquiry, is, that "the Fathers are consulted on the subject, because the fabric of the ministry which they describe, forms an historical basis for interpreting Scripture." (Answer, p. 3.) In order to understand the bearing of this rule of interpretation, it is necessary to know what it means. A "basis" is defined to be "the foundation of a thing; that on which a thing stands or lies; that on which it rests; the ground-work or first principle; that which supports." (*Webster.*) An "*historical* basis" must mean, therefore, that the opinions or facts of history—that is, in this case, the testimony of the Fathers—constitute the *foundation, the ground-work, or first principle* of the intepretation of the Bible; or that on which such an interpretation *rests*, or by which *it is supported*. It would seem to follow, therefore, that, unless we first become acquainted with this "historical basis," we are wholly in the dark about the proper interpretation of the Bible, and that our interpretation is destitute of any true support and authority. To this principle of interpretation, in this case and in all others, the objections are obvious and numerous: (1.) Our first objection lies against the supposed necessity of having any such previously ascertained *basis*, in order to a just interpretation of the oracles of God. We object wholly to the doctrine that the Scriptures are to be interpreted by historical facts to be developed long after the book was written. The great mass of men are wholly incompetent to enter into any such "historical" inquiry; but the great mass of men are not unqualified to understand the general drift and tenor of the New Testament. (2.) The statement is, "that the fabric of the ministry which they describe" is to be the basis of such interpretation. But who knows what the fabric of the ministry which they describe is? It is to be remembered, that the question is not respecting the ministry in the fourth century and onward. But the inquiry—and the only one of material value on any supposition—pertains to the Fathers previous to that period. And there every thing is unsettled. Prelacy claims the Fathers in that unknown age. The Papacy claims the Fathers there. Presbyterianism claims the Fathers there. Congregationalism and Independency, too, claim them there. Every thing is unsettled and chaotic. And this is the very point which has been the interminable subject of contention in this whole inquiry, and from which we hoped we had escaped, by the principles laid down in the Tract. Yet the position *now* advanced would lead us again into all the difficulties, and controversies, and jostling elements, and contradictory statements which have always attended the appeal to the Fathers. If we are to wait until we have ascertained "the fabric of the ministry" which these Fathers describe, before we have a "basis" for interpreting Scripture, we may close the New Testament in despair. (3.) This canon of interpretation is contrary to the rule which Dr. Onderdonk has himself laid down in the Tract itself, (p. 3.) In that instance, the authority of the Scriptures was declared to be ample and final. And throughout the Tract, there is a manifest indication of a belief, that the Bible is susceptible of interpretation on the acknowledged rules of language, and the principles of common sense. We hailed such a manifestation, not only as auspicious to the cause of truth in regard to the claims of Episcopacy, but because it evinced the spirit to which the church *must* come,—of a direct, unqualified, and final appeal to the word of God,—to determine religious doctrine. To that standard we mean to adhere. And, as far as in us lies, we intend to hold it up to the view of men, and to insist on the great truth, from which nothing shall ever divert us, and from which we fervently pray the church may never be diverted, that we are not to look for the discovery of truth, by ascertaining *first* an "historical basis," or a set of instruments by which we are to measure and adjust the proportions of truth which we find in the revelation of God. Without any design to disparage or undervalue the Fathers, whom we sincerely reverence, as having been holy, bold, and venerable men; without any blindness, as we believe, to the living lustre of that piety which led many of them to the stake; without any apprehension that their testimony, when examined, would be found to be on the side of Episcopacy,—for it remains yet to be seen that the Fathers of the first two centuries ever dreamed of the pride and domination which subsequently crept into the church, and assumed the form of Prelacy and

Popery; without any thing to influence us, so far as we know, from any of these "extraneous" sources, we intend to do all in our power to extend and perpetuate the doctrine that the ultimate appeal in all religious inquiry, is to be the Bible, and the Bible only. "The Bible," said Chillingworth, "is the religion of Protestants." We rejoice to hear this sentiment echoed from the assistant bishop of Pennsylvania. And, without meaning to insinuate that this sentiment is not as honestly acted on by Episcopalians as by any other denomination of Christians, we may add, that we deem the first sentence of the Tract worthy to be written in letters of gold on the posts of every Episcopal sanctuary, and over every altar, and on the cover of every "Book of Common Prayer." "*The claim of Episcopacy to be of divine institution, and, therefore, obligatory on the church, rests fundamentally on the one question,—Has it the authority of Scripture? If it has not, it is not necessarily binding.*" (4.) Our fourth objection to this rule of interpretation is, that it is, substantially, that on which rests the Papal hierarchy. We do not know that the Papist would wish to express his principles of interpretation in stronger language than that "the Fathers are consulted on this subject, because the fabric of the ministry which they describe forms an historical basis for interpreting Scripture." To us it seems that it would express all that they ask; and, as we doubt not that Dr. Onderdonk would shrink from any approximation to the Papacy quite as firmly as ourselves, we deem it necessary merely to suggest the consideration, to render the objection at once satisfactory to his own mind.

We object, also, to the principle of interpretation advanced on p. 18 of the Answer, which we have already quoted. The fact there assumed, is, that various orders of men are observable in civil governments, etc.; and hence, that there is presumptive evidence that such orders are to be found in the Scriptures. We are not ignorant of the purpose for which this fact is adduced. It is to show that the "burden of proof" does not lie so entirely on the Episcopalian, as we had affirmed in the review. We admit, to some extent, the modifying force of the circumstances, so far as the "burden of proof" is concerned. But it merely *lightens* the burden; it does not *remove* it. Presumption, in such a case, is not proof. When the fact affirmed relates to a doctrine of the Bible, it is not sufficient to say that that fact occurred elsewhere, and, *therefore*, it must occur in the Bible. It is still the business of the Episcopalian to *prove* his affirmation from the New Testament itself, that bishops are superior to other ministers of the gospel, in ministerial power and rights. This is *his* affirmation; this is the point which he urges; this is to be made out from the Bible *only;* and assuredly the fact that there are dukes, and earls, and emperors, and admirals, and nabobs, forms at best a *very slight* presumption in favour of the affirmation, that the ministry of the gospel consists of three "orders." But our objections may be further stated. *So far as the presumption goes, it is not particularly in favour of Episcopacy, as consisting in* THREE *orders of the clergy.* For, (1.) The fact is not, that there are three orders observable everywhere. It is, that there are many orders and ranks of civil officers and of men. (2.) The presumption drawn from what has taken place, would be rather in favour of despotism, and the Papacy. (3.) The presumption is equally met by the doctrine of Presbyterianism as by Prelacy. Presbyterians hold equally to a division of their community into various ranks,—into bishops, and elders, and people. The presumption, drawn from the fact that civil society is thus broken up, is as really in their favour, as in favour of Episcopacy. (4.) The Congregationalist may urge it with the same propriety. His community registers the names of his minister, *and* deacons, *and* church, *and* congregation,—each with distinct privileges and rights. If Dr. Onderdonk should reply to this, that his remark referred only to the distinction of "*systems of office*, both religious and civil," (p. 18,) and "that among *officers*, there is a difference of power and rights," (p. 19,) we reply, that the distinction of *officers* pertains to other churches, as well as the Episcopal. No non-Episcopalian, perhaps, can be found who holds to a *parity* of *office*. He will refer, at once, to his minister, to his elders, to his deacons, as evincing sufficient *disparity*, to meet the full force of the *presumption* alleged by Dr. Onderdonk. But our main objection here, as before, is to the principle of interpretation. We respectfully insist that it should be laid aside, as an "extraneous consideration" in the inquiry whether Episcopacy "has the authority of Scripture."

In our review we stated that the burden of proof, in this inquiry, was laid wholly on the friends of Episcopacy, (p. 209.) This point was so obvious, that we did not think it necessary to illustrate it at length. Nor do we now intend to do more than merely, by adverting to it, to recall it to the attention of our readers. The author of the "Answer" has endeavoured to *remove* this burden from himself and his friends, (p. 4 and p. 18.) This he has done, by attempting to show that there is a *presumptive* argument in favour of Episcopacy; which presumption throws the task of *proving* the parity of the clergy on those who advocate it. Now we are not disposed to enter into a controversy on this point. To us it seemed, and still seems, to be a plain case, that where it was affirmed that the clergy of the Christian church was separated by divine authority, into three grades, or orders, and that *one* of those orders had the *exclusive* right of ordination, of discipline, and of general superintendence; it could not be a matter requiring much deliberation, to know where rested the burden of proof. If a man assumes authority over an army, demanding the subordination of all other officers to his will, it is not a very unreasonable presumption that the burden of proof lies with him; nor would it be the *obvious* course to expect the entire mass of officers to show, that he had *not* received such a commission. We shall, therefore, feel ourselves to be pursuing a very obvious course, if we do not recognise the authority of Episcopal bishops, unless there is proof positive of their commission. We may add, further, that in the supposed case of the commander of the army or the navy, we should not regard that as a very satisfactory proof which was pursued with as little directness and explicitness as are evinced in the argument to establish the original domination and perpetuity of the prelatical office. And in this connection we may remark, that it is perfectly immaterial, as to the main point, what may be the opinion of the man who calls the claim in question, or what may be the particular denomination to which he is attached. Whether he is an Independent, a Presbyterian, or a Congregationalist, it may be equally true that the bishop of the Episcopal Church is unable to make out his claims from the New Testament. The only material point, in which *all* other denominations are agreed, is, that the ministers of the New Testament are on an *equality* in the respect under consideration; that the power of ordaining and administering discipline, and of superintending the concerns of the church, is intrusted to them, as equals, in opposition to the exclusive and exalted assumptions of a few who claim the right to deprive them of these powers, and to make their ministrations null and void. And when claims of this order are advanced—claims designed to dispossess the great mass of the ministry throughout the world, of the right of transmitting their office to others; of exercising government and discipline in their own pastoral charges; of superintending and controlling the affairs of the particular portion of the church universal with which they are specifically intrusted; when claims like these are presented, tending to degrade them from their office, to annihilate their authority, and to leave their charges without a ministry;—we may respectfully insist that the proof of this should be drawn, by no circumlocution, from the Bible. We wish to see, with an exact specification, the chapter and the verse; we would respectfully urge that, in such a claim, it should be done *totidem verbis*, or at least so nearly so that there could be no possibility of mistake.

We may here remind our readers of the precise points which Episcopacy is called upon to make out. The *first* is, that the apostles were "distinguished from the elders, because they were *superior* to them in ministerial power and rights." (Tract, p. 15.) The *second* is, that this distinction "was so persevered in, as to indicate that it was a *permanent* arrangement." (Tract, p. 23.) These are independent propositions. One by no means follows from the other. Should the first be admitted, yet the second is to be established by equally explicit and independent proof. Nay, the second is by far the most material point, and should, as we shall show, be fortified by the most irrefragable arguments. The *third* point, indispensable to the other two, is, that there is no evidence in the New Testament that presbyters or elders discharged the functions which are now claimed for bishops; that is, that they either (1) ordained, or (2) administered discipline, or (3) exercised a general supervision. (Tract, p. 11.) Unless, then, it is shown that not *one* of these functions was ever performed by presbyters, the Episcopal claim fails of support, and must be abandoned. These are independent positions, and a failure in one is a failure in the whole.

To a cursory review of what can be said on these points, we now propose to call the attention of our readers.

The *first* claim asserted is, that the apostles were "distinguished from the elders, because they were *superior* to them in ministerial power and rights." (Tract, p. 15.) The points of their alleged superiority are, exclusive ordination, exclusive discipline, exclusive confirmation, and exclusive right of general superintendence. The question is, whether this is the nature of the superiority with which the apostles were intrusted; or, which is the same thing, *Were these the purposes for which they were set apart to the apostolic office, and for which they were called apostles?* Dr. Onderdonk affirms it; we take the liberty, most respectfully, of calling for explicit proof of it from the New Testament.

His direct proof is contained in a nutshell. It consists of *one* expression of Scripture, (Acts xv. 2, 4, 6, 22; xvi. 4:) "Apostles *and* elders," "apostles, *and* elders, *and* brethren;" and a note on p. 12 of the Tract, and in the reply, expanded to more than two pages, showing that, in his apprehension, they administered discipline. As this is the basis on which the whole fabric is reared, and as it embraces the very gist of the "Answer," we shall be pardoned for adverting to it with some particularity.

We may then inquire, why the apostles were distinguished from the elders or presbyters. Dr. Onderdonk affirms that it was because they were "superior in ministerial power and rights." The argument on this subject, from the New Testament, is, that the two classes of men are *distinguished* from each other, (Acts xv. 2, 4, 6, 22; xvi. 4,) by the following expressions: "apostles *and* elders," "apostles, *and* elders, *and* brethren." Now, in regard to this *proof*, we beg leave to make the following remarks:

(1.) That it is the *only* direct passage of Scripture which Dr. Onderdonk is able to adduce on the subject of the alleged superiority of the apostles. Its importance, in his view, may be seen from the fact, that it is not merely the *only* proof, but that it is repeated not less than five times in the space of less than a single page of the Tract, (pp. 14, 15;) and that it occupies a similar prominence in the Answer. The Tract has been written four years. Diligent research during that time, it would be supposed, might have led to the discovery of some *other* text that had a bearing on the point. But the matter still rests here. There *is* no other text; and the fabric is to be sustained on the solitary expression, "apostles *and* elders," "apostles, *and* elders, *and* brethren."

(2.) What does this passage prove? It proves this, and no more, that there was a distinction, of *some sort*, between the apostles *and* elders,—which is a point of just as much importance as when we affirm, that one class were called apostles, *and* another called elders. But it is difficult for us to see how this determines any thing respecting the *reasons* of the distinction. In Ephesians iv. 11, the apostle affirms, that God gave "some, apostles; *and* some, prophets; *and* some, evangelists; *and* some, pastors and teachers." Here *a* distinction is made out. But is the *nature* of the distinction thereby ascertained? I speak of guineas, *and* doubloons, *and* guilders. I affirm a distinction, indeed; but is its *nature* ascertained? Have I determined that the guinea is, *therefore*, superior in weight or value to the others?

(3.) We have never denied that there was a distinction between the apostles, *and* elders, *and* brethren. The very fact that they had the same apostles, shows, that there must have been some distinction, or some reason why they were so called. Unusual discernment, or laboured argument, surely, are not necessary to perceive this. But the very point is, *what* is the *nature* of this distinction? And this is to be settled, not by the use of the word, but by the statement in the New Testament; and it is incumbent on the Episcopalian to show, by *proof-texts*, that it was *because* the apostles were superior, in the power of ordination, of confirmation, of discipline, and of general superintendence of a diocese. Dr. Onderdonk *affirmed* that the name was not so given, because they were appointed by Christ personally; nor because they had seen the Lord after his resurrection; nor because they had the power of working miracles; and then observed, that "it followed, OR would not be questioned, that it was because they were superior in ministerial power and rights." (Tract, p. 15.) It seems not to have occurred to him, that they could be appointed to be WITNESSES *of his entire ministry, including the fact of his resurrection, as a main point.* We took the liberty, therefore, of examining this matter, as very material to the argument. We proved, (1.) That in the original appointment of the apostles, there was no reference to their superiority, in the powers of ordination, discipline, etc. This position we supported by the three separate accounts of Matthew, Mark, and Luke. (2.) That no such thing occurred in the instructions of our Lord, after his resurrection from the dead. This also we confirmed by an examination of the testimony of Matthew, Mark, and Luke, in neither of whose gospels was there found a vestige of such instructions. (3.) That there was nowhere else, in the New Testament, any account that what Dr. Onderdonk affirmed, as the peculiarity of the apostolic office was known to the writers. This conclusion we rested upon our own examination, and the fact that Dr. Onderdonk had not adduced any such passage. (4.) That the reason of the appointment to the apostolic office *was expressly affirmed;* and, that it was *not* that which Dr. Onderdonk supposed it to be. We showed, (*a*) that it was expressly affirmed, in the original appointment, (Luke xxiv. 48; Matt. xxviii. 18, 19,) that they should be WITNESSES *of these things;* (*b*) that this was expressly provided for, in the case of the election of one to fill the place vacated by Judas, (Acts i. 21, 22;) (*c*) that this was the account which the apostles uniformly gave of the design of their appointment, (see p. 217;) (*d*) that the same thing was again expressly provided for in the case of the Apostle Paul, and that, *in order* to a qualification for that office, he was permitted to "SEE the Just one," the Lord Jesus, (Acts xxii. 14;) and, (*e*) that he himself expressly appeals to the fact, as a proof that he was fully invested with the apostolic office. 1 Cor. ix. 1, 2. In the course of the argument, we adduced not less than *twenty* explicit passages of Scripture bearing directly on the point, and proving, beyond dispute, that this was the design of the appointment to the apostolic office. Our purpose, in this, was evident. It was to show that the peculiarity of the apostolic office was of such a nature, that it could not be transmitted to distant generations; but that it had a specific, yet very important design, which, as a matter of course, must cease.

With deep interest, therefore, we opened the "Answer," to ascertain how this array of scriptural argument was met. We did not deem it unreasonable to suppose, that there would be some new attempt to show, that the peculiarity of the apostolic office was to ordain; that the passages of Scripture on which we had relied, were irrelevant; or, that other passages might be adduced in proof of what Dr. Onderdonk had affirmed to be the peculiarity of the apostolic office, and which we had respectfully denied. Our readers will join with us in our "*amazement*," to find the following as the result of an examination of the "Answer:"

(1.) A solemn, and somewhat pompous, readducing of the expression, (Acts xv.,) "the apostles *and* elders," "the apostles, *and* elders, *and* brethren," (Answer, p. 7;) a passage, maintaining still its solitary dignity, and reposing in the "Answer," as it had in the "Tract," in its own lonely grandeur. We could not restrain our "amazement," that no other passages were even referred to, on this material point; and we came to the conclusion, that we had reached an end of the argument, so far as direct Scripture proof was concerned.

(2.) We found a notice of our extended array of proof-texts, showing what was the design of the apostolic appointment, of a character so remarkable, that we shall quote it entire :—

"The reviewer, in order to show what *he* thinks was the point in which the apostles excelled the elders, in the matter in question, dwells largely on the fact, that they were *special* witnesses of our Lord's resurrection,—and with the help of CAPITAL and *italic* letters, he has certainly made a showy argument. But nobody denies that they were the special witnesses,—or, that they were distinguished from the elders, as well as from others called apostles,—the Tract gave due attention to both these particulars. The point is,—was *this* distinction the one that led to the expression 'apostles *and* elders?' Surely not. Among *those* apostles was Barnabas, and perhaps Silas,* neither of whom was a special witness of the resurrection. Besides, the expressions 'apostles *and* elders,' 'apostles, *and* elders, *and* brethren,' are used with immediate reference to the council at Jerusalem,—and the reviewer is more acute than we pretend to be, if he can say why, in a council, acting on questions concerning 'idols, blood, things strangled, and licentiousness,' the special witnesses of the resurrection should, *as such*, have peculiar authority. We really think the Tract argues with more consistency, when it says, that the apostles were *ministerially* above the elders." Answer, p. 16.

Here, it will be observed, there is no notice taken of the texts which he had adduced, as irrelevant, or unsatisfactory in number, or as unfairly interpreted. Dr. Onderdonk, if he was the writer of the Answer, deemed it an ample notice of those texts to remark that, "with the help of CAPITAL and *italic* letters, he (the reviewer) had certainly made a showy argument." (Answer, p. 16.) That our agument was *thus* noticed, was, indeed, to us a matter of "amazement." It was, however, an indication—of which we were not slow to avail ourselves, and the hold upon which we shall not be swift to lose—that our proof-texts were *ad rem*, and that they settled the question. When all that the assistant-bishop of Pennsylvania deems it proper to say, of our array of more than twenty explicit declarations of the word of God, is,

---

* Acts xiv. 14; xv. 2, 4, 22; 1 Thess. i. 1; ii. 6.

that by the help of capitals and italics, they constitute a "SHOWY argument," (we mean no disrespect, when we display the word in a *showy* form,) we deem the conclusion to be inevitable, that our texts are just what we intended they should be—that they settled the question—and, to use an expression from the favourite chapter of the Acts of the Apostles, we "rejoice for the consolation." Acts xv. 31.

(3.) Though we were not met by any new proof-texts, or by answer to our own, we were referred to the sentiments of the following distinguished men, viz., the late Dr. Wilson, Dr. Miller, Dr. Campbell, Matthew Henry, "the *divines* who argued with Charles I. in the Isle of Wight," and Calvin, to prove that the apostles were superior to the elders and the evangelists. (Answer, p. 10.) Respecting these authorities, we may be permitted to remark (1) that we shall probably not yield, out of regard to their names, to any persons. With us, they have all the authority which uninspired men can ever be allowed to have. The writer of the review may be permitted to remark, perhaps, that he has occasion of peculiar respect for two of those venerable men. By one—whose superior, in profound powers of reasoning, in varied and extensive learning and in moral worth, he believes is not now to be found among the living in any American church—he was preceded in the office which he now holds. At the feet of the other, it has been his privilege to sit, for nearly four years, and to receive the instructions of wisdom from his lips; and, whatever skill he may have in conducting this argument, on the government of the churches, he owes to the "basis" which was laid by those instructions. Whatever may be said, therefore, of these authorities adduced in the "Answer," will not be traced to want of respect for these venerable names. But (2) we may remark, that, in *this* argument, the authorities of uninspired men are to be laid out of the account. With all due deference to them and to Dr. Onderdonk, we must be permitted to believe that their authority belongs to the "extraneous considerations," as well as that of the opinion of Cranmer, (Answer, p. 5,) which, by common consent, it had been agreed to lay out of the controversy. (See Tract, pp. 3–10.) Our wonder is, that, after the disclaimer of relying on these extraneous considerations, in the Tract, the author of the Answer should have occupied nearly two pages with the statements of these distinguished men. (3) Their authority, even when adduced, does not bear on the point before us. The question is, whether the apostles were superior to other ministers of the gospel in ministerial power and rights; that is, the power of ordination, confirmation, discipline, and general superintendence. Their authorities adduced prove only that, in the judgment of these venerable men, they were superior, in some respects, to evangelists and teachers; or, that there was *a* distinction between them—a point on which we make no denial. On the only question in debate, they make no affirmation. On the claim set up by Episcopalians, that the apostles were superior in *ordination*, etc., they concede nothing, nor did they believe a word of it.

Having thus noticed the "Answer" on this part of our argument, we shall dismiss it. We do it by simply reminding our readers, that the solitary text, which undisputed learning, talents, and zeal have discovered, during a period of more than four years, since the discussion first commenced, —the lonely Scripture proof of the sweeping claims that the apostles *only* had the power of ordination, and that this was the peculiarity of the office,—stands forth in the Tract and in the Answer: "the apostles *and* elders," "apostles, *and* elders, *and* brethren!"

But the author of the "Answer" complains, (p. 11,) that we did not give the "whole" of his argument on the subject; and he refers to a note on p. 12 of the Tract, designed to show that the apostles had the power of administering discipline, and that, therefore, they were superior to the presbyters, or held a more elevated grade of office. The note is this :—

"That the apostles alone *ordained*, will be proved. In 1 Cor. iv. 19–21; v. 3–5; 2 Cor. ii. 6; vii. 12; x. 8; xiii. 2, 10; and 1 Tim. i. 20, are recorded inflictions and remissions of *discipline* performed by an apostle, or threatenings on his part, although there must have been elders in Corinth, and certainly were in Ephesus."

This note he expands into an argument, which constitutes the most material part of the "Answer." It is incumbent upon us to examine it, and to ascertain how far it goes to settle the point under discussion. Before examining the particular cases referred to, we would remind our readers, that the purpose for which they are adduced, is to show that the apostles were *superior to presbyters in powers and rights;* and the alleged proof is, that *they administered discipline.* To bear on the case, therefore, the passages must prove not only that *they exercised discipline,* but (1) that they did it *as apostles,* or in the virtue of the apostolic office; (2) that they did it in churches where there were presbyters; and (3) that presbyters *never* administered discipline themselves. The *second* point here adverted to, is all that the author of the "Answer" feels himself called upon to make out. (Answer, pp. 11–13.) Now in regard to this point of the proof, we make the following general remarks: (1.) There were certainly, in all, fourteen apostles; and, if we may credit the writer of these pamphlets and reckon Timothy, and Barnabas, and Sylvanus, and Apollos, and Andronicus, and Junia, and Titus, and perhaps half-a-dozen others, there were somewhat more than a score invested with this office; yet it is remarkable that the only cases of discipline referred to, as going to prove the superiority of the whole college of apostles, are cases in which the Apostle Paul only was concerned. (2.) There are accounts in the New Testament of perhaps some hundreds of churches; and yet we meet with no instance of the kind of discipline relied on, except in the single churches of Corinth and Ephesus. It is incredible that there should have been no other cases of discipline in these churches. But if there were, the presumption is, that they were settled without the intervention of an apostle. (3.) These very cases, as we shall presently show, were cases in which Paul administered the rod of discipline in the churches where Titus and Timothy—apostles also and bishops—were present, by the showing of the author of the "Answer," and thus were acts of manifest disrespect for the authority of those prelates. And if the fact that the discipline was administered where there were presbyters, (Answer, pp. 11, 12,) proves that the apostle was superior to them, the same fact proves that he was superior to Timothy and Titus. The course of the argument urged by the author of the "Answer," would be, that Paul was disposed to assume the whole power into his own hands, and to set aside the claims alike of bishops and presbyters. It has a very undesirable looking toward the authority claimed by the Papacy.

The two cases alleged as proof that the apostles *only* had the power of administering discipline, are those at Corinth and at Ephesus. Paul wrote fourteen epistles, and wrote them to eight churches. In all these epistles, and in all the numerous churches of which he had the charge, (2 Cor. xi. 28, "the care of all the churches,") these are the only instances in which he was called, so far as appears, to exercise discipline. We now inquire, whether he did it for the purpose of showing that the apostles *only* had this power.

The first case alleged is that at Corinth. "In 1 Cor. iv. 19–21, etc., are recorded inflictions and remissions of *discipline* performed by an apostle, or threatenings on his part; although there must have been elders at Corinth." (Note *z*, Tract, p. 12.) The *argument* here is, that there must have been elders at Corinth, and yet that Paul interposed over their heads to inflict discipline. This is the whole of the argument. (See Answer, p. 11.)

In reply to these we observe: That there were elders, teachers, ministers, instructors in Corinth, we think it placed beyond a question, by the argument of the "Answer" and by the nature of the case. This fact we do not intend to call in question. The *argument* of the "Answer" from this fact, we state in the author's own words:—

"Yet, without noticing these elders in the matter, so far as the epistles show—though they doubtless were noticed and consulted, as much as courtesy and their pastoral standing made proper—without putting the matter into their hands, or even passing it through their hands, Paul threatens, inflicts, and remits *discipline* among the people of their charge. This is a 'ministerial act.' And Paul's doing it himself, instead of committing it to the elders, shows that he, an apostle, was '*superior* to them in ministerial power and rights.'" p. 11.

Further, if there were elders there, there was an "apostle;" a prelatical bishop, according to the Tract, there also. This is shown by a quotation from the Epistle itself, relating to this very time, and in immediate connection with the case of discipline. (1 Cor. iv. 17.) "For this cause, [that is, on account of your divided and contending state,] have I sent unto you Timotheus, who is my beloved son and faithful in the Lord, who shall bring you into remembrance of my ways which be in Christ, as I teach everywhere in every church." Now, as it will not be pretended by Episcopalians that Timothy was not an "apostle," and, as it is undeniable that he was at that time at Corinth, the argument will as well apply to set aside *his* right to administer discipline in the case, as that of the elders. Borrowing, then, the words of the Answer, we would say: "Yet without noticing" this apostle "in the matter, so far as the epistles show—though" he was "doubtless noticed and consulted, as much as courtesy and his" apostolical "standing made proper, without putting the matter into" his "hands, or even passing it through" his "hands,—Paul threatens, inflicts, and remits *discipline*. This is a 'ministerial' act. And Paul's doing it himself, instead of committing it to" Timothy, "shows, that he, an apostle, was *superior* to" him "in ministerial power and rights." Now no Episcopalian will fail to be at once deeply impressed with the fallacy of this reasoning, in regard to the "apostle" and "bishop" Timothy. And yet, it is manifestly just as pertinent and forcible in his case, as it is for the purpose of the Answer in regard to the elders of Corinth. It cannot be pretended that a difference existed, because the "elders" were *permanently* located there, and Timothy not; for the argument of the "Tract" and the "Answer" is, that the apostles were superior, *as apostles*, and, therefore, it made no difference on this point, whether they were at Corinth, or at Crete, or at Antioch; they were invested with the apostolic office everywhere. *Our* conclusion, from this instance, and from the fact which we have now stated, is, that there was some peculiarity in the case at Corinth, which rendered the ordinary exercise of discipline by presbyters difficult; which operated equally against any interference by Timothy; and which called peculiarly for the interposition of the founder of the church, and of an inspired apostle,—for one clothed with authority to inflict a heavy judgment, here denominated "delivering unto Satan for the destruction of the flesh," (1 Cor. v. 5,)—a power which could be exercised by none then in Corinth. Our next inquiry is, whether there are any reasons for this opinion. The following we believe satisfactory:—

(1.) Paul had founded that church, (Acts xviii. 1–11,) and his interference in cases of discipline would be regarded as peculiarly proper. There would be a natural and obvious deference to the founder of the church, which would render such an interposition in the highest degree appropriate. We are confirmed in this view, because he puts his authority *in this very case* on such a fact, and on the deference which was due to him as their spiritual father, (1 Cor. iv. 15:) "For though ye have ten thousand instructors in Christ, yet have ye not many FATHERS; for in Christ Jesus *I* have begotten you through the gospel."

(2.) The circumstances of the church at Corinth were such, evidently, as to render the ordinary exercise of discipline, by their own elders, impossible. They were distracted; were rent into parties; were engaged in violent contention; and the authority, therefore, of one portion of the "teachers" and "instructors" would be disregarded by the other. Thus no united sentence could be agreed upon; and no judgment of a party could restore peace. An attempt to exercise discipline would only enkindle party animosity and produce strife. (See chap. i. 11–17.) So great, evidently, was the contention, and so hopeless the task of allaying it by any ordinary means, that even *Timothy*, whom Paul had sent for the express purpose of bringing them into remembrance of his ways, (1 Cor. iv. 17,) could have no hope, by his own interference, of allaying it. It was natural that it should be referred to the founder of the church, and to one who had the power of punishing the offender.

(3.) It is material to remark, that this was not an ordinary case of discipline. It was one that required the severest exercise of authority, and in a form which was lodged only with those intrusted with the power of inflicting disease, or, as it is termed, "of delivering to Satan for the destruction of the flesh." 1 Cor. v. 5. Such cases would inevitably devolve upon the apostles, as clothed with miraculous power; and such, beyond all controversy, was this case. It therefore proves nothing about the *ordinary* mode of administering discipline. This case had reached to such a degree of enormity; it had been suffered to remain so long; it had become so aggravated, that it was necessary to interpose in this awful manner, and to decide it. Yet,

(4.) The apostle supposes that they *ought* to have exercised the usual discipline themselves. This is evident, we think, from a comparison of the following passages: 1 Cor. v. 9, 10, 11, 12, with v. 2. In these verses it is supposed that they did themselves *usually* exercise discipline. Paul (ver. 9) gave them the general direction not to keep company with fornicators; that is, to exercise discipline on those who did. In ver. 11, he asks them,—in a manner showing that the affirmative answer to the question expressed their usual practice,—whether they did not "judge those that were within?" —that is, whether they did not ordinarily exercise discipline in the church? And in ver. 2, he supposes that it *ought* to have been done in this case; and as it had *not* been done by them, and the affair had assumed special enormity, he exercised the miraculous power intrusted to him by inflicting on the offender a grievous disease, (ver. 4, 5; comp. 1 Cor. xi. 30.)

(5.) It is evident that other churches did, in ordinary cases, exercise discipline without the intervention of an apostle. Thus, the church in Thessalonica—where Episcopacy, with all its zeal, has never been able even to *conjecture* that there was a diocesan bishop—was directed to exercise discipline in any instance where the command of the inspired apostle was not obeyed. (2 Thess. iii. 14.) We shall soon make this point incontestable.

(6.) The circumstances of the early churches were such as to make this apostolic intervention proper, and even indispensable, without supposing that it was to be a permanent arrangement. They were ignorant and feeble. They had had little opportunity of learning the nature of Christianity. In most cases their founders were with them but a few weeks, and then left them under the care of elders ordained from among themselves. (Comp. Acts xiii. xiv., *et passim.*) Those elders would be poorly qualified to discharge the functions of their office; and they would be but little elevated, in character and learning, above the mass of the people. The churches must be imperfectly organized; unaccustomed to rigid discipline; exposed to many temptations; easily drawn into sin, and subject to great agitation and excitement. Even a great many subjects which may now be considered as settled, in morals and religion, would appear to them open for debate; and parties, as at Corinth, would easily be formed. (Comp. Acts xiv. xv.; Rom. xiv.; 1 Cor. vii.) In these circumstances, how natural was it for these churches to look for direction to the inspired men who had founded them; and how natural, that such persons should interpose and settle important and difficult cases of discipline. And after these obvious considerations, are we to suppose that the fact that the Apostle Paul, in *two* cases,—and two such cases only are recorded,—exercised an extraordinary act of discipline is to be regarded as proof that this power appertained *only* to the apostolic office, and was to be a permanent arrangement in the church? We confess our "amazement" that but *two* cases of apostolic interference are mentioned, during the long and active life of Paul; and we regard this as some evidence that the churches were expected to exercise discipline, and actually did so, on their own members.

(7.) We are confirmed in our views on this point, from what is known to take place in organizing churches in heathen countries at the present day. Since we commenced this article, we were conversing with one of the American missionaries, stationed at Ceylon.* In the course of the conversation, he incidentally remarked that the missionaries were obliged to retain the exercise of discipline in their own hands;

* Rev. Mr. Winslow.

and that, although the mission had been established more than fifteen years, yet the exercise of discipline had never been intrusted to the native converts. He farther observed that the missionaries had been endeavouring to find persons to whom they could intrust the discipline of the church as elders, but as yet they had not found one. The native converts were still so ignorant of the laws of Christianity; they had so little influence in the church; they were so partial to each other, even when in fault, that, thus far, discipline—though somewhat frequent acts of discipline were necessary—was retained in the hands of the missionaries. Substantially the same thing must have occurred in the early churches in Asia Minor, in Syria, and Greece. Will Dr. Onderdonk infer that because Mr. Winslow, Mr. Poor, and Dr. Scudder, in Ceylon, have found it necessary to retain the power of administering discipline, that therefore they are diocesan bishops, and that they do not contemplate that the churches in Ceylon shall be other than prelatical? If not, his argument in the case of the church in Corinth can be allowed no weight.

We have now done with *this* instance of discipline. We have shown that all the circumstances of the case can be accounted for, without any such conclusion as that to which the author of the Tract is desirous to conduct it. We turn, therefore, to his other case of discipline, in the church at Ephesus.

The case is thus stated in 1 Tim. i. 20: "Of whom is Hymeneus and Alexander; whom *I* have delivered *unto Satan*, that they may learn not to blaspheme." His argument is, that "it is the apostle who inflicts the discipline; the elders do not appear in the matter. And discipline is a ministerial function, and excommunication its highest exercise." (Answer, p. 13.) In reply to this case, we make the following observations:

(1.) It occurs in a charge to Timothy,—Timothy, on the

supposition of Episcopalians, an apostle co-ordinate with Paul himself; Timothy, prelate of Ephesus. If Timothy was an apostle and diocesan bishop, and if the exercise of discipline pertained to the apostle and bishop, why did Paul take the matter into his own hands? Why not refer it to Timothy, and repose sufficient confidence in him to believe that he was competent to fulfil this part of his Episcopal office? Would it now be regarded as courteous for the bishop of Ohio to interpose and inflict an act of discipline on some Hymeneus or Alexander of the diocese of Pennsylvania? And would there be as cordial submission of the bishop of Pennsylvania, as there was of the bishop of Ephesus? If Timothy was at Ephesus, and if the case of discipline occurred at the time which Dr. Onderdonk supposes, this case appears, to our humble apprehension, very much as if Paul regarded Timothy as neither an apostle nor a prelate.

(2.) If the exercise of the authority in this case of discipline by Paul proves that the presbyters at Ephesus had no right to administer discipline, for the same reason it proves that Timothy had not that right. By the supposition of Episcopalians, Timothy was there as well as the presbyters. The assumption of the authority by Paul proves as much that it did not belong to Timothy, as that it did not belong to the presbyters.

(3.) This was a case such as occurred at Corinth. It was not an ordinary act of discipline; it was one which supposed the infliction of the judgment of God by a miraculous agency: "Whom I have delivered *unto Satan*, that they may learn not to blaspheme." Compare this account with the record of the case in Corinth, (1 Cor. v. 5,) and it is evident that this was not an *ordinary* act of discipline, but was such as implied the direct infliction of the judgment of the Almighty. That such inflictions were intrusted to the hands of the apostles, we admit; and that Paul, not Timothy, inflicted this, proves that the latter was neither an apostle nor a prelate.

(4.) Dr. Onderdonk supposes that this occurred at Ephesus, and while Timothy was there. But what evidence is there of this? It is neither affirmed that the transaction was at Ephesus, nor that Timothy was there. His argument proceeds on the assumption that Timothy was bishop there when this Epistle was written, and that the case of discipline occurred there. And the *proof* of this would probably be, the subscription at the end of the *second* Epistle, and the "tradition of the elders." But that subscription has no authority; and it is not to be *assumed, but proved*, that Timothy was there in the capacity of a prelate, or there at all, when this Epistle was written to him. The demonstration that a bishop only exercised discipline, it must be admitted, rests on slender grounds, if this be all.

(5.) But if this case *did* occur at Ephesus, what evidence is there that it occurred at the *time* that Bishop Onderdonk supposes? The account in the Epistle to Timothy by no means fixes the time of the transaction. "Whom I have delivered (παρέδωκα) unto Satan," etc. It was already done; and the presumption is that it was done when Paul was himself present with them. It is morally certain that it was *not* an act of discipline that was then *to be done.*

Our readers have now the whole case before them. Episcopacy affirms that prelates *only* have the power of administering discipline. It affirms that the churches are prohibited from exercising it on their own members; that those appointed to preach the gospel, to administer the sacraments, and to be pastors of the flock, and who may, therefore, be supposed to understand the cases of discipline, and best qualified to administer it, have no right to exercise this act of government over their own members; but that this exclusive prerogative belongs to a stranger and a foreigner, a prelatical bishop, whom the churches seldom see, and who must be, in a great degree, unacquainted with their peculiar wants and character. All power of discipline, in an entire diocese of some hundreds of churches, is to be taken away from the members themselves, and from the pastors, and lodged in strange hands, and committed to a solitary, independent man, who, from the nature of the circumstances, can have little acquaintance with the case, and possess few of the qualifications requisite for the intelligent performance of his duty. And does the reader ask what is the authority for this assumption of power? Why are the churches and their pastors disrobed of this office, and reduced to the condition of humble dependents at the feet of the prelate? Let him, in astonishment, learn. It is not because there is any *command* to this effect in the New Testament; it is not because there is any declaration implying that it *would* be so; it is not by any affirmation that it ever *was* so. This is the reason, and this is all:—The Apostle Paul, in two cases, and in both instances over the heads of presbyters, (and over the head of Bishop Timothy, too,) delivered men "to Satan for the destruction of the flesh, that they might learn not to blaspheme;" and, THEREFORE, Bishop Onderdonk, and Bishop Griswold, and Bishop Doane, *only* have power to administer discipline in all the churches in Pennsylvania, and in the Eastern diocese, and in New Jersey; and, THEREFORE, all the acts of discipline exercised by Presbyterians, Methodists, Baptists, etc., in Pennsylvania and New Jersey, and by the Congregationalists of New England, are null and void. The disposal of *such* antecedents and consequents may be safely left to all who hold that "no argument is worth taking into the account that has not a *clear* and *palpable* bearing on the naked topic,—the scriptural evidence of Episcopacy." (Tract, p. 3.)

But we have not done with this subject. We are now prepared to show not only that there is no evidence that the apostles exclusively exercised discipline, but that there *is* positive proof that all the acts of discipline were, *in fact*, exercised by the presbyters of the churches. To put this matter to rest, we adduce the following passages of Scripture:

Acts xx. 17, 28: "From Miletus, Paul sent to Ephesus, and called for the PRESBYTERS of the church, and said unto them: Take heed unto yourselves, and to all the flock over which the Holy Ghost hath made you BISHOPS, (ἐπισκόπους,) to feed (ποιμαίνειν, like good shepherds, to provide for, watch over, and govern) the church of God." It would be easy to show that the word translated *feed* includes the whole duty which a shepherd exercises over his flock, including all that is needful in the supervision, government, and defence of those under his care. Proof of this may be found in the following passages of the New Testament, where the word occurs in the sense of ruling or governing, including of course the exercise of discipline; for how can there be government, unless there is authority for punishing offenders?—Matt. ii. 6; John xxi. 16; 1 Peter v. 2; Rev. ii. 27: "And he shall *rule* them (ποιμανεῖ αὐτοὺς) with a rod of iron;" an expression which will be allowed to imply the exercise of discipline. Rev. xii. 5; xix. 15. Comp. Ps. ii. 9; xxiii. 1; xxvii. 12; xlvii. 13. And the Iliad of Homer may be consulted, *passim*, for this use of the word. See particularly I. 253; II. 85.

1 Pet. v. 2, 3: "The PRESBYTERS who are among you I exhort, who am also a PRESBYTER. FEED (ποιμάνατε) the flock of God which is among you, taking the OVERSIGHT (ἐπισκοποῦντες, discharging the duty of BISHOPS) thereof, not by constraint, but willingly," etc. Here the very work which is claimed for prelates is enjoined on presbyters, the very name which prelates assume is given to presbyters; and *Peter ranks himself as on a level with them in the office of exercising discipline, or in the government of the church.* It is perfectly obvious that the presbyters at Ephesus, and the pres-

byters whom Peter addressed, were intrusted with the pastoral care to the fullest extent. It is obvious that they were required to engage in all the work requisite in instructing, directing, and governing the flock. And it is *as* obvious that they were intrusted with a power and an authority in this business, with which presbyters are *not* intrusted by the canons of the Episcopal Church. We respectfully ask, Whether the bishop of Pennsylvania, or New Jersey, would now take 1 Pet. v. 2, 3, for a text, and address the "priests," or "second order of clergy," in these words, without considerable qualification: "The PRESBYTERS who are among you I exhort, who am also a PRESBYTER. *Feed* (ποιμάνατε) the flock of God, ἐπισκοποῦντες, discharging the duty of BISHOPS, over it, not by constraint, neither as being LORDS *over God's heritage.*"

Heb. xiii. 7: "Remember them which have the rule over your: τῶν ἡγουμένων ὑμῶν, YOUR RULERS." Verse 17: "Obey them that have the rule over you." (Πείθεσθε τοῖς ἡγουμένοις ὑμῶν.) That bishops are here referred to no one will pretend. Yet the office of *ruling* certainly implies that kind of government which is concerned in the administration of discipline.

1 Thess. v. 12: "We beseech you, brethren, to know them which labour among you, *and are over you in the Lord.*" (καὶ προϊσταμένους ὑμῶν ἐν κυρίῳ.) 1 Tim. v. 17: "Let the PRESBYTERS that rule well (προεστῶτες) be counted worthy of double honour." There can be no question that *these* passages are applied to presbyters. We come, then, to the conclusion that the terms which *properly* denote government and discipline, and on which alone *any* claim for the exercise of authority can be founded,—the terms expressive of governing, of feeding, of ruling, of taking the oversight, are all applied to presbyters; that the churches are required to submit to them in the exercise of that office; and that the

very term denoting *episcopal jurisdiction* is applied to them also. We ask for a solitary passage which directs apostles, or prelates, to administer discipline; and we leave the case of *discipline*, therefore, to the common sense of those who read the New Testament, and who believe that presbyters had any duties to perform.

We have now examined the essential point in Episcopacy; for, if the claims which are arrogated for bishops are unfounded, the system, as a system, is destroyed. We have examined the solitary passage urged directly in its favour, "the apostles *and* elders," "the apostles, *and* elders, *and* brethren;" and the claims set up in favour of their exclusive right to administer discipline; and, if we mistake not, we have shown that hitherto, so stupendous claims have never been reared on so narrow a basis.

The next point which it is indispensable for Episcopalians to make out from the Bible, is, *that it was intended that the superiority in ministerial rank and power should be a permanent arrangement.* This, it will be perceived, is a distinct and independent inquiry. It by no means follows of necessity, even if all that the Episcopalians claim for the apostles had this superiority, and yet, that it was designed merely as a temporary arrangement. As the "Answer" has added nothing material to the argument of the Tract on this subject, we shall not long be detained on this point. The *sole* argument in the "Tract" is drawn from the claim that Timothy was bishop of Ephesus, and Titus of Crete; and that the "angels" of the seven churches were prelatical bishops. (pp. 23–29.) In our review, we examined these several claims at length, (Review, pp. 223–242.) As the writer of the Answer has not thought proper to notice our argument here, we are left to the presumption, that an obvious or satisfactory reply was not at hand. The train of our reasoning, then, we shall take the liberty of regarding as unbroken and untouched.

The only *appearance* of argument on this subject, in the Answer, is found on p. 14, and it is this: that its author supposes our argument to have been that Timothy and Titus had a temporary and extraordinary office, because they were "migratory;" and, as many of the presbyters—Apollos, for example—were migratory, hence it would follow that the office of presbyter also was temporary. Now, in reply to this, we observe, that although we *did* affirm the appointment of Timothy and Titus to have been "temporary," yet we were not so weak as to suppose that it was *because* they were migratory. That this fact *indicated* that they had not a permanent prelatical office, we assuredly did, and still do believe. But we showed—in a manner which we marvel the author of the Answer did not notice—that Timothy was sent to Ephesus for a *special* purpose, and that he was to execute that office *only* until Paul returned. (Review, pp. 230, 233; 1 Tim. i. 3; iv. 13; 1 Tim. iii. 14, 15.) The same thing we showed, from the New Testament, to be the case with regard to Titus, (Review, p. 236. See Titus i. 6–9; iii. 10, 12.) We never so far forgot ourselves, as to suppose that *because* Timothy and Titus were "migratory," that, therefore, they were not bishops. We put the matter on wholly different ground; and in the course of our argument, we quoted no less than *forty-six* passages of the New Testament, containing, we believe, all that can be supposed to bear on the point. We cannot withhold the expressions of our "amazement," that an author whose express object was to "test Episcopacy by Scripture," should have left unnoticed this argument. Never was there invented a shorter and more convenient mode of avoiding such an argument, than by saying of something which we never intended to urge, that the whole of it was founded on the fact of their being "migratory." We would now remind the author, that our argument was *not* of such a character; but it was, (1) That Timothy is not even called an apostle; (2) that he is expressly distinguished *from* the apostles; (3) that there is no evidence that he was bishop of Ephesus; (4) that the Scripture *affirms* he was sent to Ephesus for a *special* and *temporary* purpose; and (5) that the Epistles to Timothy contain full proof of the falsehood of any such supposition as that he was a prelatical bishop; because (*a*) there are but two orders of officers in the church spoken of in those Epistles; (*b*) they contain no description of his own office as a prelate; (*c*) they contain full and explicit directions on a great variety of other topics, of far less importance than the office which, according to Episcopacy, was to constitute the very *peculiarity* of the church; and not a word respecting his brother bishops then existing, or any intimation that such an order of men ever *would* exist.

In regard to Titus, we proved, (1) That he was left in Crete for the *special* purpose of completing a work which Paul had begun; (2) that Paul gave him express directions, when he had done that to come to him; and (3) that he obeyed the command, left Crete, and became the travelling companion of Paul; and that there is not the slightest reason to suppose that he ever returned to Crete.

In regard to the "angels" of the seven churches, we showed that the whole of Dr. Onderdonk's argument was a mere assumption, that there was an inferior body of the "clergy at large;" that they were in each of those cities more churches than one,—a fact which should be proved, not assumed;—also, that the style of the address to the "angel," was that of the "angel of *the church*," evidently referring to an individual congregation, and not to such a group of churches as constitute a modern diocese; and that the application of the term "angel," to the pastor of a single church, was more obvious, and much the more probable supposition, than to "the formal, unfrequent, and in many instances, stately and pompous visitations of a diocesan bishop."

To this argument there is no reply, except by an assumption that Timothy was bishop of Ephesus; that the same thing must be presumed to exist in the year 96; and that the "elders" at Ephesus being there also, and being ministers, any direction to the "angel," must suppose that he was superior to the presbyters. (Answer, p. 17.) Now the whole of this argument proceeds on the supposition that the elders at Ephesus were ordained ministers of the gospel, a distinct rank of the clergy, and sustaining the same office as the "second order" in the Episcopal Church. But this is assuming the very point in debate. In our review, we showed, (p. 232,) that all the facts in the case of the elders at Ephesus (Acts xx. 17, etc.) are met by the supposition that they were ruling elders, or persons appointed to govern, guide, and secure, the spiritual welfare of the church. Our argument is, (1.) That Dr. Onderdonk admits, that the word rendered "feed," (ποιμαίνειν,) may mean to rule, (Tract, pp. 24, 37.) (2.) That the idea of *ruling* is the one which is there *specifically* dwelt on. That he directs them to "feed," or exercise the office of a shepherd over them,—that is, to guard, defend, provide for them, as a shepherd does in the care of his flock. He directs them to watch against the grievous wolves which should come in, and against those who should rise up from among themselves, to secure parties, etc. (3.) There is no counsel given them about the proper mode of administering the sacraments, the peculiar duty of the "second order" of clergy. (4.) There is no expression of lamentation that they had not a prelatical bishop; or any intimation that they should soon be furnished with one. (5.) It is evidently implied that the *number* of these elders was considerable. They are addressed as such; and yet they are addressed as in charge of one "flock," over which they had been placed. Now it is incredible that any considerable body of the "second order of clergy" should have been ordained in an infant church like Ephesus. And it is equally incredible, that *if* Paul had so ordained them, he should have set them over *one* flock, in a single city,—collegiate "rectors" in a single church in Ephesus,—under a "diocesan" also, of the single "flock," or church; a diocesan not then present, and concerning whom not the slightest hint was dropped by Paul, either of lamentation or promise. So that, on the whole, one knows not at which to be most surprised—the number of *assumptions* indispensable to the purpose of "enthroning" the Bishop Timothy at Ephesus, or the singular coolness with which Episcopalians urge all these assumptions, as if they were grave matters of historical record.

In reference to the term "angel," as used in the Apocalypse, we have only to remark, further, that the interpretation which makes it refer to a prelatical bishop, is so unnatural and forced, that Episcopalians are, many of them, themselves compelled to abandon it. Thus Stillingfleet, than whom an abler man, and one whose praise is higher in Episcopal churches, is not to be found among the advocates of prelacy, says of these angels: "If many things in the epistles be denoted to the angels, but yet so as to concern the whole body, then, of necessity, the angel must be taken as a *representative* of the whole body; and then, why may not the word *angel* be taken by way of representation of the body itself, either of the whole church, or, *which is far more probable*, of the *consessors*, or order of presbyters in that church? We see what miserable, unaccountable arguments those are, which are brought for any kind of government, from metaphorical or ambiguous expressions, or names promiscuously used."—*Irenicum.*

In regard to this second point, which it is incumbent on Episcopalians to make out, we are now prepared to estimate the force of these arguments. The case stands thus:—(1.) There is no *command* in the New Testament to the apostles to transmit the peculiarity of the apostolic office. If there *had* been, the industry of Dr. Onderdonk would have called it to our attention. If the peculiarity of the office was to be transmitted, it was required that such a command should be given. (2.) There is no affirmation that it would be thus transmitted. If there had been, Dr. Onderdonk's Tract would not have been so barren on this point. And we ask him whether it is credible that the apostles were bishops of a superior order, and that it was designed that all the church should be subject to an order of men "superior in ministerial rank and power," deriving their authority from the apostles; and yet not the slightest command thus to transmit it, and not the slightest hint that it would be done? We say again, *Credat Judæus Apella!* (3.) It was *impossible* that the peculiarity of the apostolic office *should be* transmitted. We have shown, not by assumptions, but by a large array of passages of Scripture, what that peculiarity was,—to bear witness to the great events which went to prove that Jesus was the Messiah. We have been met in this proof by the calm and dignified observation that this was a "showy" argument; and we now affirm that the peculiarity of that office, as specified by Jesus Christ, by the chosen apostles, by Paul, and by the whole college, COULD NOT be transmitted; that no bishop is, or can be a *witness*, in the sense and for the purpose for which they were originally designated. (4.) We have examined the case of Timothy, of Titus, and of the angels of the churches, —the slender basis on which the fabric of Episcopal pretension has been reared. We now affirm, (5.) That, should we admit all that Episcopalians claim, on each of these points, there is not the slightest proof, as a matter of historical record, that the Episcopal office has been transmitted from prelate to prelate; but that the pretended line has been often broken, and that no jury would give a verdict to the amount of five dollars, on proof so slender as can be adduced for the uninterrupted succession of prelates. As satisfactory evidence on this point, we repeat the following passage, contained in the September number of this journal:

"We are informed by many ancient historians, and very expressly by Bede, in his famous Ecclesiastical History, 'that at the request of Oswald, King of Northumberland, certain *presbyters* came (in the seventh century) from Scotland into England, and ordained bishops; that the abbot, and *other presbyters* of the island of Hy, sent Aydan for this express purpose, declaring him to be worthy of the office of bishop, and that he ought to be sent to instruct the unbelieving and the unlearned.' He informs us, that 'those presbyters ordained him and sent him to England on this errand; and that Finan, sent from the same monastery in the same island, succeeded him in the episcopal office, after having been ordained by the Scottish presbyters.'

"Upon this testimony of Bede, Baxter remarks: 'You will find that the English had a *succession* of bishops by the *Scottish presbyter's ordination;* and there is no mention in Bede of any dislike or scruple of the lawfulness of this course. The learned Dr. Doddridge refers us to Bede and Jones to substantiate the fact that 'the ordination of English bishops cannot be traced up to the Church of Rome as its original; that in the year 668, the successors of Austin, the monk, (who came over A. D. 596,) being almost extinct, *by far the greater part* of the bishops were of Scottish ordination, by Aydan and Finan, who came out of the Culdee monastery of Columbanus, and were no more than *presbyters*.'

"And is it verily so, that the Episcopal blood was thus early and extensively contaminated in England? Is it verily so, that when the effects of pious Austin's labours had become almost imperceptible, the sinking church was revived again, by sending to Scotland or *presbyters* to come and *ordain* a *multitude* of bishops? Then it is verily a fact that presbyterian ordination is one of the sturdiest pillars that support the vast fabric of the Church of England. No matter if only *ten* bishops were thus ordained, the contamination (if it be one) having been imparted more than *eleven hundred years ago*, has had a long time to diffuse itself, and doubtless has diffused itself so extensively from bishop to bishop, that not a single prelate in Great Britain can prove that he has escaped the infection. For what one of them can tell, if he was not consecrated by bishops, who were themselves consecrated by bishops, and they by other bishops, to whom all the ordaining power they ever had, was transmitted from the *presbyters of Scotland?* But this is not the whole of the evil. As no one bishop can trace his episcopal pedigree farther back, perhaps, than two or three centuries, so he cannot certainly know that any presbyter, on whose head he has imposed hands, has received from him any thing more than presbyterian ordination. Nor is this all the evil. The Protestant Episcopal bishops and presbyters in America are in the same plight; for I am told that all their authority came from England. But as the English bishops who gave it to them, could not *then*, and cannot *now*, certainly, tell whence it came, so who knows but all the Episcopal clergy in the United States of America are originally indebted to the hands of the *Elder Aydan* and *Elder Finan* for all their ministerial powers? I tremble for all Protestant Episcopal churches on both continents, if Presbyterian ordination be not VALID and SCRIPTURAL.' " pp. 486, 487.

One point more, in the argument for Episcopacy, remains. It is, *that none but prelates ordained.* It is incumbent on Episcopalians to prove this, as essential to their argument. For if presbyters or elders exercised the office of *ordaining*, then the main point claimed for the superiority of bishops is unfounded. We aim, therefore, to show that there is positive proof that presbyters *did* ordain. We have shown in the course of our argument, that they exercised the office of *discipline*, one of the things claimed peculiarly for bishops; we now proceed to show that the office of *ordaining* was one which was intrusted to them, and which they exercised. If this point be made out, it follows still further, that the peculiarity of the office of the apostles was not that they ordained, and that the clergy of the New Testament are not divided into "three orders," but are equal in ministerial rank and power. The argument is indeed complete without this; for, unless Episcopalians can show, by positive proof, the superiority of their bishops to the right of ordination and discipline, the parity of the clergy follows as a matter of course.

The writer of these articles is a Presbyterian. But the argument does not require that he should go largely into the proof of his own views on church polity. The object is to *disprove* Episcopacy. If *this* is disproved, it follows that the clergy are on an equality. If it is shown that the doctrine of the New Testament is, that presbyters were to ordain, it is a sufficient disposal of the "feeble claims of lay-ordination," and of all other claims. It will follow that a valid ordination is that which is performed in accordance with the direction that *presbyters* should ordain. What particular churches, *besides* the Presbyterian, accord in their practice with the direction, it is not our business to inquire. It is sufficient for our purpose that the *Presbyterian* churches accord with that requirement, and follow the direction of the New Testament, in the ordination of their ministry by presbyters, and in their ministerial equality. This is all the reply that is necessary to the train of reflections in the "Answer," (pp. 5, 6.) We have seen, also, that Episcopal ordination is valid, not because it is performed by a prelate, but because it is, in fact, a mere Presbyterian performance.

In proof of the point now before us, therefore, we adduce 1 Tim. iv. 14: "Neglect not the gift that is in thee, which was given thee by prophecy, with the laying on of the hands of the presbytery." Of this passage, which, to the common sense of mankind, affirms the very thing under discussion, it is evidently material for Episcopalians to dispose; or their claims to exclusive rights and privileges are forever destroyed. We shall, therefore, examine the passage, and then notice the objections to its *obvious* and *common-sense* interpretation, alleged by Dr. Onderdonk.

We observe, then, (1.) That the translation of the passage is fairly made. Much learned criticism has been exhausted, to very little purpose, by Episcopalians, to show that a difference existed between "with," (μετὰ,) in this place, and "by," (διὰ,) in 2 Tim. i. 6. It has been said "that such a distinction may justly be regarded as intimating that the *virtue* of the ordaining act flowed from Paul, while the presbytery, or the rest of that body, if he were included in it, expressed only *consent.*" (Tract, p. 22.) But it has never been shown, nor can it be, that the preposition "with" does not fairly express the force of the original. The same observation may be applied to the word "presbytery," (πρεσβυτερίον.) It denotes properly a body, or assembly of elders, or presbyters. In Luke xxii. 66, it is applied to the body of elders which composed the Sanhedrim, or great council of the Jews, and is translated "the elders of the people," (το πρεσβυτέριον τοῦ λαοῦ.) See also Acts xxii. 5: "The estate of the elders." The word occurs nowhere else in the New Testament, except in the passage under consideration. Dr. Onderdonk has endeavoured to show that it means "the *office* to which Timothy was ordained, not the *persons* who ordained him; so that the passage would read, 'with the laying on of hands to confer the *presbyterate*,' or presbytership, or the clerical office;" and appeals to the authority of Grotius and Calvin in the case. (Tract, pp. 19, 20.) In regard to this interpretation, we observe, (1.) That if this be correct, then it follows that Timothy was not *an apostle*, but *an elder*,—he was ordained to the office of the *presbyterate*, or the eldership. Timothy, then, is to be laid out of the college of the apostles, and reduced to the humble office of a presbyter. When prelacy is to be established by showing that the office of apostles was transmitted, Timothy is an apostle; when it is necessary to make *another* use of this same man, it appears that he was ordained to the *presbyterate*, and Timothy becomes a humble *presbyter*. But (2) if the word "presbytery" (πρεσβυτέριον) here means the *presbyterate*, and not the *persons*, then it doubtless means the same in the two other places where it occurs. In Luke xxii. 66, we shall receive the information, that "the presbyterate," "the presbytership," or "the clerical office" of the people,—that is, the body by which the people conferred "the presbyterate,"—came together with the scribes, etc. In Acts xxii. 5, we shall be informed, that "the presbyterate," or the "clerical office," would bear witness with the high-priest to the life of Paul. Such absurdities show the propriety of adhering, in interpretation, to the obvious and usual meaning of the words. (3.) The word is fixed in its meaning in the usage of the church. Suicer (Thesaurus) says, it denotes "an assembly, congregation, and college of *presbyters* in the Christian church." In all the instances which he quotes from Theodoret, (on 1 Tim. iv. 14,) from Chrysostom, (Homil. xiii. on this Epistle,) from Theophylact, (in locum,) and from Ignatius, (Epis. to Antioch and to the Trallians,) there is not the slightest evidence that it is *ever* used to denote the *office*, instead of the *persons*, of the presbytery. (4.) As the opinion of Grotius is referred to by Dr. Onderdonk, we beg leave to quote here a passage from his commentary on this place:—"The custom was, that the presbyters who were present placed their hands on the head of the candidate, at the same time with the presiding officer of their body," *cum cœtus sui principe.* "Where the apostles, or their assistants, were not present, ordination took place by the presiding officer (*præsidem*) of their body, with the concurrence of the presbytery." We were particularly surprised that the authority of CALVIN should have been adduced, as sanctioning that interpretation, which refers to the word *presbytery* to *office*, and not to *persons.* His words are: "They who interpret *presbytery*, here, as a collective noun, denoting the college of presbyters, are, in my opinion, right." Our first argument, then, is, that the word "presbytery," denoting the persons who composed the *body* or *college of elders*, is the proper, obvious, and established sense of the passage.

(2.) It is evident from this passage, that whoever or whatever else might have been engaged in this transaction, a material part of it belonged to the presbytery or eldership concerned. "*Neglect not the gift that is in thee, which was given thee by prophecy;* WITH THE LAYING ON OF THE HANDS OF THE PRESBYTERY." Here it is evident that the presbytery bore a material part in the transaction. Paul says that the gift was in Timothy, was given him by *prophecy*, with the laying on of the hands *of the presbytery*. That is, that prophecy, or some prophecies relating to Timothy, (comp. 1 Tim. i. 18, "according to the prophecies which went before thee,") had designated him as a proper person for the ministry, or that he *would* be employed in the ministry; but the prophecy did not invest him with the office—did not confer the gift. *That* was done—that formal appointment fulfilling the prophecy—by the imposition of the hands of the presbytery. It was necessary that that act of the presbytery should thus concur with the prophecy, or Timothy had remained a layman. The presbyters laid their hands on him; and he thus received his office. As the prophecy made no part of his ordination, it follows that he was ordained by the presbytery.

(3.) The statement here is just one which would be given now in a *Presbyterian* ordination; it is *not* one which would be made in an Episcopalian ordination. A Presbyterian would choose these very words to give an account of an ordination in his church; an Episcopalian would not. The former speaks of ordination by a *presbytery;* the latter of ordination by a *bishop*. The former can use the account of the Apostle Paul here, as applicable to ordination, without explanations, comments, new versions, and criticisms; the latter cannot. The passage speaks to the common understanding of men in favour of Presbyterian ordination—of the action of a *presbytery* in the case: it never speaks the language of Episcopacy, even after all the torture to which it may be subjected by Episcopal criticism. The passage is one, too, which is not like the "apostles *and* elders," "the apostles, *and* elders, *and* brethren,"—the *only* direct passage on which Episcopacy relies—a passage which has no perceptible connection with the case; but it is one that speaks on the very subject; which relates to the exact transaction; and which makes a positive affirmation of the very thing in debate.

(4.) The supposition that this was not a *presbyterial* transaction renders the passage unmeaning. Here was present a body of men called a presbytery. We ask the Episcopalian, why they were present? The answer is, *not* for the purpose of ordination, but for "concurrence." Paul, the bishop, is the sole ordainer. We see Timothy bowing before the presbytery. We see them solemnly impose their hands on him. We ask, Why is this? "*Not* for the purpose of ordination," the Episcopalian replies, "but for 'concurrence.' Paul is the ordainer." But, we ask, Had they no share in the ordination? "None at all." Had they no participation in conferring the gift designated by prophecy? "None at all." Why then present? Why did they impose hands? For "concurrence," for form, for nothing! It was an empty pageantry, in which they were mistaken, when supposing that their act had something to do in conferring the gift; for their presence really *meant* nothing, and the whole transaction could as well have been performed without as with them.

(5.) If this ordination was the joint act of the presbytery, we have here a complete scriptural account of a Presbyterian ordination. It becomes, then, a very material question, how the Episcopalians dispose of this passage of Scripture. Their difficulties and embarrassments on this subject will still farther confirm the obvious interpretation which Presbyterians suggest and hold. These difficulties and embarrassments are thus presented by Dr. Onderdonk:

He *first* doubts whether this transaction was an *ordination*. (Tract, pp. 18–19.) To this we answer, (1) That, if it were not, then there is no account that Timothy was ever ordained; (2) that there is no specific work mentioned in the history of the apostles, to which Timothy was designated, unless it was ordination; (3) that it is the *obvious* and fair meaning of the passage; (4) that if *this* does not refer to ordination, it would be easy to apply the same denial to all the passages which speak of the "imposition of hands," and to show that there was no such thing as ordination to the ministry in any case; (5) that it accords with the common usage of the term "imposition of hands," (ἐπιθέσις τῶν χειρῶν,) in the New Testament. The phrase occurs but four times: Acts viii. 18; 1 Tim. iv. 14; 2 Tim. i. 6; Heb. vi. 2. In all these places it evidently denotes conferring some gift, office, or favour described by the act. In 2 Tim. i. 6, it denotes, by the acknowledgment of all Episcopalians, ordination to the ministry. Why should it not here? (6.) If, as Dr. Onderdonk supposes, it refers to "an inspired designation of one already in the ministry, to a particular field of duty," (Tract, p. 19,) then, (*a*) we ask, why we have no other mention of this transaction? (*b*) we ask, how it is to be accounted for that Paul, while here evidently referring Timothy to the duties and responsibilities of the ministerial office in general, should not refer to his *ordination*, but to *a designation to a particular field of labour?* His argument to Timothy, on such a supposition, would be this: "Your office of minister of the gospel is one that is exceedingly important. A bishop must be blameless, vigilant, sober, of good behaviour, given to hospitality, apt to teach, not given to wine, etc. (chap. iii.) In order to impress this more deeply on you, to fix these great duties in your mind, I refer you—not to the solemnity of your ordination vows—but *I solemnly remind* you of '*an inspired separation of one already in the ministry to a particular field of duty.*'" We need only observe here, that this is not a strain of argument that looks like Paul. But,

Secondly. Dr. Onderdonk supposes that this was not a *Presbyterian* ordination. (Tract, pp. 19–21.) His first supposition is, that the word "presbytery" does not mean *persons*, but the office, (p. 19.) This we have already noticed. He next supposes, (pp. 20, 21,) that, if "the presbytery" here means not the office given to Timothy, but a body of elders, that it cannot be shown "of whom this ordaining presbytery was composed," (p. 21.) And he then proceeds to state that there are "seven modes" in which this "presbytery" might be composed. It might be made up of "ruling elders;" or, it might be composed of the "grade called presbyters;" or, as Peter and John called themselves "elders," it might be made up of "apostles;" or, "there may have been ruling elders *and* presbyters; or presbyters *and* one or more apostles; or, ruling elders and one or more of the apostles; or, ruling elders, *and* presbyters, and apostles," (p. 21.) Now, as Dr. Onderdonk has not informed us *which* of these modes he prefers, we are left merely to conjecture. We may remark on these suppositions, (1.) That they are *mere* suppositions. There is not the shadow of proof to support them. The word "presbytery"—"a body of elders"—does not appear to be such a difficult word of interpretation, as to make it necessary to envelop it in so much mist, in order to understand it. Dr. Onderdonk's argument here is such as a man always employs, when he is pressed by difficulties which he cannot meet, and when he throws himself, as it were, into a labyrinth, in the hope that amid its numerous passages, he may escape detection and evade pursuit. (2.) If this "body of elders" was made up of "ruling elders," or, "of the grade called presbyters," then the argument of Episcopacy is overthrown. Here is an instance, on *either* supposition, of Presbyterian ordination, which is fatal to the claims that bishops only ordain. Or, if it be supposed that this was not an ordination, but "an inspired separation of one already in the ministry to a particular field of duty," it is an act equally fatal to the claim of prelates to the general "superintendence" of the church; since it is manifest that these "elders" took upon themselves the functions of this office, and designated "the bishop of Ephesus" to his field of labour. Such a transaction would scarcely meet with Episcopal approbation in the nineteenth century.

But in regard to the other suppositions,—that a part of all the "presbytery" was composed of apostles,—we remark: (1.) That it is a *merely gratuitous* supposition. There is not an instance in which the term "presbytery," or "body of elders," is applied, in the New Testament, to the collective body of the apostles. (2.) On the supposition that the "presbytery" was composed entirely of apostles, then we ask, how it happens that, in 2 Tim. i. 6, Paul appropriates to himself a power, which belonged to every one of them in as full a right as to him? How came they to surrender their power into the hands of an individual? Was it the *character* of Paul thus to assume authority which did not belong to him? We have seen already how, on the supposition of the Episcopalian, he superseded Bishop Timothy in the exercise of discipline, in Corinth and in his own diocese at Ephesus: we have now an instance in which he claims all the virtue of the ordaining power, where his fellow-apostles must have been equally concerned.

But if a *part* only of this "presbytery" was composed of apostles, and the remainder presbyters, either ruling elders or "the second grade," we would make the following inquiries:

(1.) Was he ordained as a *prelate?* So the Episcopalians with one voice declare,—prelate of Ephesus. Then it follows that Timothy, a prelate, was set apart to his work by the imposition of the hands of elders. What was then his prelatical character? Does the water in the cistern rise higher than the fountain? If laymen were concerned, Timothy was a layman still. If presbyters, Timothy was a presbyter still. And thus all the power of prelates, from him of Rome downward, has come through the hands of humble presbyters,—just as we believe, and just as history affirms. (2.) Was he ordained as a *presbyter?* Then his Episcopal character, so far as it depends on his ordination, is swept away; and thus we have not a solitary instance of the consecration of a prelate in all the New Testament.

Which of these suppositions of Dr. Onderdonk he is disposed to receive as the true one, we are unable to say. All of them cannot be true; and whichever he chooses is, as we have seen, equally fatal to his argument, and involves a refutation of the claims of prelacy.

The only other reply, with which Dr. Onderdonk meets the argument for Presbyterian ordination, from this passage, is, by the supposition that the *virtue* of the ordaining act was derived from the Apostle Paul. The passage on which he rests the argument is, (2 Tim. i. 6:) "That thou stir up the gift of God which is in thee, by the putting on of MY hands." On this passage we observe, (1.) Paul does not deny that *other* hands were also imposed on Timothy; nor that his authority was derived *also* from others, in conjunction with himself. (2.) That, by the supposition of Episcopalians, as well as Presbyterians, other hands were, in fact, imposed on him. (3.) It was perfectly natural for Paul, in consequence of the relation which Timothy sustained to him, as his adopted son, (1 Tim i. 2;) as being selected by him for the ministry, (Acts xvi. 3;) and as being his companion in the ministry and in travels, to remind him, near the close of his own life, (2 Tim. iv. 6,) that he had been solemnly set apart to the work by himself,—to bring his *own* agency into full view,—in order to stimulate and encourage him. That Paul had a part in the act of the ordination, we admit; that others also had a part,—the "presbytery,"—we have proved. (4.) The expression, which is here used, is just such as an aged Presbyterian minister would now use, if directing a farewell letter to a son in the ministry. He would remind him, as Paul does in this Epistle, (2 Tim. iv. 6,) that he was about to leave the ministry and the world; and, if he wished to impress his mind in a peculiarly tender manner, he would remind him, also, that *he* took part in his ordination; that, under his own hands, he had been designated to the work of the ministry; and would endeavour to deepen his conviction of the importance and magnitude of the work, by the reflection that he had been solemnly set apart to it by a *father*. Yet who would infer from this, that the aged Presbyterian would wish to be regarded as a *prelate?*

Dr. Onderdonk remarks on this case, (Tract, p. 22,) that, if *Paul* was engaged in the transaction, it was the work of an *apostle*, and was "an apostolic ordination." We admit that it was an "*apostolic* ordination;" but when will Episcopalians learn to suppose it possible, that an "apostolic ordination" was not a *prelatical* ordination? Did not Dr. Onderdonk see that this was *assuming* the very point in debate, *that the peculiarity of the apostolic office was the power of ordaining?* We reply, further, that whoever was engaged in it, a "presbytery" was concerned, and it was a *Presbyterian* ordination.

We have now considered all the objections that have been made to the obvious interpretation of this passage; and we are prepared to submit it to any candid mind, as a full and unqualified statement of an instance of Presbyterian ordination.

Whichever of the half-dozen suppositions—assuming a hue, chameleon-like, from the nature of the argument to be refuted—which Episcopalians are compelled to apply to the passage, is adopted, we have seen that they involve them in all the difficulties of an unnatural interpretation, and conduct us, by a more circuitous route, only to the plain and common-sense exposition of the passage, as decisive in favour of Presbyterian ordination.

Having thus shown that there was one Presbyterian ordination, in the case of Timothy, claimed by Episcopalians as a prelate, and this, too, in perhaps the only instance of ordination to the ministry recorded in the New Testament; we now proceed to adduce the case of a *church* that was *not* organized on the principles of Episcopalians, with three orders of clergy. We refer to the church at Philippi. "Paul and Timothy, servants of Jesus Christ, to all the saints in Christ Jesus, who are at Philippi, with the bishops and deacons." (σὺν ἐπισκόποις καὶ διακόνοις.) In regard to this church, we make the following observations: (1.) It was organized by the Apostle Paul himself, in connection with Silas, and was, therefore, on the truly "primitive and apostolic" plan. (Acts xvi.) (2.) It was in the centre of a large territory, the capital of Macedonia, and not likely to be placed in subjection to a diocesan of another region. (3.) It was surrounded by other churches; as we have express mention of the church at Thessalonica and the preaching of the gospel at Berea, (Acts xvii.) (4.) There is mention made of but two orders of men. What the *deacons* were, we know from the appointment in Acts vi. 1–6. They were designated, not to preach, but to take care of the poor members of the church, and to distribute the alms of the saints. As we have there, in the original appointment of the office, the express and extended mention of its functions, we are to infer that the design was the same at Philippi. If we admit, however, the supposition of the Episcopalians, that the deacons were *preachers*, it will not at all affect our argument. The other class, therefore, the "bishops," constitute the preaching order, or the clergy,—those to whom were committed the preaching of the word, the administration of the sacraments, and of the discipline of the church. Now, either these bishops were *prelates*, or they were the *pastors*, the *presbyters* of the church. If Episcopalians choose to say that they were *prelates*, then it follows, (*a*) that there was a plurality of such prelates in the same diocese, and the same city, and the same church; which is contrary to the fundamental idea of Episcopacy. It follows, also, (*b*) that there is entirely wanting, in this church, the "second order" of clergy; that an Episcopal church is organized, defective in one of the essential grades, with an appointment of a body of prelates, without presbyters; that is, an order of "superior" men, designated to exercise jurisdiction over "priests" who had no existence. If it be said that the "presbyters," or "second order," might have been there, though Paul did not expressly name them, then we are presented with the remarkable fact, that he specifies the *deacons*, an inferior order, and expresses to them his Christian salutations; that he salutes and addresses also the saints, and yet entirely disregards those who had the special pastoral charge of the church. Paul thus becomes a model of disrespect and incivility. In the Epistles to Timothy, he gives him directions about every thing else, but no counsel about his brother prelates: in the epistles to the churches, he salutes their prelates and their *deacons*, but becomes utterly regardless of the "second order of clergy," the immediate pastors of the churches.

But if our Episcopal brethren prefer to say that the "bishops," here, mean, not prelates, but presbyters, we, so far, shall agree with them; and then it follows, (*a*) That here is an undeniable instance of a church, or rather a *group* of churches, large enough to satisfy the desire of any diocesan bishop for extended jurisdiction, organized without any prelate. None is mentioned; and there are but two orders of men to whom the care of the "saints at Philippi" is intrusted. (*b*) If there was a prelate there, then, we ask, why Paul did not refer to him, with affectionate salutations? Why does he refer to "the second and the third orders of clergy," without the slightest reference to the man who was "superior to them in ministerial rank and power?" Was Paul jealous of the prelate? or have we here *another* instance of indecorum and incivility? (*c*) If they had had a prelate, and the see was now vacant, why is there no reference to this fact? why no condolence at their loss? why no prayer that God would send them a man to enter into the vacant diocese? (*d*) Episcopalians have sometimes felt the pressure of these difficulties to be so great, that they have supposed the prelate to have been absent when this Epistle was addressed to the church at Philippi; and, that this was the reason why he was not remembered in the salutation. Of this solution, we observe only, that, like *some* other of their arguments, it is mere assumption. And even granting this assumption, it is an inquiry of not very easy solution, why Paul did not make some reference to this fact, and ask their prayers for the absent prelate. One can scarcely help being forcibly reminded, by the ineffectual efforts of Episcopalians to find a prelate at Philippi, of a remarkable transaction mentioned 1 Kings xviii. 27, 28, to which we need only refer our readers. It is scarcely necessary to add, that if a single church is proved to have been organized without the "*three* orders of clergy," the parity of the ministry is made out by apostolic appointment, and the Episcopal argument is at an end.

We may add, that our view of the organization of the church in Philippi, is confirmed by an examination of the organization of the church in its immediate neighbourhood, in Thessalonica. In the two epistles which Paul directed to that church, there is not the slightest reference to any prelatical bishop; there is no mention of "three orders of clergy;" there is no hint that the church was organized on that plan. But *one* order of ministers is mentioned, evidently as entitled to the same respect, and as on an entire equality. They were men, clearly of the same rank, and engaged in discharging the functions of the same office: "And we beseech you, brethren, to know them which labour among you, and are over you in the Lord, and admonish you; and to esteem them very highly in love, for their work's sake." 1 Thess. v. 12, 13. Will our Episcopal friends be kind enough to inform us why there is no mention of the prelate, whether present or absent?

We are here prepared to estimate the force of the undeniable fact that there is no distinction of grade or rank by the *names* which are given to the ministers of the gospel in the New Testament. It is admitted by Episcopalians themselves that the names bishop, presbyter, etc. in the Bible, do not denote those ranks of church officers to which they are now applied, but are given indiscriminately to all. On this point we have the authority of Dr. Onderdonk. "The *name* 'bishop,'" says he, "which now designates the highest grade of the ministry, *is not appropriated to this office in Scripture.* That name is given to the middle order, or presbyters; and ALL THAT WE READ IN THE NEW TESTAMENT CONCERNING 'BISHOPS,' (including, of course, the words 'overseers' and 'oversight,' which have the same derivation,) IS TO BE REGARDED AS PERTAINING TO THIS MIDDLE GRADE." (Tract, p. 12.) "Another irregularity of the same kind occurs in regard to the word 'elder.' It is sometimes used for a minister, or clergyman of any grade, higher, middle, or lower; but it more strictly signifies a presbyter." Tract, p. 14.

In accordance with this fact, which is as remarkable as it is true, we have seen that Peter applies to himself the name of presbyter, and puts himself on a level with other presbyters:

"The presbyters which are among you I *exhort*, (not, I *command*, or *enjoin*, as a prelate would do,) who am also a presbyter." 1 Pet. v. 1. And in the very next verse, he exhorts them (the elders or presbyters) to "feed the flock of God, taking the oversight, (ἐπισκοποῦντες, exercising the office of bishop,) not by constraint," etc.

Now let these conceded facts be borne in mind. The term presbyter is applied to the apostles: "All that we read of in the New Testament concerning 'bishops,' is applied to the middle grade." The apostles address each other, and their brethren, by the same terms—by no words or names that indicate rank, or grade, or authority. We maintain that this fact can be accounted for, only on the supposition that they regarded themselves as ministers, as *on a level*. If they meant to teach that one class was superior in rank and power to others, we maintain that they would *not* have used terms *always* confounding such distinctions, and *always* proceeding on the supposition that they were on an equality. It will not be pretended that they *could* not employ terms that would have marked the various grades. For if the term "bishop" can now do it, it could have done it then; if the term presbyter can now be used to denote "the middle grade," it could then have been so used. We maintain, too, that if such *had* been their intention, they would have thus employed those terms. That the sacred writers were *capable* of using language definitely, Dr. Onderdonk will not doubt. Why, then, if they *were* capable, did they choose *not* to do it? Are Episcopal bishops, now, ever as vague and indefinite in their use of the terms "bishop" and "presbyters," as were the apostles? Why were the latter so undesirous of having "the pre-eminence?" 3 John, 9.

It is remarkable that the mode of using these terms in the New Testament is precisely in accordance with the usage in Presbyterian and Congregational churches. *They* speak, just as the sacred writers did, of their ministers indiscriminately as "bishops," as "pastors," as "teachers," as "evangelists." *They* regard their ministers as on an equality. Did not the sacred writers do the same?

It is *as* remarkable, that the mode of using these terms in the Episcopal churches is NOT, *ex concessis*, that which occurs in the Bible. And it is *as* certain that *were* they thus to use those terms, it would *at once* confound their orders and ranks, and reduce their ministers to equality. Do we ever see any approximation, in their addresses and in their canons, in this respect, to the language and style of the New Testament? Do we ever hear of Bishop Tyng, or Bishop Hawkes, or Bishop Schroeder, or Bishop Croswell? Do we ever hear of Presbyter Ives, or Doane, or Onderdonk? How would language like this sound in the mouth of a prelatical bishop? Would not all men be amazed, as if some new thing had happened under the sun, in the Episcopal Church? And yet, we venture to presume that the terms used in the New Testament, to designate any office, may be used still. We shall still choose to call things by their true names, and to apply to all ranks and orders of men the terms which are applied to them by the spirit of inspiration. And as the indiscriminate use of these terms is carefully avoided by the customs and canons of the Episcopal Church; as there seems to have been a presentiment in the formation of those canons, that such indiscriminate use would reduce the fabric to simple "parity" of the clergy; and as these terms *cannot* be so used, without reducing these "ranks and orders" to a scriptural equality, we come to the conclusion that the apostles *meant* to teach that the ministers of the New Testament are equal in ministerial rights and powers.

We have now gone through this entire subject. We have examined, we trust, in a candid manner,—we are sure with the kindest feelings towards our Episcopal brethren,—every argument which they have to adduce from the Bible in favour of the claims of their bishops. We have disposed of these arguments, step by step. We have done this, remembering that these are ALL the arguments which Episcopacy has to urge from the Bible. There is nothing that remains. The subject is exhausted. Episcopacy rests here. And it is incumbent on Episcopacy to *show*, not to *affirm*, that our interpretation of those passages is not sustained by sound principles of exegesis.

The burden of proof still lies on them. They assumed it, and on them it rests. They affirm that enormous powers are lodged in the hands of the prelate—every thing pertaining to ordination, to discipline, to the superintendence of the Christian church. They claim powers tending to degrade every presbyter in the world to the condition of a dependent and inferior office; stripping him of the right of transmitting his own office, and of administering discipline among his own flock. They arrogate powers which go to strip all other presbyters, except Episcopalian, of any right to officiate in the church of God; rendering their ordination invalid, their administrations void, and their exercise of the functions of their office a daring and impious invasion of the rights of the priesthood, and a violation of the law of Christ. The foundation for these sweeping, and certainly not very modest claims, we have examined with all freedom. At the conclusion we may ask any person of plain, common sense, to place his finger on that portion of the book of God which is favourable to Prelacy.

The argument for Prelacy having been met and disproved, we have produced an instance of express Presbyterian ordination, in the case of Timothy. Two churches we have found that were organized without prelates. We are thus, by another train of argument, conducted to the same result—that prelates are unknown in the New Testament. And to make our argument perfectly conclusive, we have shown that the *same titles* are applied indiscriminately to all.

Our argument may be stated in still fewer words. The Episcopal claims are *not* made out; and, of course, the clergy of the New Testament are equal. The Episcopalian has failed to show that there were *different* grades; and it follows that there must be *parity*. We have examined the only case of ordination specified in the New Testament, and the constitution of the churches, and find that it *is* so; and we are conducted inevitably to the conclusion that Prelacy is not in the Bible.

We now take our leave of the Episcopal controversy. As Episcopacy has nothing which it *can* add to the scriptural argument, we regard our labours in this department as at end. The whole *scriptural* argument is exhausted, and here *our* inquiry ends, and here *our* interest in this topic ceases. We take leave of the subject with the same kind feelings for that church, and the same respect for the author of the "Tract," with which we began the inquiry. We remember the former services which the Episcopal Church rendered to the cause of truth, and of the world's redemption; we remember the bright and ever-living lights of truth which her clergy and her illustrious laymen have, in other times, enkindled in the darkness of this world's history, and which continue to pour their pure and steady lustre on the literature, the laws, and the customs of the Christian world; and we trust the day will never come when our own bosoms, or the bosoms of Christians in any denomination, will cease to beat with emotions of lofty thanksgiving to the God of grace that he raised up such gifted and holy men, to meet the corruptions of the Papacy and to breast the wickedness of the world.

In our view of ecclesiastical polity, we can have no unkind feelings toward any branch of the true church of God. We strive to cherish feelings of affectionate regard for them all, and to render praise to the common Father of Christians, for any efforts which are made to promote the intelligence, the purity, and the salvation of mankind. In our views of the nature of mind and of freedom, we can have no unkind feelings toward any denomination of true Christians. "There are diversities of gifts, but the same spirit. And there are differences of administrations, but the same Lord. And there are diversities of operations, but it is the same God which worketh all in all." We have no expectation that all men in this world will think alike. And we regard it as a wise arrangement that the church of God is thus organized into different sections and departments, under the banner of the common captain of their salvation. It promotes inquiry. It prevents complacency in mere forms and ceremonies. It produces healthy and vigorous emulation. It affords opportunities for all classes of minds to arrange themselves according to their preferences and their habits of thought. And it is not unfavourable to that kindness of feeling which the Christian can cherish, and should cherish, when he utters in the sanctuary the article of his faith—"I believe in the holy catholic church, the communion of saints." The attachment of a soldier to a particular company or squadron need not diminish his respect for the armies of his country, or extinguish his love of her liberty. Being joined to a company of infantry, need not make me feel that the cavalry are useless, or involve me in a controversy with the artillery.

We ask only that Episcopacy should not assume arrogant claims; that she should be willing to take her place among other denominations of Christians, entitled to like respect as others, to all the tender and sympathetic affections of the Christian brotherhood; and willing that others should walk in the liberty wherewith Christ has made his people free. We shall have no contest with our Episcopal brethren for loving the church of their choice, and the church in which they seek to prepare themselves for heaven. We shall not utter the language of unkindness, for their reverencing the ministerial office in which the spirits of Cranmer and Leighton were prepared for their eternal rest. Content that other denominations should enjoy like freedom, while they do not arrogate to themselves unholy claims, and attempt to "lord it over" other parts "of God's heritage," we shall pray for their success, and rejoice in their advancement. But the moment they cross this line; the moment they make any advances which resemble those of the Papacy; the moment they set up the claim of being the only "primitive and apostolical church;" and the moment they speak of the "invalid ministry" and the "invalid ordinances" of other churches, and regard them as "left to the uncovenanted mercies of God,"—that moment the language of argument and of Christian rebuke may properly be heard from every other denomination. There *are* minds that can investigate the Bible as well as the advocates for Episcopacy; there are pens that can compete with any found in the Episcopal Church; and there are men who will not be slow to rebuke the first appearance of arrogance and of lordly assumption, and who will remind them that the time has gone by when an appeal to the infallible church will answer in this controversy. Arrogant assumptions, they will be at once reminded, do not suit the present state of intelligence in this land, or the genius of our institutions. While the Episcopal Church shall seek, by kind and gentle means, to widen its influence, like the flowing of a river, or like the dews of heaven, we shall hail its advances; when she departs from this course, and seeks to utter the language of authority and denunciation,—to prostrate other churches as with the sweepings of the mountain-torrent,—she will be checked by all the intelligence and piety of this land; and she will be reminded by a voice uttered from all the institutions of these times, that Episcopacy has had its reign of *authority* in the dark ages and at the Vatican; and that the very genius of Protestantism is, *that one church is not to utter the language of arrogance over another; and that not authority or denunciation, but* SCRIPTURAL EXPOSITION, *is to determine which is in accordance with the book of God.*

VII.

[NEW ENGLANDER, 1844.]

The Position of the Evangelical Party in the Episcopal Church.

It is from no desire to intermeddle with the internal affairs of another denomination of Christians, that we introduce to our readers the subject which we have placed at the head of this article. Nor is it from any wish to take advantage of the present troubles and growing dissensions of the Episcopal Church to make converts to our better faith, or to make reprisals for the accessions which they have sought to gain from the disputes and divisions of other denominations. We have listened in calmer times with proper interest to their proclamations of their own unity, while other churches have been rent into factions or threatened with schism. We have seen a few from other churches, charmed with this proclamation of unity, and professedly won by the hope of peace, leave the connections in which they were trained, and attach themselves to Episcopacy. But they have not been men whose departure the churches have had occasion to regard as a serious calamity, or whose recovery would be worth any very serious effort. We are content that they should minister in their new connection, we hope with greater success than was promised in their former relations, and with all the peace and comfort which it may be possible for them now to obtain.

We feel that we have a right to advert to this subject only so far as it pertains to the cause of our common Christianity. In their internal affairs; their questions of precedency and order; their family affections or alienations; their domestic difficulties, troubles, or joys; their questions about the relative rights and powers of bishops, priests, deacons, or laymen, we claim no right and have no disposition to interfere. The limits of courtesy and propriety on such matters are settled. With the domestic concerns of a neighbour—the family jars, loves, alienations, modes of living, style of dress, or intercourse—we have no right to intermeddle. It is their own concern, and they have a right to manage it their own way. We are not to be "busybodies in other men's matters." We are not to attempt to foment divisions; or to aggravate a family quarrel; or to utter the note of triumph over their dissensions—though it should be to meet and ward off reproaches on account of our own; nor are we to interfere with a view of encouraging a feebler party against a stronger, in order to prolong the strife and rend the family asunder, or to make needless proclamation of what we may happen to know of the family jar. We go even farther than this. We should not feel ourselves at liberty in such a domestic difficulty to lend our aid or to give our counsel to one of the parties that we regarded as indubitably right, and that held opinions in accordance with our own, in order to prolong the difficulties there, or to prevent a reconciliation in any way which they might regard as proper.

But there is a sense in which this becomes a matter of common interest, and in reference to which there is common ground. If the community is to be affected by this difference, we have a right to express our views. If there are common interests pertaining to the good order of society that are in danger of suffering, we have a right to lift up the voice in their defence. If principles are advanced by either party which may affect the welfare of the community, we are not at liberty to be silent. If the difficulty is the regular and inevitable result of certain views which both parties publicly proclaim that they hold, we have a right to say so. And if one party is aiming at an impracticable thing; endeavouring, though in the most peaceful manner, and with the purest motives, to maintain principles and to accomplish objects which are in their nature wholly at variance with those on which the family has been uniformly administered, and to which that party also has solemnly expressed its assent, we do not suppose that we are forbidden by any law of courtesy to express our convictions on these points, and to endeavour to derive from this inevitable want of harmony lessons that shall be of value to the common cause.

Such we consider to be the present condition of the Episcopal Church. A crisis has occurred in that communion such as it could have been foreseen, by a moderate measure of sagacity, must sooner or later occur, and which, however it may be for a time suppressed, we venture to foretell will in some form continue to break out, until "the church" is thoroughly reformed and Prelacy abandoned.

In the controversy now waging there, the great interests of our common Christianity are affected. There are momentous questions at stake in which all who love the religion of the Saviour are interested. There are points of much more importance than any which can be raised about the qualifications of Mr. Arthur Carey for the "diaconate." There are questions respecting the working of the system; its fitness to promote unity; the measures which are adopted to secure harmony; the effect of those measures in suppressing the truth, preventing free discussion, and fostering error; and, above all, the general effect of the system of Episcopacy on evangelical religion, which it is the duty of every man who conceives it possible—as it may be—that he or any one of his friends should be invited to become an Episcopalian, to examine, and which the present outbreak furnishes an appropriate opportunity to examine. We have never had any sympathy for Prelacy. We have never believed that it was the form of religion prescribed in the New Testament. We have always regarded it as a system adapted to cramp and crush the free spirit of the gospel. But we have had no doubt that there were many of the intelligent and the good among the followers of the Lord Jesus who regarded it conscientiously as the system prescribed in the Bible; and we have supposed that there *were* minds so formed that they would be better edified in connection with that form of religion than under a different method of organization. We think the time now has come to examine the influence of that system on evangelical religion; and in order to make our inquiry definite, we propose to inquire into the present position of the evangelical, or as it is often called, the low-church party in the Episcopal Church. We shall inquire whether the objects at which they aim can be secured in that communion, or whether they do not necessarily meet with obstructions in the organization of the Episcopal Church which will certainly prevent the accomplishment of those objects; whether there are not in their forms of worship things which will inevitably cramp and crush the free spirit of religion; and whether the Episcopal Church is not so organized as effectually to secure the ultimate ascendency of the objects aimed at by the high-church party. In other words, the question is, whether Tractarianism is not a fair development of the system, and whether those views, if the present organization of that church should be continued, are not destined to be ultimately triumphant.

It is well known that there have been, perhaps from the commencement of its existence in this country, two parties in the Episcopal Church. These parties are generally known by the names of the high and the low church—or, as the latter prefer, we believe, to be called, the evangelical—party. These parties have grown up, not from the nature of Prelacy, or by any tendency in the Episcopal Church to foster the aims sought by the evangelical party, but from the contact of Episcopacy with the spirit of our age, and with the free developments of Christianity among the other denominations with whom Episcopalians come necessarily in contact. It is possible that the germs of these parties existed in the Episcopal Church in its incipient state in this country; but that which has now grown up into the evangelical party, we suppose would have been suppressed by the overshadowing of the religion of forms, if it had not been excited and kindled by the reflected influence on the Episcopal Church of the views and objects of evangelical Christians in other denominations. It has been apparent that other denominations greatly surpassed the Episcopal communion in zeal for those things specially commended in the New Testament; that they sought a more spiritual religion than had been common in the Episcopal communion; that they aimed more to convert and save the souls of men; and that they sought in methods that had the undoubted sanction of the New Testament, to spread the gospel around the globe. The question arose whether these objects could not be grafted on Episcopacy, and whether without producing schism, and with the maintenance of the highest respect for Prelacy and for the forms of religion, it was not possible to introduce the evangelical spirit into the bosom of the Episcopal Church, and to add to what was regarded as the nobleness, venerableness, and authority of her ancient forms, the life and vigour, and elastic energy which reigns with such power in other denominations. If so, it seems to have been supposed that there might be urged in favour of Prelacy all that is now urged from the necessity of the "apostolic succession;" all the authority of the Fathers; all its boasted power to preserve the unity of the church; and all the advantages derived from a staid and regular organization, united with all that commends evangelical religion to the hearts and consciences of men. It is not to be denied that there have been and are still in the bosom of the Episcopal Church men who strive sincerely, and with a zeal not surpassed by those of other denominations, for the conversion of souls. They are men who would do honour to any cause, and whose life and labours would be a blessing to any communion. It is this party which has endeavoured to engraft the spirit of evangelical religion on the forms of Prelacy; and it is to their holy and devoted efforts that the result has already more than once occurred that the Episcopal Church has been in danger of being rent in twain. It is not that they have *aimed at* such a disruption, but it has been the kind of danger which would exist in a statue of marble that a fissure would be caused by applying intense heat to one portion and not to the other. It has required all the power of numbers, influence, and prelatical authority on the part of the high-church party, united with all the veneration of the low-church party for the church and her forms, to prevent such a rupture. Thus far this has been successful, and in every controversy of this kind the high-church party has secured the victory, and the unity of the church has been preserved. We think the history thus far furnishes an omen of most portentous character in regard to the issue of such contentions at present and in all time to come. We have no expectation that the low-church party will ever gain the ascendency, or carry ultimately a single point. Our reasons for this opinion will be seen in the progress of our remarks.

The present position of the parties in the Episcopal Church is not determined precisely by the different views which characterize the high church and the evangelical party. There has been to some extent a breaking up of the old lines of demarcation, and a somewhat modified arrangement. The controversy respecting Puseyism is not precisely the same as the controversy which has hitherto prevailed. To a superficial observer it might have been anticipated, perhaps, that the low-church party would have been found, without an exception, arrayed against the doctrines of the Tractarians, and that the high-church portion would have been as uniformly friendly to the Oxford theology. But this, if we correctly understand the matter, has not been precisely the case. A portion of those who have been regarded as high church have made as strenuous opposition to the advances of this system as have been witnessed in any other quarter; and some who have been regarded as leaders of the evangelical party have shown a decided inclination to vindicate the most arrogant form in which the spirit of the Oxford theology could manifest itself in this free country. Those of the high church, moreover, who have resisted these aggressions, have shown no more affinity for the evangelical portion than they did before. In the possible, but not probable, event of a rupture in the Episcopal Church, they would undoubtedly be found ranged with the friends of the Tractarian cause—no matter what their arrogance, and no matter how near they approximate to Rome, rather than with the evangelical party. This they would do, not because they love Puseyism *more*, but because they love the low-church principles *less*. We apprehend also, that, if the question of a possible rupture should actually come up in the Episcopal Church, it would be found that rather than such a crisis should occur, what there is of the evangelical spirit in the other party would be suppressed or crushed, rather than that matters should come to such a result. Such is the inborn horror in the mind of a genuine Episcopalian at the very word *schism*—though the whole system of Episcopacy is a schism of the worst kind from the proper sense of the unity of the church; such the love of forms and of order; such the desire not to expose themselves to the possible danger of vitiating the "succession;" and such the belief, in spite of experience, that the free-born spirit of

Christianity *may* live and breathe under all the incumbent pressure of these antiquated forms, and may move on to the conquest of the world, fettered and manacled as it must be, that these difficulties with Puseyism would be greatly diminished in their view, and that no one would dare to mention the word *separation.*

But our business now is not directly with Puseyism. We wish to refer to the lines which existed before the slight irregularity in the ranks of the parties, caused by the prevalence of the Tractarian theology, occurred. The characteristics of the two parties before the present difficulties arose in the Episcopal Church, we shall proceed to state as we understand them.

The views of the high-church party are accurately defined, and the points in which they differ from their low-church brethren, as well as from all the denominations of evangelical Christians, are well understood. They have never made any secret of them, and have never propounded them as if they wished to practice any concealment, or regarded them as mysteries to be made known only to the initiated. They hold, if we understand them aright, to the necessity of an actual, uninterrupted succession from the apostles, in order to the validity of the ministry. They hold, that the ministry of the church consists of three orders, and that the supremacy is in the bishop; that all the power of ordaining is in him, and that no one has any right to officiate as a minister of religion in any form, except in virtue of the imposition of his hands. They hold, that to him alone appertains the right of confirmation; and that grace, quite desirable, if not essential to salvation, is conveyed by that rite. They hold, that there is no church but the Episcopal Church, and that in any other body of persons there is no valid ministry, and that there are no valid sacraments. They hold to the doctrine of baptismal regeneration, and to the efficacy of the sacraments by some kind of *opus operatum.* They hold, that those who have been baptized in a proper manner are to be brought to the bishop and confirmed, as soon as they can say the creed, the Lord's prayer, and the catechism, and are to be admitted to the church without any special inquiry into their spiritual state, or without giving any distinct evidence of a change of heart. They hold, that such is the efficacy of baptism thus administered, of confirmation, of the observance of the eucharist, and of a connection with the true apostolical church, that by this process their salvation will be secure.

They are opposed to revivals of religion, as the term is commonly employed; to prayer-meetings; to "night-services," and to all "voluntary" societies for the spread of the gospel. They utterly refuse, as a body, to give the Bible without the Prayer-book, and religiously abstain from all connection with any association for promoting any religious object out of "*the* church." They take no part in a Bible, Sunday-school, tract, or missionary society, where persons of other denominations are concerned in the directorship, or where their appearance could be construed as an admission that other denominations appertain to the church of Christ. They are seen on no platform mingling with other Christians in the promotion of the common cause; and neither by their contributions, their presence, nor their names, do they lend any countenance to any meeting or association which can be construed as a union of different denominations of Christians for any object whatever. As members of the church of Christ, as ministers of his religion, they hold that there can be no common ground on which they can meet others. As citizens, as neighbours, as friends of literature, as those who may be engaged in the business of mending a road, or building a bridge, they may be connected with others, because these things cannot be Episcopally done; but they go no farther.

Not even in the temperance cause will they associate with others. Of this we know not exactly the reason, whether they are unfriendly to temperance principles themselves, or whether they regard temperance as a part of religion, and consider that it is not desirable to promote it except somehow through the apostolic succession. We do not recollect that they have given to the public an opportunity of forming an opinion on these points.

As a consequence of these views, they regard all other associations of men, however numerous and respectable, as left "to the uncovenanted mercies of God." They are in this respect on the same platform with the Jew and the Mussulman; the Japanese and the Caffrarian. From the true church they are "dissenters." They are without valid ordinances, without a valid ministry, and without the promises. They meet in conventicles, not in churches; they listen to the arguings of laymen, not to the teachings of the authorized ministers of religion. They are sprinkled in infancy, or immersed in riper years, by those who have no authority for doing either; they partake of bread and wine which in nowise differs from common bread and wine, except that they are taken in smaller quantities and in a "meeting-house;" they are ministered unto by those who would commit sacrilege by putting on the surplice or by going into a pulpit duly consecrated; and they are buried in ground that has never been consecrated, and by those who, as they have no right to address the living in the name of Christ, have no right to officiate at the graves of the dead. They *may* indeed be saved—but who may not be? God is merciful, and they have the same chance of salvation that the better part of the heathen have—and no other. These, if we understand them, are the leading views of the high-church party. We have designed not to do injustice to them, and we have the means of substantiating the correctness of this representation by the highest authorities in the Episcopal Church.*

The views of the low-church or evangelical party are not less accurately defined. In most of those things which characterize the high church they are united with them. They are not "a whit behind the chiefest" of that party in the belief of the apostolic succession; in glorifying the Prayer-book; in attachment to "*the* church;" in the faith that a valid ministry is found only in connection with Prelacy; and in strenuous endeavours to promote the interests of the Episcopal sect. They do no more than the highest Puseyite would do in recognising the ministers of another denomination as authorized to preach the gospel, or to administer the sacraments. They never invite them to preach, and never appear with them in any such connection as to show that they regard them as the ministers of the Lord Jesus. They

---

* To the view here presented, that the tendency of the high-church opinions is to "unchurch" all others, justice requires that we should notice one exception. It is the only one which has fallen under our observation. It is that of the Rev. H. U. Onderdonk, D.D., of the diocese of Pennsylvania. He says, (Tract on Episcopacy,) "By the present writer this consequence" [that of unchurching other denominations] "is not allowed." He states no reasons why it is *not* allowed, nor does he attempt to show how this admission of the fact that others are not unchurched, is consistent with certain principles which he has laid down. We have never been able to make out the consistency of the admission with the views which he defends in that "Tract," and we merely record it as a *fact* which we regard as an exception to the general views of that party. We see no way of explaining it, except by ascribing it to the promptings of a heart of kindness, which shrank from the conclusion to which his reasoning was tending, and which led him to express the feeling of charity even at the sacrifice of logic. Such an expression of feeling we will always honour, wherever we find it. We only wish, as the feeling is undoubtedly right, that the logic in the Tract had been such as would have been consistent with it. Is that logic likely to be correct, which would require a man either to suppress such a feeling, or to give vent to it in the face of all his reasoning?

recognise their baptism no more, we believe, than they would that of laymen, and, in common with their high-church brethren, they expect that those who come among them from other churches, if private members, will submit to the rite of confirmation; if ministers, that they will abjure their former ordination, and submit to the imposition of the hands of the prelate. We do not know that in a single instance they have ever protested against this as improper, or even hinted that they regarded the previous ordination as differing in any way from lay-ordination. While they allow one who has been ordained by papal hands to minister at their altars without being reordained, and offer no remonstrance against it, we suppose that there is not a low-church minister in this land who would not be shocked if a Presbyterian minister should be admitted to the rank of a "priest," or even of a "deacon," without being reordained. We think, too, that they are *as* zealous for the Episcopal Church, and for its up-building, as any high churchman can be. It is an object never lost sight of by an Episcopalian; and whatever may be the place in which he is ranked in his controversy between the high and low church, or in the disputes respecting the Oxford theology; and whatever may be the style of his inter-course with other denominations, the obligation to remember the interests of the Episcopal Church is never for a moment forgotten.

But with these views the low churchman has endeavoured to blend certain others, in which he greatly diverges from his high-church brethren, and in which he assimilates himself to other denominations. He does not believe in the efficacy of forms for justification. He does not believe in baptismal regeneration. He holds to the doctrine of regeneration by the agency of the Holy Spirit; to justification solely by faith; to sanctification, not by any *opus operatum* of the sacraments, but by the word and Spirit of God; to the necessity of spiritual religion; to the duties of a holy life; to the obligations of steady self-denial and a separation from the world. He believes that they who come to the Lord's table *should be* converted as a qualification, not that they should come *to be* converted. He claims the right of *not* "bringing those to the bishop to be confirmed" whom he does not regard as having evidence of true conversion. He would guard the church from the admission to its ordinances of any who do not give evidence of true piety.

The low churchman is, in general, a Calvinist, and frequently of the highest order. He preaches the humbling doctrines of the cross, and advocates the lofty themes of Divine sovereignty in the salvation of men.

The low churchman believes in the necessity of special efforts for the salvation of men. He believes that prayer-meetings are adapted to promote the edification of believers, and to secure the salvation of sinners. He is no enemy of "night meetings," and is so much the friend of "protracted efforts," that he unites cheerfully in "associations" with his own brethren, and in Episcopal churches, and seeks to turn the bad and unauthorized arrangements of his own church, for the observance of saints' days, and especially of Lent, into a series of protracted preaching efforts to promote revivals of religion.

The low churchman is one who is willing to act with the friends of religion, where he can meet them on common ground. He is willing to engage in the circulation of the Bible, though it have not the Prayer-book attached to it—reserving his zeal for the latter to be manifested through a society in his own church specially organized for that purpose, and reserving to himself the right to manifest as much zeal for that as shall seem to him to be meet. He is willing to act with others in the distribution of tracts on the common topics of religion, and in the establishment of Sabbath-schools, even should they not be connected with the Episcopal denomination.

In the cause of temperance, of the Sabbath, of promoting the gospel among seamen—and in opposition to the arrogancy and the aggressions of the Papacy, he will meet with other Christians in the same committee-room, or on the same platform, but never *as* clergymen, or in such a way as to imply that those with whom he associates are to be regarded as authorized ministers of the gospel.

We see thus in the Episcopal Church two distinct classes of men—classes that must, from the nature of the case, come into frequent collision. We propose now to examine the position of the latter class, especially in regard to their relation to their own church, and to the question whether they can ever succeed in the objects at which they aim. We regard the question as one of great interest and importance, not doubtful in our minds as to the issue, but as a struggle throwing light on the nature of religion, and as adapted to aid us in determining whether Prelacy is the form of religion that is revealed in the New Testament. If the experiment should be successful, it would do something to make us less doubtful whether the ministry was organized with "the three orders;" —if it always has been and must be a failure, it is to us a clear demonstration that the church was organized on some other foundation.

We need not say that in the main our sympathies are wholly with the low-church party. With the aim of the other party we have none; but the low-church party, so far as they differ from their brethren in the Episcopal communion, are aiming at the same objects as all the rest of the evangelical world, and are endeavouring to promote those views of religion which, we believe, will ultimately triumph. The question with us is not whether the objects at which they thus aim are right, and will ultimately be somehow secured on the earth, but whether the Episcopal Church can be imbued with these principles, and whether they will triumph in the controversies which inevitably arise in their own denomination. Now, in reference to this question, we shall state freely some views which seem to us to put this question to rest.

The first is, that the object at which they aim has never yet been accomplished. The experience of the world has been against it. We state a position here which we think is the result of all experiments, and which we challenge the advocate of Episcopacy to refute. It is, THAT IT HAS NEVER BEEN POSSIBLE PERMANENTLY TO CONNECT THE RELIGION OF FORMS WITH EVANGELICAL RELIGION; or, what amounts to the same thing, that the Episcopal mode of worship has been permanently blended with the objects at which the low churchman aims. We will first refer to a few facts sustaining this position. We shall then take occasion to show why it is so.

The attempt to unite the religion of forms with the gospel, has often been made. There have been good men connected with every form of worship. There have been in all ages of the church men who have held to the doctrines of grace; men who believed in all that constitutes evangelical religion; men holding to the entire depravity of man, the doctrine of regeneration by the agency of the Holy Spirit, the necessity of holy living and of a close walk with God—who have endeavoured to unite these things with the religion of forms. There have been, as there are now, those who have been warm friends of prayer-meetings, and of revivals, and of efforts to spread the gospel around the world, who have sighed for the spirit of freedom amid the pompous and imposing ceremonials of the worship of forms. They have loved sincerely the forms of religion; and they have loved, with an ardour which nothing could extinguish, the pure doctrines of grace and the holy aspiration of Christianity. Trained in the bosom of a church prescribing pomp and splendour in public worship, they have brought to its favour all the prejudices of education; accustomed to use a Prayer-book from childhood, they love it as they do the home and the companions of their youth; sincerely believing that Episcopacy is the form of worship prescribed in the New Testament, they have become bound to it by all the strength of conscience; or in lands where this is prescribed by statute, and where it is the religion of the state, they have felt that every thing of a temporal nature depended on adhesion to it, and have sincerely desired its perpetuity. At the same time they have loved evangelical religion. They have believed that it is the religion of the Bible. They have not doubted that it would finally prevail. They have sought, therefore, to spread its spirit in the bosom of the Episcopal Church. What now has been the lesson which history has taught us in regard to the relation of the religion of forms to evangelical religion?

The Jewish religion, in the time of the Saviour, was a religion of forms. It had a strong resemblance, in many respects, to Episcopacy; and indeed Episcopacy has avowedly borrowed much from it, and often defends itself by a reference to the divinely-appointed pomp and pageantry of the temple service. There were, in the time of the Saviour, as there always had been, some pure worshippers of God in connection with that system; for Zecharias and Simeon, Anna, Elizabeth, and Mary were of that number. But the Saviour originated the evangelical system, and detached it at once, wholly and forever, from the Jewish forms. He severed his whole church from it; required his people to come out of it; pronounced his gospel to be free, and never meant that its freedom should be cramped by the religion of forms. The rites which he appointed for his religion were as few as possible, and the most simple that can be conceived. He designated but two as permanent in the church, nor did he appoint any other that can with any propriety be designated as "sacraments," even if these should be. The two which he specified are baptism and the Lord's supper, and we venture to say that if every form of religion ever propounded among men were examined, two more simple or unostentatious rites could not be found. As the rites themselves, also, are the extreme of simplicity, so he made every thing about them as plain as they possibly could be. He prescribed no baptismal font of massive gold, silver, or marble; but the water taken from a running stream, or from a fountain bursting forth in the desert, would answer all the purposes of the emblem. He ordained no splendid communion-service to contain the symbols of his body and blood; but the plainest cup and platter would suit the design. As these rites are as simple as possible, so it was reasonable to suppose that they would be as remote as any could be from abuse. They are the last things on which it could be conceived to be possible to rear a gorgeous superstructure of spiritual pomp and power. Who could have imagined that the simple rite of water baptism could ever be magnified into the doctrine of baptismal regeneration, or could become the instrument of giving dignity and supremacy to the holy hands that were appointed to administer it, and thus of sustaining the arrogant claims of a priesthood in the religion of forms, and be so tortured by the "cunning craftiness" of men, as to be a substitute for the regenerating influences of the Holy Spirit? And what finite mind could have anticipated the history of the Lord's supper? Who could have foreseen what the simple emblems of bread and wine would be made to become when attached to a religion of forms, and what use would be made of them in banishing evangelical religion from the world? Who could have imagined that they would become the principal support of the most extraordinary claims ever set up by a priesthood over men; that the doctrine would be gravely taught and believed, that by words of ceremony they would be changed into "the very body and blood, soul and divinity of the Son of God;" that they would be borne along in gorgeous procession, and that princes and kings would prostrate themselves before them; and that the power of making this wonderful transmutation would be supposed to give to any one class of men a sanctity above all others, and a mysterious connection with the Deity elsewhere unknown among mortals? If rites so simple, and so little susceptible of abuse, have been thus made the means of excluding the agency of the Holy Spirit from the soul, and of establishing the power of the most mighty hierarchy on earth, we see one reason why Christ established no more, and why his whole arrangement was such as most effectually to detach his religion from all connection with the religion of forms. The Jewish religion, eminently a religion of forms, accomplished its object in separating that people from all others, and in adumbrating a future spiritual system. It was adapted to the age of the world during which it was designed to continue, and to the purpose of preparing for a better system; and though it is undeniable that there were holy men under that system, yet its history served, among other instructive lessons, to teach its own tendency to sink into heartless ceremony, and the difficulty of maintaining spiritual religion in connection with forms—and the Saviour, therefore, detached *his* religion from it forever. As soon as possible, the Jewish altar was thrown down, the priests were disrobed of their gorgeous vestments, the smoke of incense ceased to ascend, and the temple itself was demolished to be built no more. The spirit of the gospel separated from forms then, nor was it ever to be united with the pomp and ceremonies of the ancient worship.

From the days of Constantine, Christianity became a religion of forms. But where was the spirit of the gospel? Where during the dark ages did it live? Has it ever been known in permanent connection with the papal communion, or in the Greek, the Armenian, or the Nestorian churches? In all these churches the religion of forms has prevailed, and still prevails, and their history has been characterized by an almost entire separation from the spirit of Christianity. There has been no permanent connection, and if, under the influence of the Spirit of God, there has been at any time a reviving spirit of piety, after a few efforts to diffuse itself through the cold and slumbering church, it has either died away or withdrawn where it could breathe the air of freedom. To see this, let a few facts be submitted to the attention of candid men.

Far back in the history of the papal communion, there was a reviving spirit of the gospel. Some pure spirits arose imbued with the same love of Christ, and feeling the same power of religion, which prevailed in the days of the apostles; but could they blend their religion with the prevailing religion of forms? They withdrew, and in the peaceful valleys of Piedmont the Waldenses worshipped God "in spirit and in truth," until the fires of martyrdom were lighted on all their hills and through all their vales, by the advocates of the religion of forms, and Rome succeeded in nearly exterminating them.

Again the spirit of vital piety was rekindled in the bosom of the papal church. Simultaneously, and without concert, a heavenly influence breathed upon the souls of Zuingle, of Luther, of Melancthon, and of Farel. They were all in the bosom of the papal church; all had been reared in connection with the religion of forms; all had every thing to lose and nothing to gain by a separation; and all by a separation exposed themselves to the thunders of the Vatican —the fearful power that could shake the thrones of princes and cause monarchs to turn pale in their palaces. Yet, with every inducement from education, from their belief of the heavenly origin of the Papacy, from the love of peace, and from the dread of martyrdom, to remain in the bosom of the papal communion, an attempt to blend the spirit of the gospel that now filled their hearts with holy fire, with the cold spirit of the religion of forms, was hopeless—and hence the Reformation. In Germany, in Switzerland, and in France, as far as the Reformation extended, there was a final separation of the two; nor was there any power of argument, or art, or interest, or arms, that could there unite them.

In England the experiment was to be tried in another manner, and with a much better prospect of success. It was the experiment that was made under Henry VIII., Edward VI., and Elizabeth. There was the genuine spirit of the Reformation in the Anglican church. It reigned not indeed either in the heart of Henry or Elizabeth, but it did in the heart of Edward, and more illustriously still in the hearts of Latimer, Ridley, Bradford, and Cranmer, and with these men there was a sincere effort to blend the two together. There was every facility for making the experiment in as satisfactory a manner as possible. Every thing in the protection of the laws—in the power of talent, eloquence, learning, and piety, that could be demanded for the successful prosecution of the effort, existed, nor could circumstances ever be well imagined that were more favourable to success. What was the result? It is before the world, and the world has it by heart. The Puritan spirit gradually rose and increased. It became chafed, and galled, and was impatient under the fetters of form. It sighed for freedom; and in a single day two thousand of the best men in the English church left their livings—exposed themselves to poverty, persecution, and imprisonment, only because the spirit of the gospel could not be permanently blended with the religion of forms Part of those men went to prison; all were subjected to privations and sorrows in their external circumstances;—but the evangelical spirit was free, and the "church" was left a cold, dead, dull, formal thing. The vital power of the Episcopal communion had withdrawn, and there were no earthly temptations that could ever again induce the Puritan to seek a union with the religion of forms. The experiment had been made under the most advantageous circumstances possible, and it was decisive.

A portion of the band of Puritans, driven from their country to Holland, and then across the ocean, found a refuge on the rock of Plymouth, and gave their religion to this great Western World. Here all was free and vast. A boundless territory was spread out before them, and they laid the foundation of a religious system which they intended should be forever separated from a religion of forms. Its effect is seen in the religious activity and zeal, the intelligence and order, the revivals and the efforts to spread the gospel abroad, which distinguish our republic among the nations of the earth.

But the history of the religion of forms in our father-land is not completed. The separating of the Puritans had left the church a dry, cold, dead thing. Again, however, God visited that church with the special influences of the Holy Spirit, and there was a reviving and quickening spirit of religion. God breathed upon the heart of the Wesleys, and of Fletcher, and of Whitefield, and fired them with as devoted a zeal as had ever warmed the bosom of a Puritan. They were *in* the church, and were converted when connected with it. They loved it. They shrank back from the very thought of a separation. John Wesley lived and laboured, and prayed night and day, that he might *not* separate himself from the church in which he was reared, but that there might be diffused through all that communion the spirit of evangelical religion. Never was there a more honest, vigorous, or persevering effort to unite the spirit of the gospel with the religion of forms, but in vain. That vital part of the Church of England which had been quickened by the Spirit of God, in spite of every effort to bind them together, drew off by itself, breathing the air of freedom and spreading the heavenly fire over continents.

Until the present time, the result of the experiment has been uniform. The religion of forms has never been permanently blended with the gospel. The experiment is again made in our land and in our father-land, with what result is a matter of great interest to the whole Christian world, but what that result will be no one can reasonably doubt. That there should be outbreaks and collisions; that the love of revivals and of prayer-meetings, and the purpose to mingle with other denominations in great efforts to spread the knowledge of the truth, should bring the patrons of these things into conflict with the high-church party, is to be expected. They are the regular results of the existing state of things in the Episcopal Church, and they cannot be avoided. Such conflicts will arise, and however much they may be suppressed for a time, and however all parties may unite in singing pæans to the "unity" of the church, yet the elements of collision, like the pent-up fires of the volcano, rage within. To keep these elements under; to prevent entire separation and a prostration of the whole fabric, requires all the power of authority on the one side, and all the yielding of a Christian spirit on the other, and a devout attachment to Prelacy in both. It is the spirit of the gospel struggling in bonds and sighing for freedom. The present state of the Episcopal Church is but the acting over again of scenes which have been played from the beginning. The spirit of the true faith will not be bound. It does not breathe and act freely when fettered with forms. It cannot go forth freely to the conquest of the souls of men, or to the subjugation of the world. If it lives, it *will* be the spirit of the Apostles—unfettered by forms; the spirit of the Waldenses, of Wickliffe, of Luther, of Farel; of the Puritans, of Wesley, of Whitefield. Every controversy thus far waged, where the spirit of the gospel has come in conflict with the religion of forms, has had one of two results—either the spirit of the gospel is suppressed and dies away, or the one is severed from the other, never to be united again. They never have been, they never can be permanently blended. Such, it requires little sagacity to foresee, must be the result of the present controversy between the two great parties in the Episcopal Church. It is just a struggle whether the love of Prelacy, and the cry of unity, and the power of numbers, and of wealth, and of the "bishops," shall be sufficient to crush the rising spirit of the gospel, or whether there will be vital energy, and independence, and the love of the pure doctrines of the gospel, enough to break away from all this, and be free. We should rejoice in the latter result—we anticipate the former—and we fear the Episcopal Church will still continue to be *"one."*

We have thus stated one truth, as it seems to us, of great importance in regard to the position of the evangelical party in the Episcopal Church, and to the probable result of their struggles. In illustrating the nature of their relative position, and the difficulties with which they have to contend, we now proceed to remark, that *they are compelled to use a liturgy which counteracts the effect of their teaching.* We have stated that they are no less sincerely attached to the Prayer-book, and no less disposed to laud its excellence above all other uninspired productions, than the most staunch defender of high-church principles. And yet, what is the effect of the perpetual use of this book on an attempt to diffuse evangelical doctrines through the Episcopal Church.

The prescription to use the liturgy in the worship of God is binding religiously on all the ministers and members of the Episcopal Church. The *whole* service for public worship, for marriages, for baptisms, for funerals, is prescribed. Every prayer to be offered is set down; every portion of Scripture to be read is designated; and every address, with the single exception of the sermon, is already composed. At a baptism, a marriage, or a funeral, it does not appear from the canons that a minister is to be allowed either to offer an extemporary prayer, or to make an extemporary address. Even the form of prayer in a family is prescribed, and the "master or mistress having called together as many of the family as can conveniently be present, is to *say as follows*"—morning and evening. The directions for public worship are all positive and explicit: "The minister *shall* begin the morning prayer by reading one or more of the following portions of Scripture." "Then the minister *shall* say." "The people *shall* answer here." "Then the minister *shall* kneel and say the Lord's prayer;" "then likewise he *shall* say;" "then *shall* be said or sung the following anthem;" "then *shall* follow a portion of the Psalms;" "then *shall* be read the first lesson according to the table or calendar," and "before every lesson the minister *shall* say, Here beginneth such a chapter or verse of such a chapter of such a book"—and so on to the end of the Prayer-book. All the discretion which is allowed, appears to be the following:—that he may choose some *one* of half a dozen "collects" of half a dozen lines each; that at the end of the Venite, Benedicite, Jubilate, Benedictus, Cantate Domino, etc., there "*may* be said or sung the Gloria Patri;" that he has a choice between two forms of the creed—a longer and a shorter form; and that he may introduce into the morning service more or less of the quite tedious communion service. With these quite unimportant discretionary powers, the prescriptions are absolute, and the design was undoubtedly to render the service of the church wholly uniform. There is *no* discretion given in regard to extemporary prayer. There is *no* permission on any occasion to go beyond what is written down. If there is any special emergency requiring a form of prayer different from any of those which are printed, it is necessary to wait until it can be prepared in the authorized quarter, and sent down to the inferior clergy. There is no permission to hold prayer-meetings, and the liturgy does not contemplate any such thing as a prayer-meeting. There is not even permission given to the minister to select and read a portion of Scripture that shall have any relation to the subject on which he is to preach. If his text should happen to be "God so loved the world that he gave his only-begotten Son," and the "lesson" for that day should happen to be that chapter of the book of Chronicles which commences thus, "Adam, Sheth, Enosh, Kenan, Mahalaleel, Jered, Henoch, Methuseleh, Lamech," all that the minister is to do, is to say, "here beginneth such a chapter," and read on.

We are aware that the low-church party do sometimes hold prayer-meetings, and that occasionally an extemporary prayer is offered after sermon; and we will do them the justice to say, that, so far as we have heard, their prayers are models of a simple, pure, and holy worship, and are such as to prompt irresistibly to the expression of regret that they are *not* permitted by their book to pour out their souls in this manner, and that they are fettered by forms. But we believe that they themselves regard such prayers, and such prayer-meetings, as a departure from the prescribed mode of worship. We know that the high-church party consider them a direct violation of the prescribed rules of the church. *We* consider them as wholly unauthorized by the church. We see no permission of such things; we see no latitude of discretion in regard to such things; we believe that such a thing as a prayer-meeting, where extemporary prayer should be offered, and especially by laymen, is a thing not contemplated by the canons of the Episcopal Church.

What then is the inevitable tendency of the constant use of the liturgy according to the manner prescribed? Or, which amounts to the same thing so far as the subject before us is concerned, what must be the effect of its use even as it is employed by the low-church party, in regard to the preaching of evangelical doctrines? They hold, we have conceded, the great doctrines of grace. They teach the necessity of regeneration by the agency of the Holy Spirit. They insist on the doctrine of justification by faith. They are friendly to revivals of religion. Do the arrangements in the liturgy harmonize with these efforts? So far from it, we think, that their teaching and the Prayer-book come into perpetual conflict; and where the Prayer-book is to be perpetually used, the result of such a conflict cannot be doubtful.

We do not advert now to the fact, though we might do it, that *preaching* in the Episcopal Church is quite a secondary thing, and that the arrangement is so made as to allow it to produce as little effect as possible. A whole hour of the service, if performed with any degree of deliberate solemnity, is occupied inevitably with the prayers and other forms of devotion. After this protracted and wearisome service, it cannot be supposed that the mind will be in a very desirable state to listen to a *sermon* of any considerable length. The ordinary length of Episcopal sermons—from fifteen to twenty minutes—we regard as in entire accordance with the arrangements in the Episcopal Church; a sermon of fifty minutes or an hour, becomes intolerable. In another communion—the mother of Episcopacy—the *pulpit* is placed in a corner of the church; in the Episcopal Church the *sermon* is designed to occupy the same relative position.

But the difficulties encountered by the evangelical party lie deeper than this. We mean, that they are compelled perpetually to use a liturgy which counteracts all their teaching. The liturgy is opposed to the views of the low-church Episcopalian, and to the whole influence of his teaching, and is a *constant* influence. To some of the views thus constantly brought before the people in the Prayer-book, opposed to the evangelical teaching, we will now advert.

There is, first, the doctrine of baptismal regeneration—a doctrine which we regard as the undoubted teaching of the Prayer-book, and which presents a constantly counteracting influence to the doctrine of the necessity of a change of heart by the agency of the Holy Spirit accompanying the truth. The doctrine of the Prayer-book is, that a child that is baptized in a proper manner, is "regenerated by the Holy Ghost." The language of the liturgy on this subject is as explicit as language can be, and we have never seen any explanation by the advocates of low-church views, which seemed to us to have the least degree of plausibility. The language on this subject, in respect to the public baptism of infant children, is the following:—The "minister," after the baptism and making the sign of the cross, is commanded to "say"—"Seeing now, dearly beloved, that this child is regenerate, and grafted into the body of Christ's church, let us give thanks unto Almighty God for these benefits," etc.—"We yield thee hearty thanks, most merciful Father, that it hath pleased thee to regenerate this infant *with thy Holy Spirit,* to receive him for thine own child by adoption, and to incorporate him into thy holy church." The same doctrine is expressed in reference to the "private baptism of children." After the baptism, and the sign of the cross, the "minister" is directed also to "say"—"this child is regenerate, and grafted into the body of Christ's church;" and in like manner to give thanks, "that it hath pleased thee to regenerate this infant with thy Holy Spirit, to receive him for thine own child by adoption, and to incorporate him into thy holy church." But this doctrine, that by baptism there is regenerating grace bestowed by the Holy Spirit, is held not only in reference to infants and children, but, if possible, still more clearly in reference to "those of riper years." In the canonical directions on this subject, we find in the Prayer-book the following things:—(1.) The people are told that "all men are conceived and born in sin," that "none can enter into the kingdom of God, except they be regenerate and born anew of water and of the Holy Ghost," and are exhorted to "call upon God the Father through our Lord Jesus Christ, that of his bounteous goodness he will grant to these persons that which by nature they cannot have, that they may be baptized with water *and the Holy Ghost.*" (2.) The following prayers are then directed to be offered: "Mercifully look upon these thy servants; wash them, and sanctify them *with the Holy Ghost;* that they being delivered from thy wrath, may be received into the ark of Christ's church." And again: "Give thy Holy Spirit to these persons, that they may be born again, and be made heirs of everlasting salvation, through our Lord Jesus Christ." (3.) After baptism, and the sign of the cross, the minister is directed to say: "Seeing now, dearly beloved, that these persons *are regenerate,* and grafted into the body of Christ's church, let us give thanks unto Almighty God for these benefits." The thanksgiving then follows, and then this prayer: "Give thy Holy Spirit to these persons; that, *being now born again, and made heirs of everlasting salvation through our Lord Jesus Christ,* they may *continue* thy servants," etc. Here is a regular order in the teachings, prayers, and thanksgivings, all implying the doctrine of baptismal regeneration, and all implying that that regeneration is accomplished by the Holy Ghost. There is the exhortation to the people to pray for this; then the prayer actually offered for this; and then a solemn form of thanksgiving that it has been done. And that this is the true teaching of the liturgy on this subject, and that the meaning is not, as some Episcopalians have endeavoured to show, that the word "regeneration" here means a mere "change of state," or a transition from the world into the church, seems to us to be perfectly clear; for, (1.) Such is not the meaning of the Scripture terms, "regeneration," and "being born again," employed in this service. In the Bible they cannot be understood to have this meaning, and there is no evidence that the framers of the liturgy meant to depart from the Scripture usage. (2.) The regeneration here spoken of, is not a mere "change of state or relation." It is a change of regeneration *by the Holy Ghost.* This is what is prayed for; what is taught as having been accomplished; and that for which "hearty thanks" are given when the form of baptism is passed through. Now regeneration by the agency of the Holy Ghost in the Scriptures, means a definite thing. It is not a transition from heathenism to nominal Christianity; it is not a mere profession of religion; it is a work on the heart itself, by which *that* is changed, and by which the soul begins to live anew unto God. (3.) This *cannot* be the meaning in the liturgy. Is it possible to believe that sensible men should gravely entreat a whole congregation to offer fervent prayers, that certain persons then present might be enabled *to join a church?* Is it necessary for all this parade and ceremony, and all this solemn invocation of the special aid of God's Holy Spirit, that they might be enabled *to change their relation?* Is this a work so difficult to be performed as to need the special interposition of heaven in the case, and that no one could hope to be able to do it without the particular influences of the Spirit of God? And is religion in the Episcopal Church such a solemn trifling as this representation would imply? We do not believe it; and despite all the efforts of low-church Episcopalians to explain this, we believe that the high church and the Puseyites have the fair interpretation of this part of the liturgy, that it is intended to teach the doctrine of baptismal regeneration, and that this will be the impression ever made on the great mass of those who use the Prayer-book.

Now these prayers, teachings, and thanksgivings, occur constantly. Whenever an infant or an adult is to be baptized, the low churchman, as well as the high churchman, is compelled to publish this doctrine. He has no discretion. The whole service, from beginning to end, is to be read through, and no matter what may be his public teaching as a preacher, or his private views, he is under a necessity of teaching the doctrine of baptismal regeneration. He gives public thanks in reference to every child as well as every adult that is baptized and sealed with the sign of the cross, that he *is* regenerated by the Holy Ghost and made an heir of everlasting life. What will be, then, the force of his preaching, on the subject of the new birth or the change of heart, in the proper sense of the term? What impression will be made on those already "regenerated by the Holy Ghost" in baptism, in regard to this? Can such preaching be intended for them? Can it be applicable to any but the heathen and the unbaptized; for pagans, scoffers, and "dissenters?" Are not all others already born again?

A second difficulty of a similar kind derived from the liturgy, with which the evangelical churchman is obliged to contend, relates to the doctrine of "confirmation." If we understand the views of low churchmen, they accord with our own in regard to the necessity of a change of heart, and of evidence of personal piety, as qualifications for communion. They do not suppose that regenerating grace is conferred either by confirmation or the "eucharist," nor do they hold that persons should be admitted to either without evidence of personal religion. We believe that they are sincerely aiming to guard the Lord's table from the approach of all who do not give evidence that they are truly "born again"—not of baptism, but by the Holy Spirit of God.

They are undoubtedly right in these views; but are these the views of their liturgy? Does the Prayer-book contemplate this? Have they, as Episcopalians, a right to rest in this, and to exclude from "confirmation" and the Lord's supper all who do not give *them* evidence that they are truly converted, or are truly pious? We think they have not; and that in their efforts on this subject they are not only departing from their own standards, but are in the very matter compelled to use a liturgy, the tendency of which is to counteract and render nugatory all their own instructions and efforts. We believe that the Prayer-book does not contemplate, in order to confirmation, any other regeneration than that of water-baptism, or any other qualification than that of following out the arrangement at baptism. In support of this, we turn at once to the Prayer-book itself, and find the arrangements there contemplated in reference to "confirmation" and the Lord's supper, to be the following: The minister is directed to say, not to the parents of the child, but to the "godfathers and godmothers," after baptism is administered, "Ye are to take care that this child be brought to the bishop to be confirmed by him, so soon as he can say the creed, the Lord's prayer, and the ten commandments, and is sufficiently instructed in the other parts of the church catechism set forth for that purpose." We observe here no requirement of any change of heart, or of any evidence of piety whatever. We do not believe that an acquaintance with the creed, the Lord's prayer, the ten commandments, and the church catechism, necessarily infers the possession of renewing and saving grace; and, as these are all that is specified, we do not see what right any churchman has to add thereto. To us, the only question which it would seem to be proper to propound to a candidate for confirmation would be, whether he could "*say* the creed, the Lord's prayer, the ten commandments," and the "parts of the church catechism set forth for that purpose." Why has any minister a right to require any thing more? Why is he any more at liberty to demand evidence of what *he* regards as a change of heart, than he has to insist that the candidate shall be familiar with the Westminster Confession or the Saybrook Platform? As these are all the requirements specified, we naturally turn to "the other parts of the church catechism set forth" with reference to the rite of confirmation, to inquire whether *that* contemplates a change of heart as a qualification for that rite.

The church catechism has the following title in the Prayer-book: "A Catechism; that is to say, An *Instruction*, to be learned by every person before he is brought to the Bishop to be confirmed by the Bishop." The qualification which is here specified, in accordance with that which is stated at the baptism as necessary in order to confirmation, is not that there shall be evidence of a change of heart, or any vital transformation of character after baptism, but that this catechism has been *learned;* that is, committed to memory, before he is brought to the bishop.

This catechism contains the creed, the ten commandments, the Lord's prayer, and a few questions and answers growing out of each, and on the nature of the sacraments. The inquiry now is, with what qualifications and character one would "be brought to the bishop" who should have strictly complied with the directions in the Prayer-book? Would it be necessary that he should furnish evidence of a change of heart; or would it be right to reject his application for the communion if he could "*say* the creed, the Lord's prayer, and the ten commandments, and had learned the other parts of the church catechism set forth for that purpose?" These qualifications may be learned from a few of the questions directed to be proposed to the candidate, and the answers which he is required to give. The first thing which we meet with is the odious doctrine of baptismal regeneration—the elementary idea of Episcopacy as it is in the Prayer-book, and a doctrine on which all that is required to be said by the candidate is based. "*Question.* What is your name? *Ans.* N. or M. *Quest.* Who gave you this name? *Ans.* My sponsors in baptism; *wherein I was made a member of Christ, the child of God, and the inheritor of the kingdom of heaven.*" Then *we* would propound a "question" to those Episcopalians who endeavour to show that regeneration in the Prayer-book does not mean a change of heart, but a change of state. It is this: What more can there be in the new birth, or in regeneration as effected by the Spirit of God, than to be made "a member of Christ, the child of God, and an inheritor of the kingdom of heaven?" Yet all this the candidate is to affirm was secured to him in baptism. The same doctrine we have affirmed again in still stronger terms, if possible, in this same catechism which is to be "learned." "*Quest.* What is the outward visible sign or form in baptism? *Ans.* Water; wherein the person is baptized in the name of the Father, and of the Son, and of the Holy Ghost. *Quest.* What is the inward and spiritual grace? *Ans.* A death unto sin and a new birth unto righteousness: For being by nature born unto sin, and the children of wrath, we are hereby made the children of grace." That all this is supposed to be conferred by baptism, is apparent from the previous answers on the nature of the sacraments. "*Quest.* How many sacraments hath Christ ordained in his church? *Ans.* Two only, as generally necessary unto salvation; that is to say, baptism and the Lord's supper. *Quest.* What meanest thou by this word *Sacrament?* *Ans.* I mean an outward and visible sign of an inward and spiritual grace, given unto us, ordained by Christ himself; *as a means whereby we* RECEIVE *the same and a* PLEDGE *to assure us thereof.*" The necessity of grace is not indeed anywhere denied, but it is affirmed here, as it is implied everywhere in the Prayer-book, that the grace is imparted at baptism, and the "invisible sign" and the "inward grace" go together.

With these views, and having "learned" to say these things, the candidate is to be brought to the bishop to be confirmed. We are ready to acknowledge that many or most of the questions directed to be propounded to the candidate are solemn and pertinent. On the supposition that they were propounded to one who had been *truly* converted, they are such questions as ought to be proposed to all who make a profession of religion. But what is their weight, or power, or pertinency, when addressed to one who is taught to say that by infant baptism he was "made a child of God, a member of Christ, and an inheritor of the kingdom of heaven," and that his sponsors made certain promises for him in baptism which he has come now to relieve them from, by ratifying them himself?

Now what will be the effect of this standing and stereotyped system of instruction, on the preaching of the evangelical part of the Episcopal Church? They aim to teach a different thing from this. They strive to teach, and they really believe, that water baptism, however administered, does *not* impart all the grace which is needful to the salvation of the soul. But here stands this catechism which they are to teach, and which conveys lessons so plain that it is supposed a child may understand them, and, alas! so plain that we fear they *are* understood and believed by the great mass of those who are "brought to the bishop to be confirmed." We can easily imagine what the effect would be, if, in a Congregational or Presbyterian church, all the children were to be taught that regeneration was imparted by baptism properly administered, and that all they had to do in order to be qualified for the communion, was to "learn to *say*" this. Where would be our revivals of religion?

We are aware that the evangelical party in the Episcopal Church endeavour to evade this. We know that many of them insist that the candidates for confirmation shall give evidence to them that they are truly converted, and that by the exercise of what they seem to regard as their right, they restrain those from confirmation whom *they* do not judge to be qualified for the communion. Aware of the obvious and dangerous tendency of the system as set down in the Prayer-book, they claim the right of *not* presenting to the bishop for confirmation, those whom they do not regard as qualified for it. We have no doubt that in doing this, they are acting in accordance with the New Testament, which plainly teaches that repentance and faith are indispensable qualifications for the Lord's table. But is this Episcopacy? Have they this right according to the canons of their own church? We think not. We are willing to allow that there must be some discretion allowed to the officiating minister or rector of a parish in regard to those who are to be presented, as the fair rules of interpretation seem to demand that he shall not be required to present those who are open infidels, or who are grossly immoral. But has he a right to put his own interpretation on what constitutes a proper qualification; to say that baptism does *not* mean regeneration; that the child that was baptized, was *not* "made a member of Christ, the child of God, and an inheritor of the kingdom of heaven;" that it has *not* "pleased God to regenerate him with his Holy Spirit" when he was baptized, but that another kind of regeneration is necessary, and to withhold him from confirmation until he has himself the evidence that he is born again? Has he a right to set his own views thus against the teaching of the church, and to insist that his views shall be complied with contrary to the obvious meaning of the canons, and to the almost unbroken custom of the church? We think not. We think that, by becoming an Episcopal minister, he binds himself to act in accordance with the obvious meaning of the liturgy in this respect, and that, however his soul may revolt at it, and however contrary all this may be to his convictions of what is taught in the New Testament, as long as he chooses to remain in the church, he has no discretion. He is the servant of the church. He has received this Prayer-book as his guide, and it is his to carry out its views. If he is dissatisfied with them, the way is clear. It is to leave the communion; it is not to introduce and defend practices contrary to the elementary conceptions of Episcopacy.

There is another thought. The church may be regarded as making a sort of compact with every child that is duly baptized, that, if he will comply with her regulations, he shall be entitled at the proper time to whatever advantage there may be in her full fellowship and favour. There is a pledge given, through the sponsors at baptism, that if the course of life which is then recommended is pursued, the child, as soon as he can say the creed and the ten commandments, and has been suitably instructed in the other parts of the catechism, shall be entitled to the privilege of confirmation. We believe that he may forfeit this by an unholy and wicked life, but not by any interpretation which his pastor may choose to put on the terms of the compact implying that he was *not* made a member of Christ and a child of God. On this subject, we think, the case is wholly parallel with that of one who becomes a "candidate for orders" in the Episcopal Church; and as such a candidate, if he complies with the canons in the case, has a *right* to ordination in the church, so has a youth who has been baptized, and who has learned to say what is taught him, a right to confirmation. The right in the one case is as clear as in the other. On this subject, and with reference to this principle, we shall here submit the views of a gentleman who deservedly occupies a very prominent position, not only in the evangelical portion of the Episcopal Church, but in the ministry of this country, in regard to the ordination of Mr. Arthur Carey. The reasoning, *mutatis mutandis*, applies as well to the case before us as to the ordination of Mr. Carey:

"It becomes, therefore, a very important question to consider, what are the rights of a candidate for orders. In doing this, I shall not deem it necessary to refer to particular canons, which are well-known, but to consider the course through which a candidate is led by the authority and the appointment of the church. Our canons lay open this path with great distinctness. They also guard it, and limit it, with marked and peculiar restraints. The question is, does a perfect compliance with all these directions and restraints give, from the church to the candidate, a right to expect and to claim his orders at the last, nothing appearing in any legal way to vitiate this performance of his required course? A young man is invited to become a candidate for orders, for the plan laid out for him amounts to an invitation. He obtains his certificates of personal character, and is regularly received and recorded by the bishop as a candidate. He pursues his prescribed course of studies under the direction of his bishop. He passes satisfactorily to the bishop and presbyters his required examinations. He presents his regular certificates for ordination. He subscribes the required declaration of conformity. He has thus finished and completed his prescribed course of education to the satisfaction of the authorities under which he has been placed. Now has he acquired a right upon the faith of the church, with whose prescriptions he has fully complied, to the ordination which he seeks? It must be granted, of course, that if his qualifications, mental or moral, are ultimately found insufficient, he may be justly rejected. If his examining bishop and presbyters are dissatisfied with the one, they have certainly the right to reject him there. If any persons are acquainted with moral crimes, which, if known, would actually overturn all the worth and influence of his certificates of character, they may declare them at the very last moment, and he may be arrested there. But if his examinations have been satisfactory to the persons appointed to direct them, and his character is unstained with moral crime, has he not a right secured to him to the ordination, for which he has fulfilled his appointed preparation? Or is it to be considered by him, and for him, utterly uncertain, to the very last moment, whether he shall be allowed to gain the object of his wish? May he finish his curriculum of study, and fulfil every requisition of the church under whose care he is placed, receive the approbation of the chief ministers appointed over him, gain all the required certificates of unspotted character, and be admitted to record his name in the bishop's register, to the constitutional promise of conformity to the doctrine and discipline of the church, and thus have his acceptance to orders, as it were, acknowledged to him, and his mind authorized to rest in peaceful expectation of his ordination, and yet may he be exposed to be arrested, in the very attainment of his desire, by the possible judgment of two persons in the assembled congregation, that he is deficient or erroneous in religious doctrine, or theological training? I confess this amounts in my view to extreme oppression. What young man of honourable and ingenuous feelings would be willing to expose himself to this possible disgrace, and this entire uncertainty of prospect? Or what Christian parent would be willing, in the face of such a hazard, to commit his son to the faith and guardianship of a church, whose system of law was so insecure and so destitute of all protection to his character or prospects? Yet if the principle that a final protest, founded upon the personal suspicion or conviction of any persons, that the theological attainments and preparation of the candidate are insufficient or unsound, is to be of necessity regarded, and acted upon by the bishop ordaining, to what other result than this shall we be brought? Will it not completely unsettle our whole church, in thus undermining the just prospects and rights of the ministry at the very commencement of their course? Will not the secret reservation of such arbitrary and irresponsible power, amount to a complete exclusion of desirable candidates from our ministry? I am necessarily led, therefore, from these considerations to the conviction, that there are rights secured to the candidate, upon the implied faith of the church. The connection seems to me to have the aspect of a mutual contract. The candidate voluntarily yields himself to restraints and laws, to which he was not before subject, to gain advantages and benefits, which are thus promised and secured to him. The church, therefore, comes under an obligation to bestow upon him, on the fulfilment of his part of the contract, the advantages of a ministry, to which it has encouraged him to look; and he, in consequence, has a right to the result of his labours, which cannot be justly withheld from him?"*

* Letter of the Rev. Stephen H. Tyng, D.D., in relation to the ordination of Mr. Arthur Carey, published in the Episcopal Recorder, October, 1843. This letter was understood at the time of the publication to have been written by Dr. Tyng, and in a subsequent number of the Recorder this is admitted.

Now with these principles, we do not see how a minister of the Episcopal Church can refuse to present a candidate for confirmation who has complied with the directions in the rubric, even though he should not give him evidence that his heart was changed. One of the difficulties, then, with which the evangelical party has to contend, is, that the grand, the leading object of an evangelical ministry everywhere—the conversion of the soul to God by the truth, the quickening of a spirit dead in sin by the preached gospel, the conversion and salvation of the lost by the mighty power of the Holy Spirit—meets with this counteracting, this all-pervading influence in the Prayer-book, and that despite his private convictions and all his sense of what is right and true, he is under the high obligation of his ministerial vows to act *as if* a baptized child were made "regenerate with the Holy Ghost," and was "a member of Christ, a child of God, and an inheritor of heaven."

Our next remark in regard to the position of the evangelical party, is, that there are no arrangements of provisions in the liturgy for promoting their peculiar and distinctive efforts, or which contemplate such efforts. In looking over the Prayer-book which the low churchman, in common with all other Episcopalians, is under an obligation constantly to use, the question at once occurs whether those things at which he distinctively aims are contemplated there? Do they fall in with the design of the Prayer-book? Was it the intention of the authors of the Prayer-book to promote them, and have they made arrangements for them? Or are the peculiar things which constitute the characteristics of the low-church party, and which they are endeavouring so zealously, and with so much of the spirit of the gospel, to promote—things which they have superinduced upon the liturgy, and which they are compelled to carry forward by a system of independent arrangements? We are constrained to believe that the latter is the case, for the following reasons:

1. We think that Christian missions to the heathen are not contemplated by the Prayer-book. They were not regarded as distinct objects of Christian effort at the time when the Prayer-book was made, and it has not been, and we presume could not now so be moulded, as to adapt it to the present views of Protestant Christians in their efforts to spread the gospel around the world. To say nothing of the cumbrous and unwieldy nature of the forms of Episcopacy in reference to missions—of the perplexities which must meet a missionary who should attempt to go through the liturgy in a heathen community—of the changes of vestments and postures which it contemplates, the alternations from prayer to praise, from reading now by the priest and now by the people—of the difficulties arising from the contemplated necessity of responses on the part of the people, there are other things which lead us to think that the Prayer-book was not designed to be adapted to missionary operations. There are no references to such efforts; no prayers directed to be offered for the success of missions; no allusions to churches gathered among the heathen; no petitions that the people may be imbued with the missionary spirit; no supplications that the missionary in heathen lands may be sustained in his trials, and encouraged in his work. We believe that a congregation of Episcopalians might use the Prayer-book any given time, and strictly conform to all the prescriptions of the rubric, and never have the missionary spirit excited in the least conceivable degree, and never dream, from any use of that book, that it is the duty of the Christian church to spread the gospel around the world. We have reflected with some care on the forms of prayer there prescribed, and we have been able to recall in all the petitions and all the collects only the following that has any bearing on the subject—unless the incessant repetition of the

Lord's prayer, morning, mid-day, and evening, and at all times, be an exception—a repetition amounting, as far as the use of that beautiful form can be made to, to the βαττολογια so pointedly condemned by the Saviour, (Matt. vi. 7,)—a repetition which seems to be intended to be a substitute for all sorts of petitions that ought to be offered. We find the following petitions, and those only, bearing on missions. The first occurs in the "Prayer for all Sorts and Conditions of Men:"—"O God, the creator and preserver of all mankind, we humbly beseech thee for all sorts and conditions of men, that thou wouldst be pleased to make thy ways known unto them, thy saving health unto all nations." This occurs again in the evening prayer, and this, besides the petition in the Lord's prayer, is the solitary petition which is regularly offered by the whole Episcopal Church from Sabbath to Sabbath, for the universal spread of the gospel of Christ. Beside this, in one of the "collects," for Good-Friday, designed to be used but once in the year, we find the following petition: "O merciful God, who hast made all men, and hatest nothing that thou hast made, nor desirest the death of a sinner, but rather that he should be converted and live; have mercy upon all Jews, Turks, infidels and heretics, and take from them all ignorance, hardness of heart, and contempt of thy word, and so fetch them home, blessed Lord, to thy flock, that they may be saved among the remnants of the true Israelites," etc. The fact here adverted to is the more remarkable, because in the numerous instances in which "collects" are appointed to be said, occasions are constantly occurring where it would seem almost unavoidable to make *some* allusion, and to offer *some* petition, for the spread of the gospel among the heathen, and for the success of Christian missions. Thus in the collect for "The Epiphany, or the Manifestation of Christ to the Gentiles," we have this prayer: "O God, who by the leading of a star didst manifest thy only-begotten Son to the

Gentiles, mercifully grant that *we*, who know thee now by faith, may, after this life, have the fruition of thy glorious Godhead, through Jesus Christ our Lord." Thus in the collect on the "Conversion of St. Paul:"—"O God, who through the preaching of the blessed Apostle Saint Paul, hast caused the light of the gospel to shine throughout the world, grant, we beseech thee, that *we*, having his wonderful conversion in remembrance, may show forth our thankfulness unto thee for the same, by following the holy doctrines which he taught, through Jesus Christ our Lord." So on "St. Peter's Day," and "St. James the Apostle," and "St. Bartholomew the Apostle," and "St. Matthew the Apostle," "St. Michael and all Angels," "St. Simon and St. Jude, Apostles," and "All Saints Day," we have the same utter want of allusion to the Christian duty of spreading the gospel—as if none of these apostles had ever done any thing in such a cause, or as if "St. Michael" and "All the Saints" had no interest in the universal of Christianity. It is remarkable, we think, that so many "collects" *could* have been made by Christian men, without a recollection that the "Saints" whose virtues are thus commended, were distinguished more than for any thing else in spreading the gospel among the heathen, and that the thing in which the church ought specifically to imitate them is their fidelity in obeying the Redeemer's last command. A missionary society, or a missionary effort, whether in connection with other Christians or by themselves, is a thing, we believe, unknown to the constitution of the Episcopal Church. That constitution contemplates a regularly organized congregation, and all the efforts which are made by that church in behalf of missions are efforts not contemplated by the liturgy.

2. Revivals of religion are not contemplated by the Prayer-book. We believe that this would be adverted to by the high-church party as an evidence of the excellence of the book

itself, if not as a proof of its semi-inspiration. But the evangelical party have different views of the desirableness of such works of grace. We do not doubt that they as sincerely rejoice as others do when the Spirit of God descends with power on a people, and when many are brought simultaneously to embrace the Saviour. In the proper measures for promoting such a work, they sympathize with their brethren of other churches. They would dwell on the same topics in preaching; urge with the same ardour the doctrines of depravity, of justification by faith, and of the necessity of regeneration by the Holy Spirit, and give substantially the same counsel to an inquiring sinner. They admit the efficacy of protracted services, or, as they choose to call them, "associations;" and, in addition to such services of a "voluntary" character, they propose to avail themselves of what would otherwise be the cold and benumbing influence of the long season of fasting in "Lent." But what is the relation of the Prayer-book to such efforts? What aid could be derived from that book in a work of grace? What would be the effect of the sole use of that book in endeavouring to promote a revival of religion, or in conducting it? There is nothing in that book that is adapted to promote what is commonly termed a revival of religion; and there is nothing in the book that is fitted to the thrilling scenes of such a work. There are no prayers that careless sinners may be awakened; none that inquirers may be guided to Christ; none that would express the desires of a church in behalf of those who are asking what they must do to be saved. If these things are made the object of petition in an Episcopal Church, it must be by the appointment of "prayer-meetings"—assemblages that are not contemplated, as we have already seen, by the Episcopal constitution. We have heard it said that a Presbyterian minister once went into an inquiry-meeting, and commenced the services of the evening by this question: "Can you tell me, how doth Christ execute the office of a priest?" The Episcopal Prayer-book is not as well adapted to the state of things in a revival of religion, as the use of the Assembly's Shorter Catechism would be if propounded through and through to those composing such a meeting. There is not a feature of the book that is adapted to such a work of grace. Whether this is not an advantage in favour of the book, we are aware, is a point on which many Episcopalians would differ materially from us. We say only that if there are to be revivals of religion in the church, they must be conducted in some other way than by the use of the Prayer-book.

3. The efforts for the promotion of religion among the young as a distinct class, is a thing unknown to the constitution of the Episcopal Church, and all attempts to promote Sabbath-schools, whether in the bosom of the church as a sectarian matter, or on a more general scale in union with other denominations, is a departure from the teachings and the designs of the liturgy. The Sabbath-school is an institution which has grown up some two hundred years since the Prayer-book was arranged for the use of the Anglican church, and it has never been modified in the least degree to adapt it to the grand enterprise of teaching the Bible to the young, though more than fifty years have elapsed since God began to set the undoubted seal of his blessing to the efforts of Robert Raikes. The Prayer-book, even as we now have it, is the "petrified wisdom of the age of Elizabeth," and it does not adapt itself even to the undoubted Christian institutions of an advanced period of the world. The only arrangements in the Prayer-book which contemplate the instruction of the young at all, are found in the catechism. The amount of instruction contemplated there is, the Lord's prayer, the creed, the ten commandments, a careful initiation into the mystery of baptismal regeneration, and the expression of a settled belief on the part of the child, that by baptism he was made "a member

of Christ, the child of God, and an inheritor of the kingdom of heaven." This great defect of the Episcopal Church—this fact that there is an utter forgetfulness in her forms of the young, and an utter want of adaptedness in her institutions to them, is thus candidly admitted by Archbishop Whately. He observes that the liturgy "is evidently neither adapted nor designed for children, even those of such an age as to be fully capable of joining in congregational worship, were there a service suitably composed on purpose for them. To frame and introduce such a service would not, I think, be regarded as a trifling improvement, if we could but thoroughly get rid of the *principle* of the Romish lip-service."—*Essays on Romanism*, ch. i. 5. This is a candid confession; but we do not believe that it *is* possible for the Episcopal Church, so long as her forms are used, to "get rid of the Romish principle of lip-service."

4. Prayer-meetings are not contemplated by the Episcopal service. There is no arrangement in the Prayer-book for such meetings, nor so far as we have been able to examine, is it once intimated that they would be desirable or proper. If they are ever held, they are a departure from the system, or an attempt to engraft on the system that which is no part of Episcopacy. Nothing would be more unfitted for what is ordinarily designed by a prayer-meeting, than the use of the forms of the Episcopal Church. We believe that those ministers of that persuasion who patronize such meetings, never think of using the liturgy on such occasions, unless it may be to save appearances; and we are certain that the high-church party are consistent and episcopally right in their opposition to such assemblages.

5. All union on religious subjects with other denominations, we regard as in like manner at variance with the spirit of Episcopacy. There is in the Prayer-book no recognition of any other churches as such; of any other ministers than

those who are episcopally ordained; or of any other organization for the promotion of religious objects except "*the* church," with her "bishops, priests, and deacons." In the Prayer-book, we find no admission even that others are or can be Christians. We think there is but one allusion in the forms of prayer to any Christians others than those of the Episcopal sect, and that occurs in these words: "We pray for thy holy church universal, that it may be guided and governed by thy good Spirit; that all who *profess* and *call themselves* Christians may be led in the way of truth, and hold the faith in unity of spirit, in the bond of peace, and in righteousness of life." There is no prayer offered for ministers of other denominations—no allusion whatever to them. The prayers for ministers of the gospel are always in the forms following: "Send down upon *our* bishops and other clergy, and upon the congregations committed to their charge, the healthful spirit of thy grace." "Make, we beseech thee, all bishops and pastors diligently to preach thy holy word, and the people obediently to follow the same." The recognition of another church than the Episcopal, or of other ministers of the gospel than the Episcopal, is a thing unknown to the Prayer-book. It contemplates no union with others; alludes to no common action with them; and evidently supposes that the great interests of religion in the world will not be carried forward by voluntary associations, or by union with others, but by the organization under the "three orders." We have felt grateful for the aid which some eloquent and zealous Episcopalians have rendered in the distribution of the Bible, and of Tracts, and in the support of the Sunday-school cause in connection with others; but we have never had but one feeling in regard to the consistency of this with Episcopacy. We have regarded it as a departure from the constitution of their church; and whatever independent zeal a few may show for a time in these catholic movements, we anticipate that the time is not far distant when the voice of an Episcopalian will no longer be heard at the anniversaries of our national institutions, and that the only aid which Episcopacy will render to the cause of diffusing Christianity, will be under her own distinctive organization. There is now far less disposition to unite with others, than there was a dozen years ago;—successive years will show it to be less and less.

Our next thought in regard to the efforts of low churchmen, is, that as far as we understand the subject, those efforts are all at variance with the doctrinal views of the church. We allude now to the opposition to Puseyism, or the Oxford theology. We speak here on the presumption that those who are low churchmen will be in the main opposed to that system of belief. On that controversy we have looked from the commencement with great interest, not with reference to the question whether Puseyism is in accordance with the Bible—for in regard to that we see not how a question can be raised—but with reference to the question whether it is not the true spirit of Episcopacy, and is not in accordance with the views prevailing at the time when the Prayer-book was arranged, and those expressed by the standard writers of the Episcopal Church. We do not propose now to go into an examination of these questions, but it may be of some interest to those who are in the Episcopal Church to know how these things appear to those who are without. We regard, then, the Puseyites as entirely in the right in this controversy so far as Episcopacy is concerned; wholly wrong so far as it relates to the Bible. We think that those who are opposed to the Oxford theology, are engaged in the most hopeless of all controversies ever waged, so long as they make their appeal to their own Prayer-book, or the early standard writers of the Episcopal denomination. We have no doubt that, if the views of Dr. Pusey and Mr. Newman were to prevail in the Episcopal Church, the church would be substantially in the same position in which it was in the days of Elizabeth. It was but half reformed. It retained then a large part of the offensive features of Romanism, and those views were embodied in the Prayer-book. The doctrine of baptismal regeneration, of the *opus operatum* of the sacraments, of the real presence of the intermediate state;—the veneration of saints, the appointment of festival days in commemoration of their virtues, the pomp and pageantry of worship, the sign of the cross, bowing at the name of Jesus, the holiness of the church and the altar, and the sacredness of the consecrated burying-place, all, with numerous similar things, are part and parcel of Romanism, and not of the religion of the New Testament. To bring back the Episcopal Church to the views entertained on these subjects in the time of Elizabeth, which we understand to be the declared aim of Dr. Pusey, would be to establish the sentiments advanced in the Tractarian theology. The views of Dr. Pusey in his celebrated sermon on the eucharist, which was the occasion of his suspension, we think are abundantly sustained by the quotations which he has made from the standard writers of the Episcopal Church; and, unless our evangelical brethren in that church will change their mode of argument, and appeal solely to the Bible, we are morally certain that they are destined to defeat. The Prayer-book and the Fathers of the Episcopal Church will sustain their adversaries. An honest appeal to the Bible, however, in the case, would be fatal to Episcopacy, and if persevered in, must rend the Episcopal Church in twain.

There is but one other thought which we propose to submit in reference to the present position of the evangelical party in the Episcopal Church. It relates to their own consistency in their efforts to mingle with Christians and Christian ministers of other denominations. We have already intimated that the *principles* on which this is done are well defined and understood. They never associate with the ministers of other denominations *as* Christian ministers. They never invite them to preach for them, but uniformly say when the question comes before them, that they cannot reciprocate an act of ministerial courtesy of this kind. They never recognise the right of non-Episcopal ministers to administer the sacraments of the church. They never recognise their ordination as an ordination to the Christian ministry, and never suppose that a minister from another denomination, *except the Papal*, can be suffered to officiate in an Episcopal Church without renouncing his former ordination, and perchance his baptism too, and submit to the imposition of the hands of the prelate. These and kindred acts on their part, force us almost inevitably to the conclusion that, in common with their high-church brethren, they regard the Episcopal as the only Christian church, and consider all others, ministers and people, as left to the "uncovenanted mercies of God."

Yet there is much that we cannot reconcile with this. There is a zeal for the truth, which looks as if they regarded the vital doctrines of Christianity as of more importance than its forms. There is an honest effort to promote the great objects contemplated by the gospel, which seems to rise above the narrow confinement of sectarian efforts. There is, in some things, such a hearty mingling with other Christians, and such a zeal in promoting the common objects of our religion, as to lead us for a time to forget the Episcopacy, and to rejoice in them as coworkers with all others, in the glorious efforts to spread the gospel. There is such impatience of restraint, and such a declared purpose *not* to be fettered by forms, and *not* to be limited to the narrow views of a "sect," that we begin to ask with concern, whether, in our apprehensions of their attachment to Episcopacy, we have not done them essential injustice. There are occasionally such solemn declarations made in such public places, that they "*will* not be confined within the narrow walls of a sect, nor be prevented from looking out on the broad Christian world, and sympathizing with other Christians," that we are constrained to ask, whether we have rightly understood the true interpretation of the other positions which they have taken, or whether—a conclusion which we will avoid if possible—all this is said for the purpose of effect, and is designed ultimately more and more to give Episcopacy favour in the sight of the community.

Now so antagonist and irreconcilable are these positions of the evangelical party in the Episcopal Church, that we should be glad to propound to some of the leaders of that party a few questions, and we take the liberty of submitting them here, with the hope that, through their papers, they will furnish to the community an answer.

The first would be this: Do the evangelical party regard the ministers of other denominations as in any sense authorized ministers of the gospel, and their churches as true churches? If they *do*—(which we do not believe to be the case)—then we ask of them, why they are never, in any proper way, so recognised? Why do they not come out and openly say so? Why do they never admit them to their pulpits? Why do they never protest against their being reordained when one of their number leaves the church of his fathers, and enters the service of the Episcopal denomination? Why do they submit to the gross public indignity offered to the Protestant churches by the uniform acts of the Episcopal Church—admitting a Catholic priest at once to officiate at her altars without reordination; demanding that every other minister shall be ordained?

If in reply to these questions they should say, that *they* regard the ministers of other denominations as having a right to preach and administer the sacraments, and consider the ordinances administered by them as valid, but that the "canons" of their church will not allow them to express this belief by any public act, or to reciprocate any act of ministerial fellowship, then we would ask of them as independent Christian men, how they can suffer their consciences and their hearts to be fettered and trammelled by such canons? How can they consent to remain in a position where they cannot express in any proper way the honest convictions of their minds, and act as freemen? How can they peacefully minister in a communion where the very nature of the institutions is a well-understood exclusion of all other churches as having no valid ministry and no valid sacraments? How can they, by their conduct, hold up all other churches as left to the "uncovenanted mercies of God?" The Episcopal sect, as such, is a small part of the Christian world. In this land, it is, and it will continue to be, among the "smallest of the tribes of Israel." Its communicants are few in comparison with those of other denominations. Its ministers are also comparatively few, and, in point of talent, learning, piety, and moral worth, are not eminent above all others. If it be so that other churches are true churches, and other ministers are true ministers, then they have the common rights of all Christians, to be recognised as such by all their Christian brethren. That is no desirable position for a man to place himself in, who believes that these are true churches, but who is habitually constrained to speak and act *as if* they were not, and so to act as to leave the impression that he regards them as on the same platform in regard to salvation, as the Jew, the Turk, and the infidel. And yet this is the fair interpretation of the conduct of the Episcopalian. This denomination—almost the smallest in our country—habitually acts, as if the great body of Methodists, Baptists, Presbyterians, and Congregationalists, had no claim to the character of a church, and were to be treated as those on whom the light of Christianity has never risen. The most eminent ministers of the land, living and dead, are to be regarded as preaching without authority, and as intruders in the sacred office. Of the departed, Eliot, and Edwards, and Bellamy, and Dwight, are never to be spoken of as true ministers of the gospel; of the living, that honoured appellation should not be given to Beecher, Alexander, Woods, Stuart, or Nott. Hall, in our father-land, was no true minister; Wesley was one only because he had been touched by episcopal hands; Summerfield had neither there nor here a right to preach; and nine-tenths of the effective ministry of our country are to be regarded in no other light than intruders and impostors. Now do the evangelical party in the Episcopal Church believe this? If they do not, we call upon them by every sentiment of honour and religion, *to say so.* If they cannot do this and remain in the bosom of Episcopacy, then we call upon them to act the man and the Christian, and to seek a connection where they *can* say this, and can act out the honest conviction of their souls. We do not understand the constitution of that man who can quietly remain in a connection where, by a fair interpretation, his conduct will do an enormous wrong habitually to the great mass of his Christian brethren, and where this interpretation of his conduct will express a constant falsehood in regard to his own opinions.

But if the evangelical Episcopalian should say that he does *not* regard the ministers of other denominations as having a right to preach and to administer the sacraments, then we have another question to propose. Why is not this honestly avowed? Why is there not on his part always a course of conduct entirely consistent with this? Why is there ever any such mingling with other denominations, as to leave any doubt in regard to this matter? His high-church brethren never act in such a way as to leave room for an ambiguous interpretation of their views, and we honour them for their consistency. We know where to find them. It is always *in* the Episcopal Church, and they never so far forget themselves as to convey the impression that they have ever heard that there is any other church. If the low churchman holds the same views in regard to the church and the ministry, then what means all the declamation which we hear about his own catholic and liberal views, and his determination *not* to be fettered and manacled?

We take our stand here. If the evangelical Episcopalian regards other churches as true churches, and other ministers as true ministers, we have a right to know it. If he does not, then the community has a right to know what Episcopacy is. If it is essentially narrow and exclusive; if it recognises no other communion as a true church, and regards all others as left to the uncovenanted mercies of God, then it is a *right* which the community has, to understand this. Episcopalians are everywhere endeavouring to win the young from the churches of their fathers. Let us understand fully what the system is, and let not the youth of the land, won by great professions of catholicity and zeal for the common cause, be drawn blindfold into a communion that is essentially exclusive of all others, and where the first act of faith must be the expression of a belief that a father and mother worship in a conventicle, and are baptized and buried by laymen.

We have spoken freely, but not in anger. It is not because we believe that those brethren who are endeavouring to infuse the evangelical principle into the Episcopal Church, are not good men, that we have made these remarks. We regard it as an honour that we are permitted to number some among them as our personal friends, and there are many among them at whose feet we regard it as a privilege to sit down. Among the living of this class, we doubt not there are some as holy men as the church embosoms, and among the dead, there are those whose memory will be cherished as long as piety, eloquence, and moral worth are honoured on earth. The name of Bedell will not be, and should not be, forgotten. The land has known few men who have done more honour to the ministry than he did. His silvery tones, his placid manner, his clear enunciation, his unshrinking fidelity, his indefatigable toils, his meek, pure, unobtrusive Christian spirit, his large-hearted liberality toward all who love our Lord Jesus Christ, cannot be forgotten by the multitudes who hung on his lips, as a preacher, and who loved him as a man.

But we regard these brethren as labouring in an impracticable work, and in a work which it would not be desirable to accomplish if it could be done—an attempt to blend the spirit of the gospel with the religion of forms. The experiment has now been fairly made. It cannot be hoped that it will be made under better auspices, and we regard it as destined to inevitable failure. As we love pure, evangelical religion, therefore, we think it right to state what we think must be the result of the experiment, and to set before the churches the principles which are involved in the controversy.

We think, also, that there has been an error in other denominations of Christians in this matter. There has been a feeling, the correctness of which no one seemed to regard it as proper to doubt, that the Episcopal sect was to be numbered in the family of evangelical churches, and that other churches should lend their influence to infuse the evangelical spirit more and more into that communion. Under the influence of that desire, pious and devoted young men have been advised to throw themselves into that communion, with the hope that they might do more to promote the great cause by attempting to diffuse the spirit of Christ through the religion of forms, than by ministering in connection with the church of their fathers. This, we now think, was unwise counsel. It was both *unkind* to Episcopacy, and it was morally certain that it would be a failure. It was *as* unkind as if the Methodist Church, pressed with great concern for the Presbyterian denomination, should scatter its ardent sons through all the presbyteries of the land, avowedly for the purpose of changing its policy, and diffusing the tactics of Wesley through the Presbyterian ranks. And it was an experiment which, from the nature of the case *must* fail. There *is* a way of effectually neutralizing all such influence that comes in from other denominations. Episcopacy has the means of infusing its own principles, with singular vigour, into the heart of a neophyte from another church. Let the mitre once touch the head of a low churchman, and a new light shines on his mind in regard to the apostolic succession, and on all the pomp and paraphernalia of Prelacy; and as a New-England man becomes the most cruel of all slave-drivers, if he can be made so far to forget himself as to become as a slave-driver at all, so a man from an evangelical denomination becomes the most furious for Prelacy, if he can be made so far to forget himself as to become a prelate at all. We think it time for the evangelical young men of our country to understand, that if they wish to advance the cause of the gospel, it is not to be in connection with the religion of forms. The gospel of Christ has elements of moral power in itself which are only hindered by gorgeous external rites—as the keenness of a Damascus blade is rendered useless if buried within a gorgeous scabbard.

We regard the prevailing spirit of Episcopacy, in all aspects, high and low, as at variance with the spirit of the age and of this land. This is an age of freedom, and men *will* be free. The religion of forms is the stereotyped wisdom or folly of the past, and does not adapt itself to the free movements, the enlarged views, the varying plans of this age. The spirit of this age demands that there shall be freedom in religion; that it shall not be fettered or suppressed; that it shall go forth to the conquest of the world. It is opposed to all bigotry and uncharitableness; to all attempts to "unchurch" others; to teaching that they worship in conventicles, that they are dissenters, or that they are left to the uncovenanted mercies of God. All such language did better in the days of Laud and

Bonner, than now. It might be appropriate in lands where religion is united to the state—

> "Like beauty to old age
> For interest's sake, the living to the dead,"—

but it does not suit our times or country. It makes a jar on American feelings. It will not be tolerated by this community. The spirit of this land is, that the church of Christ is not under the Episcopal form, or the Baptist, the Methodist, the Presbyterian, or the Congregational form exclusively; all are, to all intents and purposes, to be recognised as parts of the one holy catholic church, with no distinction of prerogative, with no right to the assumption of exclusive names, with no self-complacent expression of feeling that *their* form brings them nearer to heaven than others. There is a spirit in this land which requires that the gospel shall depend for its success not on solemn processions and imposing rites; not on the idea of superior sanctity in the priesthood in virtue of their office; not on genuflections and ablutions; not on any virtue conveyed by the imposition of holy hands, and not on union with any particular church, but on solemn appeals to the reason, the conscience, the immortal hopes and fears of men, attended by the holy influences of the Spirit of God:—a spirit which demands that the devotion which from age to age is to be breathed forth on our hills and along our valleys, should be that pure devotion which proceeds from the heart, worshipping God in spirit and in truth.

END OF VOL. I.

STEREOTYPED BY L. JOHNSON & CO.
PHILADELPHIA.